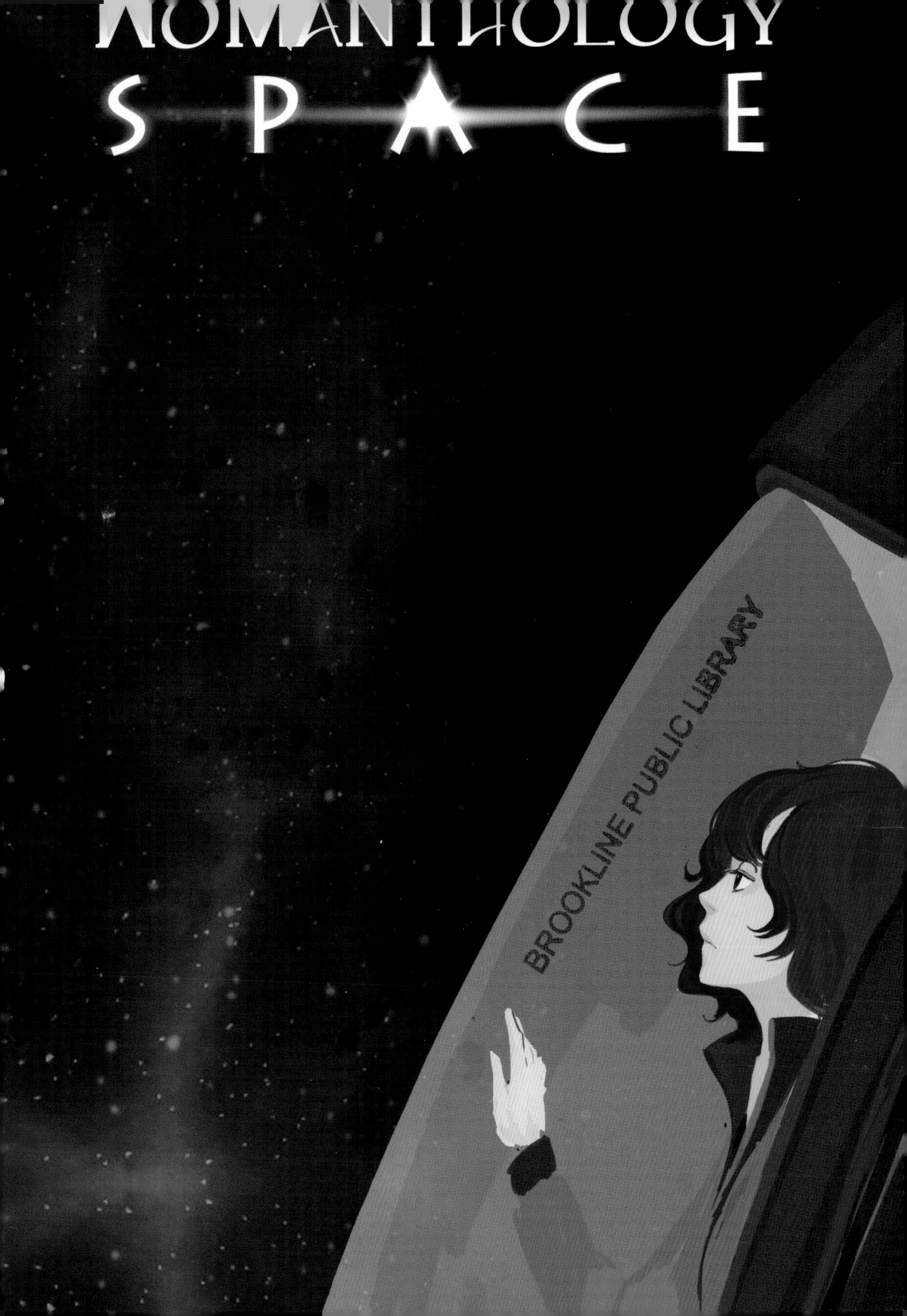
WOMANTHOLOGY
SPACE

Collection Cover by **Renae DeLiz**
Series Edits by **Mariah Huehner**
Collection Edits by **Justin Eisinger & Alonzo Simon**

manthology created by Renae DeLiz. We can't than

nded by Ted Adams, Alex Garner, Kris Oprisko, and Robbie Robbins

978-1-61377-607-0

16 1

Ted Adams, CEO & Publisher
Greg Goldstein, President & COO
Robbie Robbins, EVP/Sr. Graphic Artist
Chris Ryall, Chief Creative Officer/Editor-in-Chief
Matthew Ruzicka, CPA, Chief Financial Officer
Alan Payne, VP of Sales
Dirk Wood, VP of Marketing
Lorelei Bunjes, VP of Digital Services

Become our fan on Facebook **facebook.com/i**
Follow us on Twitter **@idwpublishing**
Check us out on YouTube **youtube.com/idwp**
www.IDWPUBLISHIN

CONTENTS

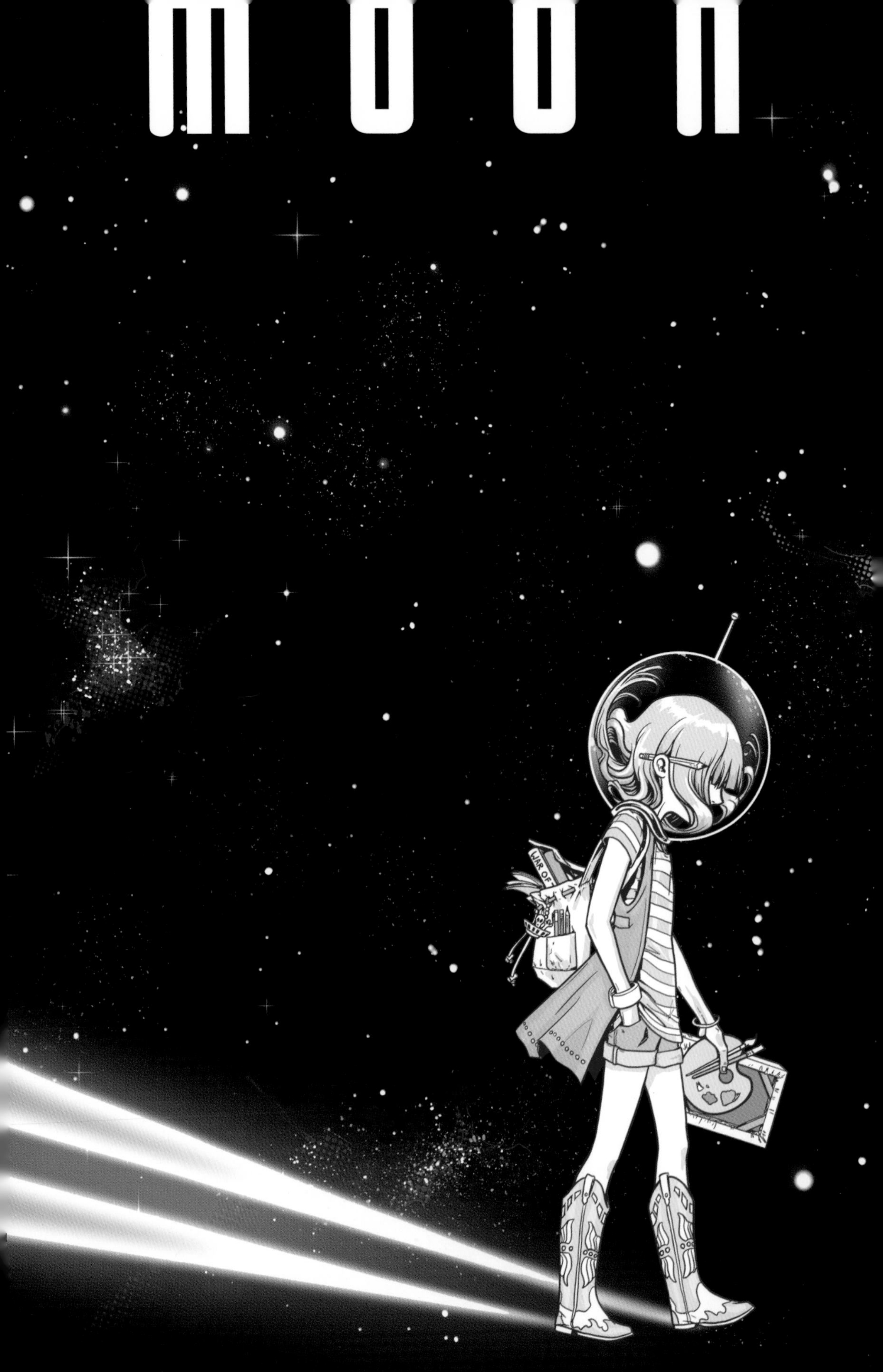
MOON

Art by Renae DeLiz

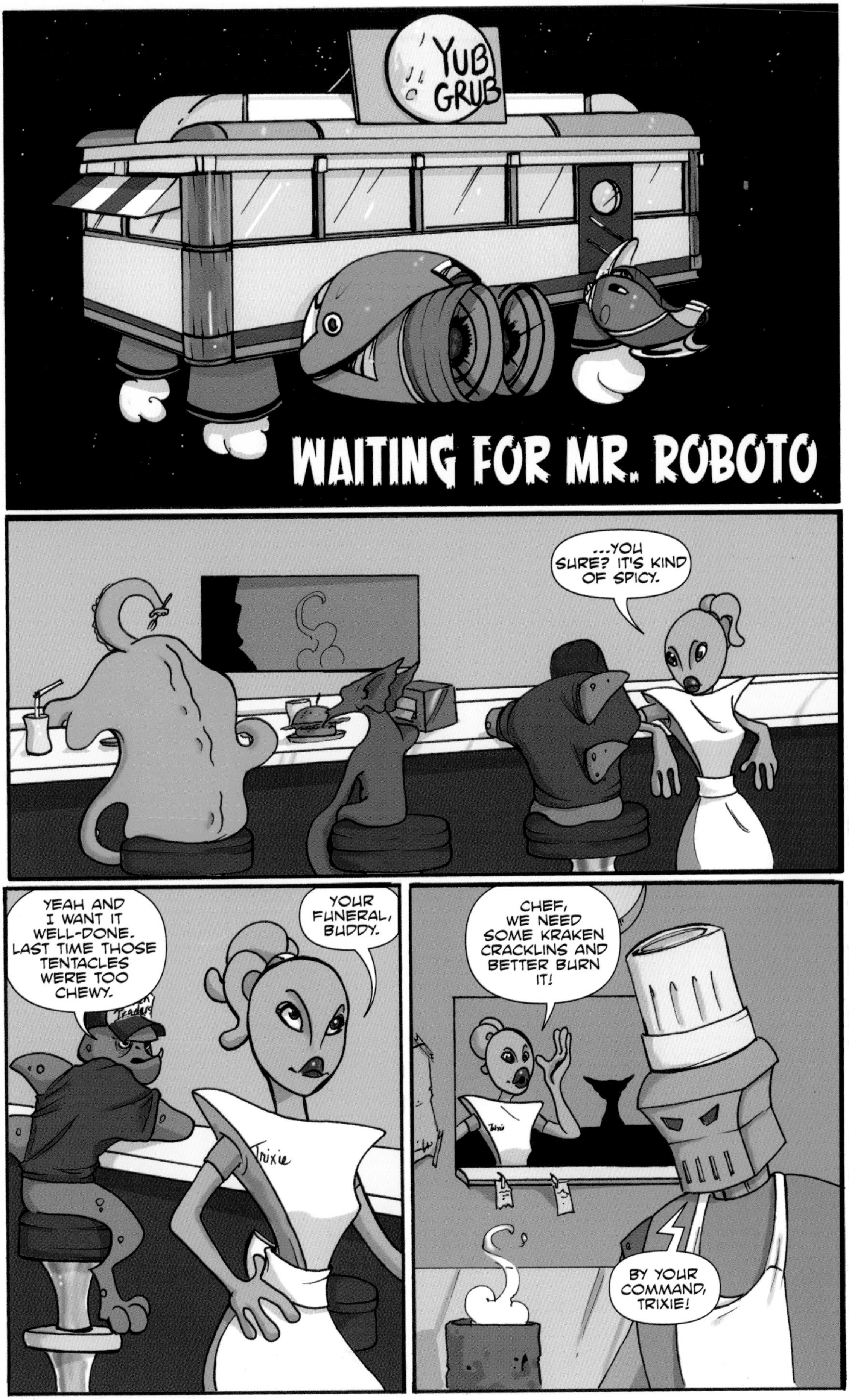
YUB GRUB
WAITING FOR MR. ROBOTO
...YOU SURE? IT'S KIND OF SPICY.
YEAH AND I WANT IT WELL-DONE. LAST TIME THOSE TENTACLES WERE TOO CHEWY.
YOUR FUNERAL, BUDDY.
Trixie
CHEF, WE NEED SOME KRAKEN CRACKLINS AND BETTER BURN IT!
BY YOUR COMMAND, TRIXIE!

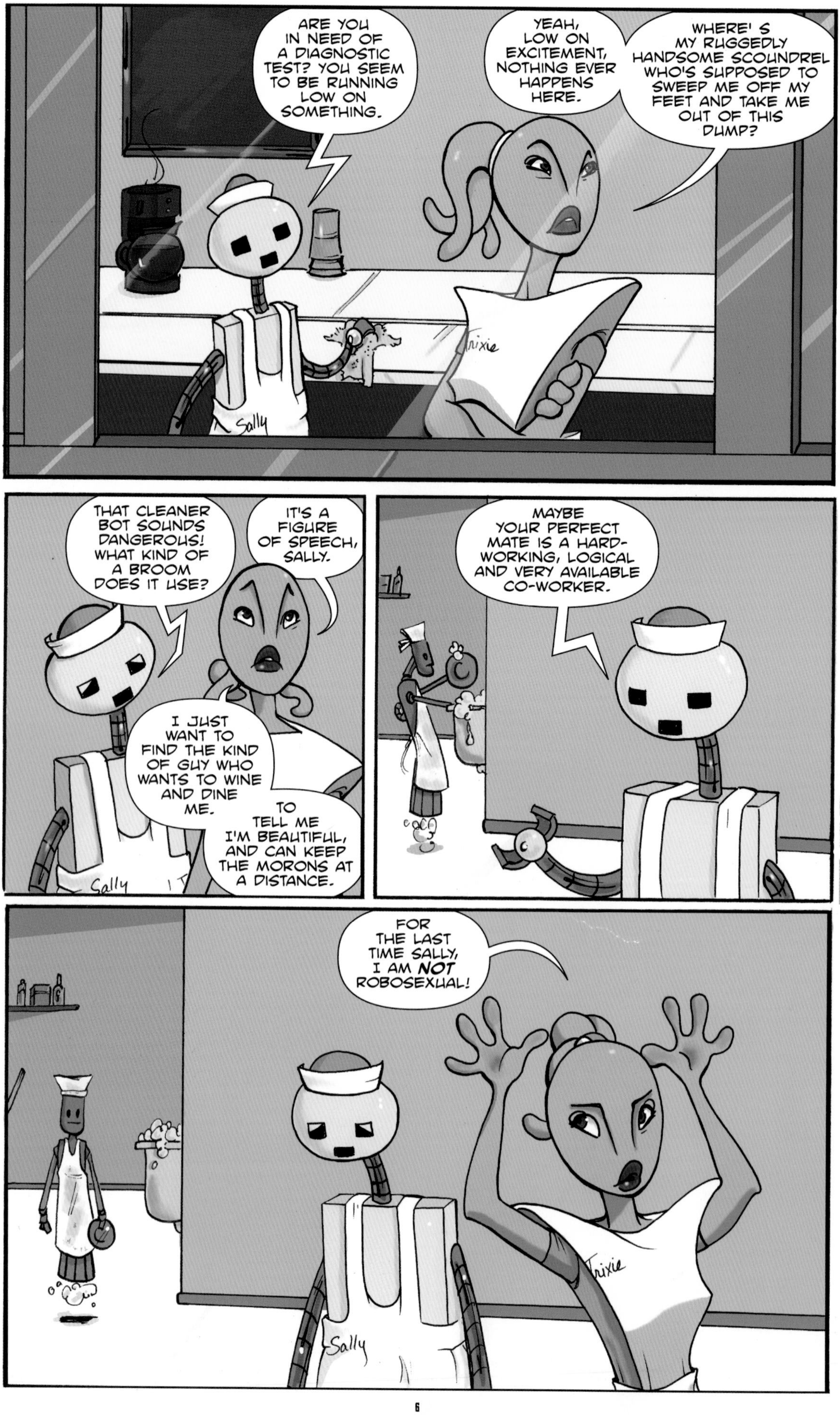
ARE YOU IN NEED OF A DIAGNOSTIC TEST? YOU SEEM TO BE RUNNING LOW ON SOMETHING.
YEAH, LOW ON EXCITEMENT, NOTHING EVER HAPPENS HERE.
WHERE' S MY RUGGEDLY HANDSOME SCOUNDREL WHO'S SUPPOSED TO SWEEP ME OFF MY FEET AND TAKE ME OUT OF THIS DUMP?
Sally
Trixie
THAT CLEANER BOT SOUNDS DANGEROUS! WHAT KIND OF A BROOM DOES IT USE?
IT'S A FIGURE OF SPEECH, SALLY.
I JUST WANT TO FIND THE KIND OF GUY WHO WANTS TO WINE AND DINE ME.
TO TELL ME I'M BEAUTIFUL, AND CAN KEEP THE MORONS AT A DISTANCE.
Sally
MAYBE YOUR PERFECT MATE IS A HARD-WORKING, LOGICAL AND VERY AVAILABLE CO-WORKER.
FOR THE LAST TIME SALLY, I AM **NOT** ROBOSEXUAL!
Trixie
Sally

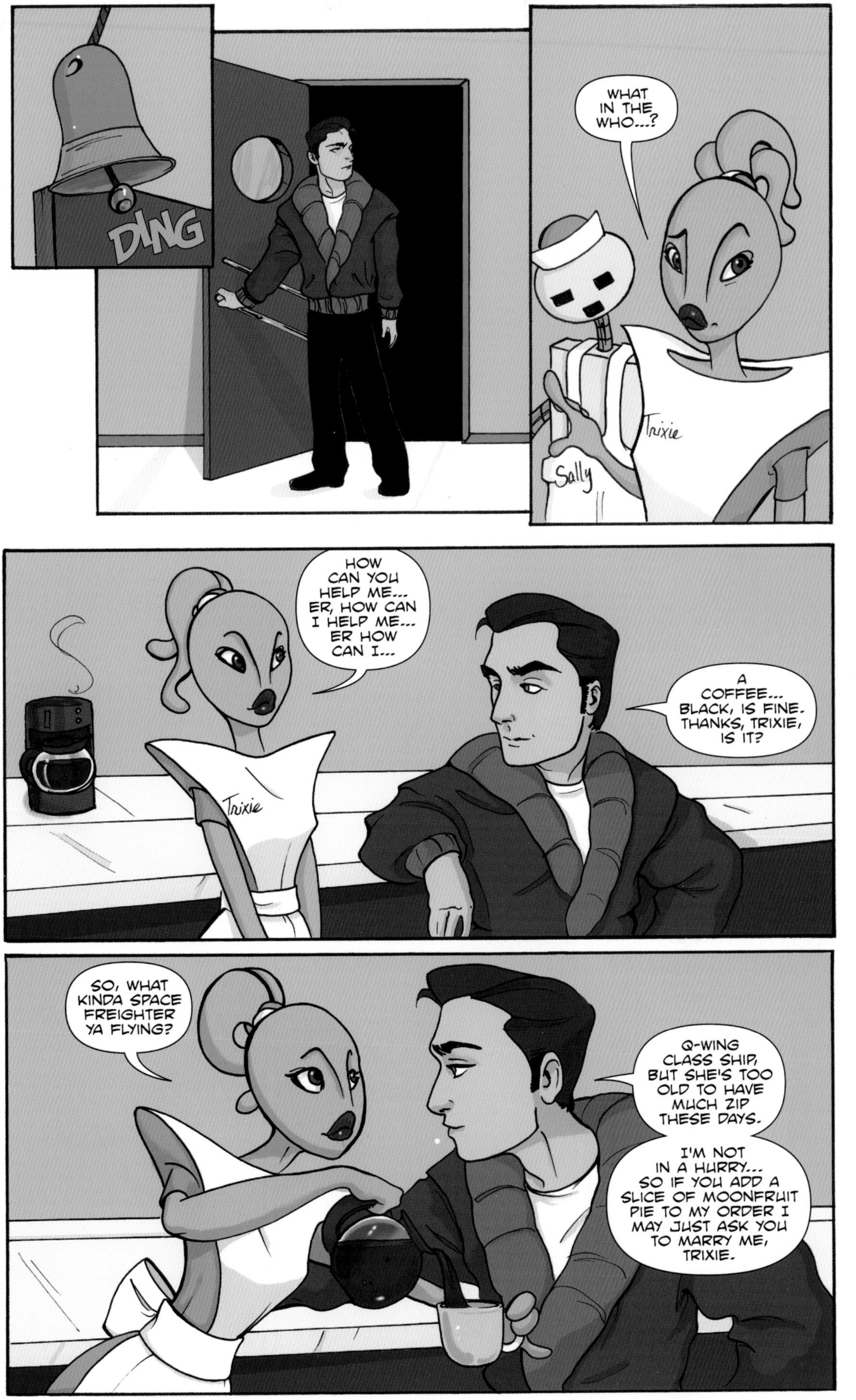
DING
WHAT IN THE WHO...?
Trixie
Sally
HOW CAN YOU HELP ME... ER, HOW CAN I HELP ME... ER HOW CAN I...
A COFFEE... BLACK, IS FINE. THANKS, TRIXIE, IS IT?
Trixie
SO, WHAT KINDA SPACE FREIGHTER YA FLYING?
Q-WING CLASS SHIP, BUT SHE'S TOO OLD TO HAVE MUCH ZIP THESE DAYS.
I'M NOT IN A HURRY... SO IF YOU ADD A SLICE OF MOONFRUIT PIE TO MY ORDER I MAY JUST ASK YOU TO MARRY ME, TRIXIE.

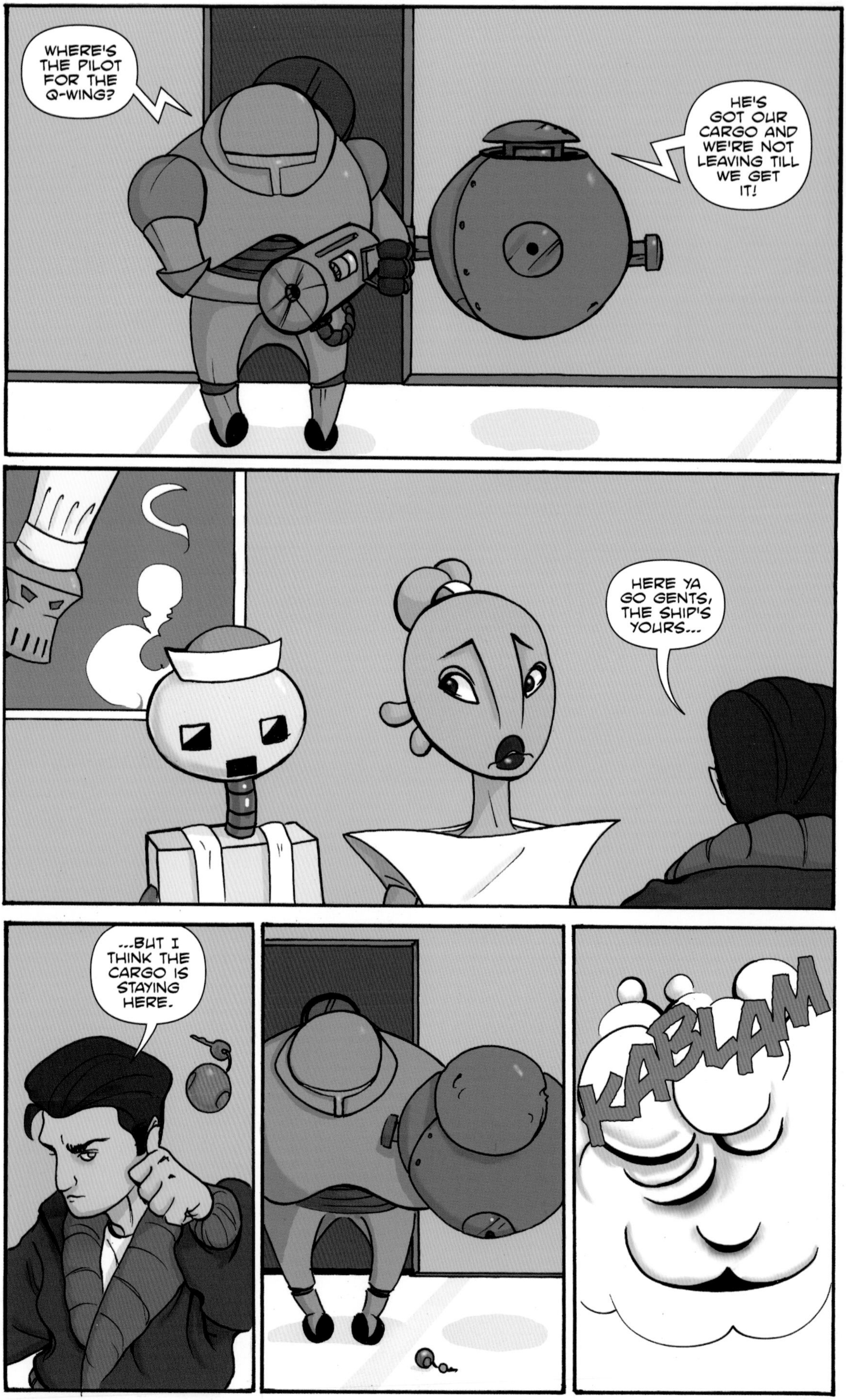
WHERE'S THE PILOT FOR THE Q-WING?
HE'S GOT OUR CARGO AND WE'RE NOT LEAVING TILL WE GET IT!
HERE YA GO GENTS, THE SHIP'S YOURS...
...BUT I THINK THE CARGO IS STAYING HERE.
KABLAM

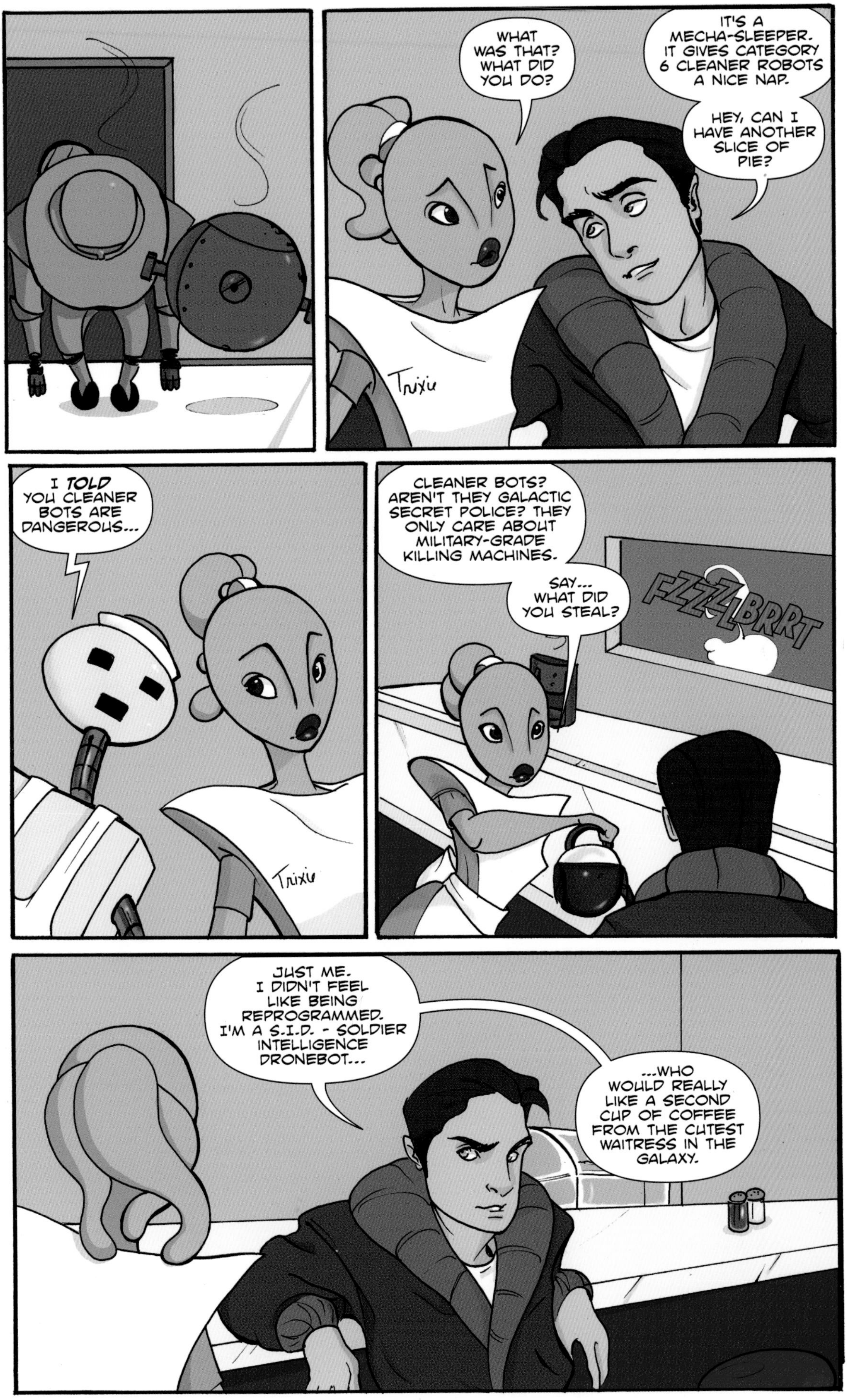
WHAT WAS THAT? WHAT DID YOU DO?
IT'S A MECHA-SLEEPER. IT GIVES CATEGORY 6 CLEANER ROBOTS A NICE NAP.
HEY, CAN I HAVE ANOTHER SLICE OF PIE?
Trixie
I *TOLD* YOU CLEANER BOTS ARE DANGEROUS...
Trixie
CLEANER BOTS? AREN'T THEY GALACTIC SECRET POLICE? THEY ONLY CARE ABOUT MILITARY-GRADE KILLING MACHINES.
SAY... WHAT DID YOU STEAL?
FZZZZLBRRRT
JUST ME. I DIDN'T FEEL LIKE BEING REPROGRAMMED. I'M A S.I.D. - SOLDIER INTELLIGENCE DRONEBOT...
...WHO WOULD REALLY LIKE A SECOND CUP OF COFFEE FROM THE CUTEST WAITRESS IN THE GALAXY.

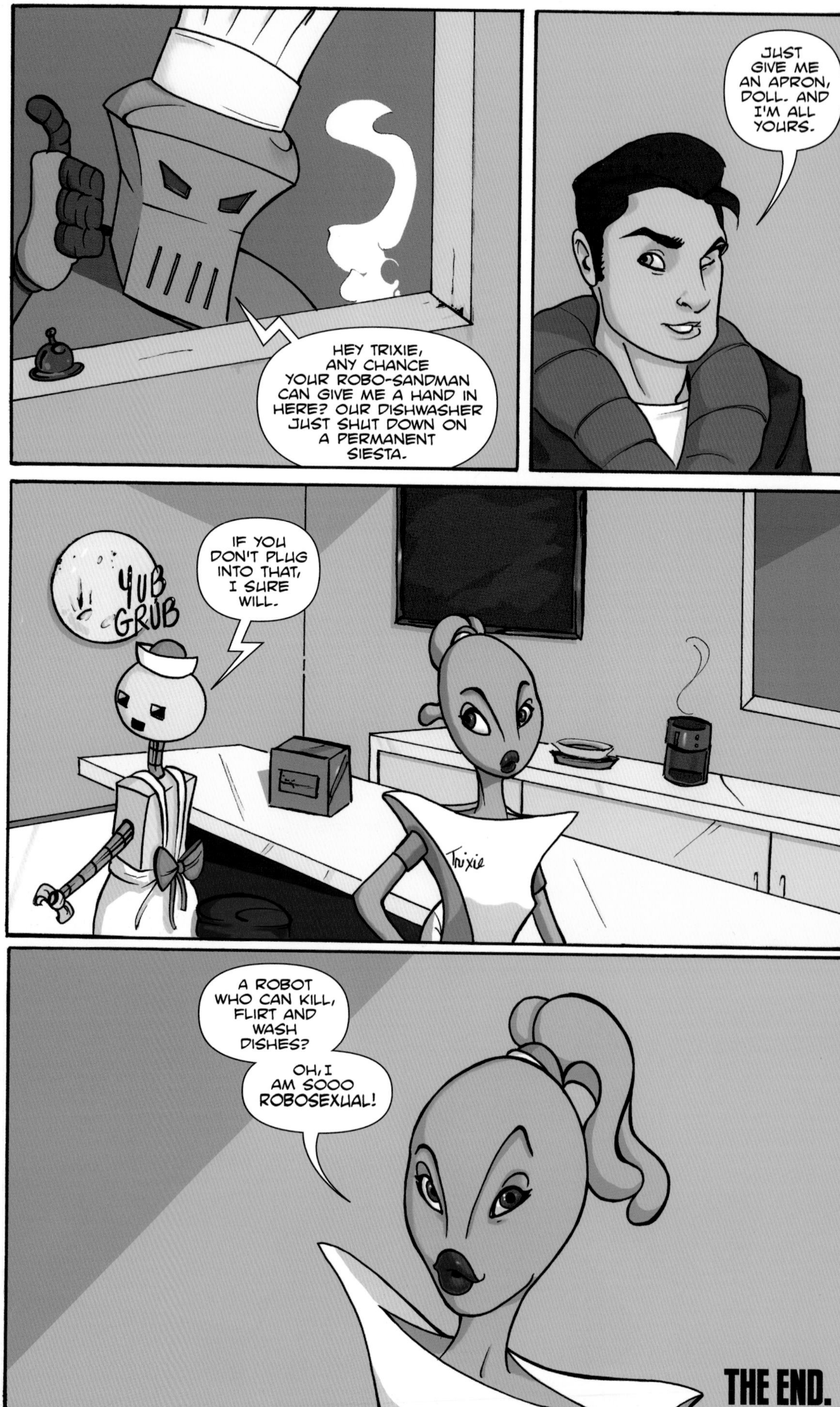
HEY TRIXIE, ANY CHANCE YOUR ROBO-SANDMAN CAN GIVE ME A HAND IN HERE? OUR DISHWASHER JUST SHUT DOWN ON A PERMANENT SIESTA.
JUST GIVE ME AN APRON, DOLL. AND I'M ALL YOURS.
YUB GRUB
IF YOU DON'T PLUG INTO THAT, I SURE WILL.
Trixie
A ROBOT WHO CAN KILL, FLIRT AND WASH DISHES?
OH, I AM SOOO ROBOSEXUAL!
THE END.

DEAD AGAIN

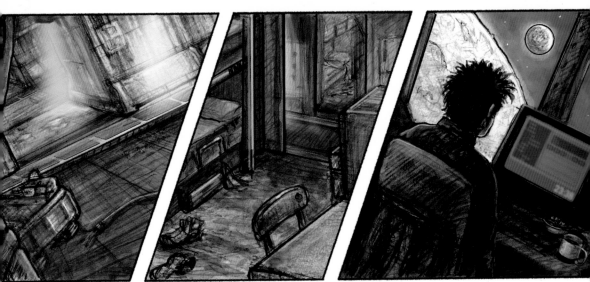

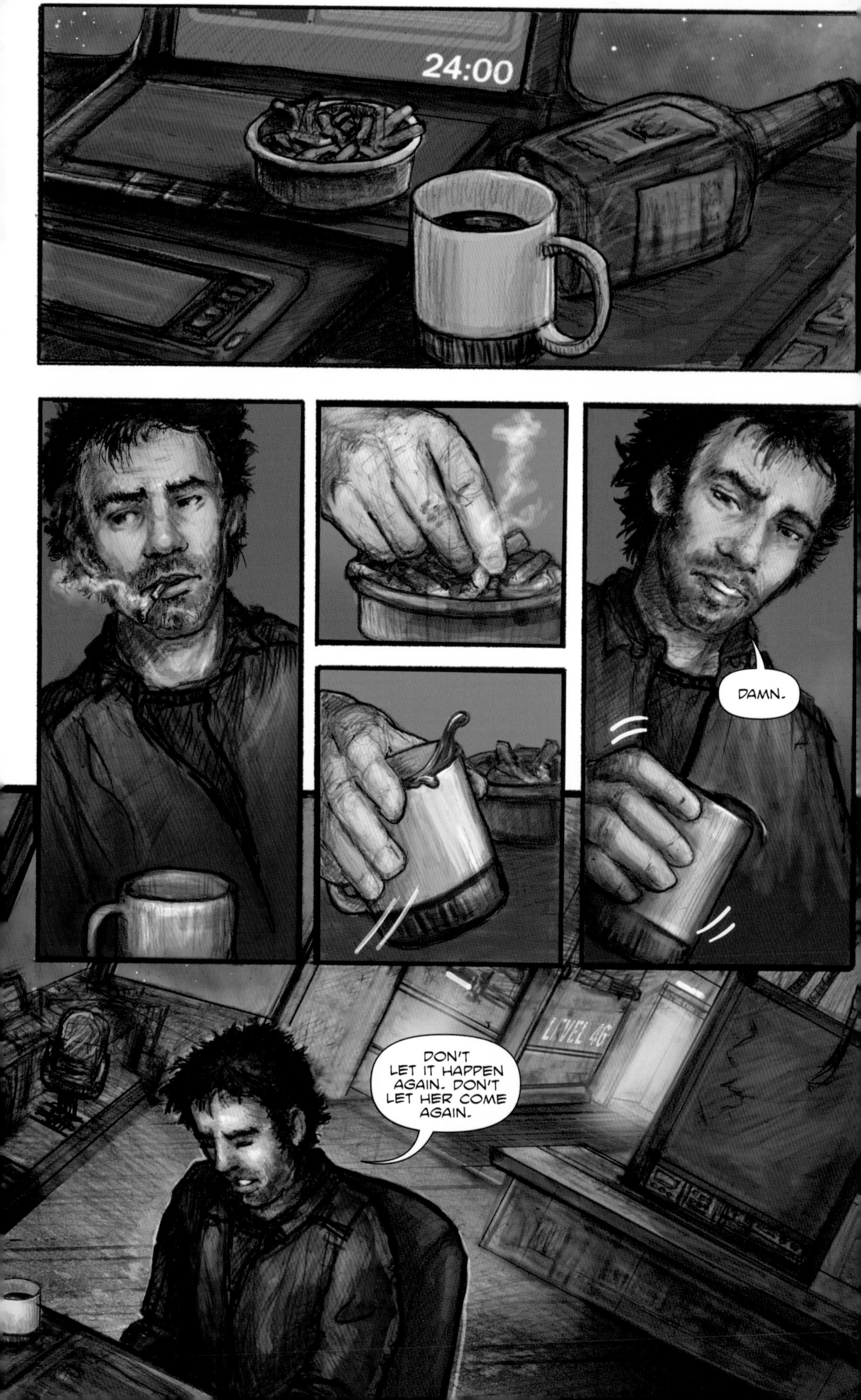
24:00
DAMN.
DON'T LET IT HAPPEN AGAIN. DON'T LET HER COME AGAIN.
LEVEL 46

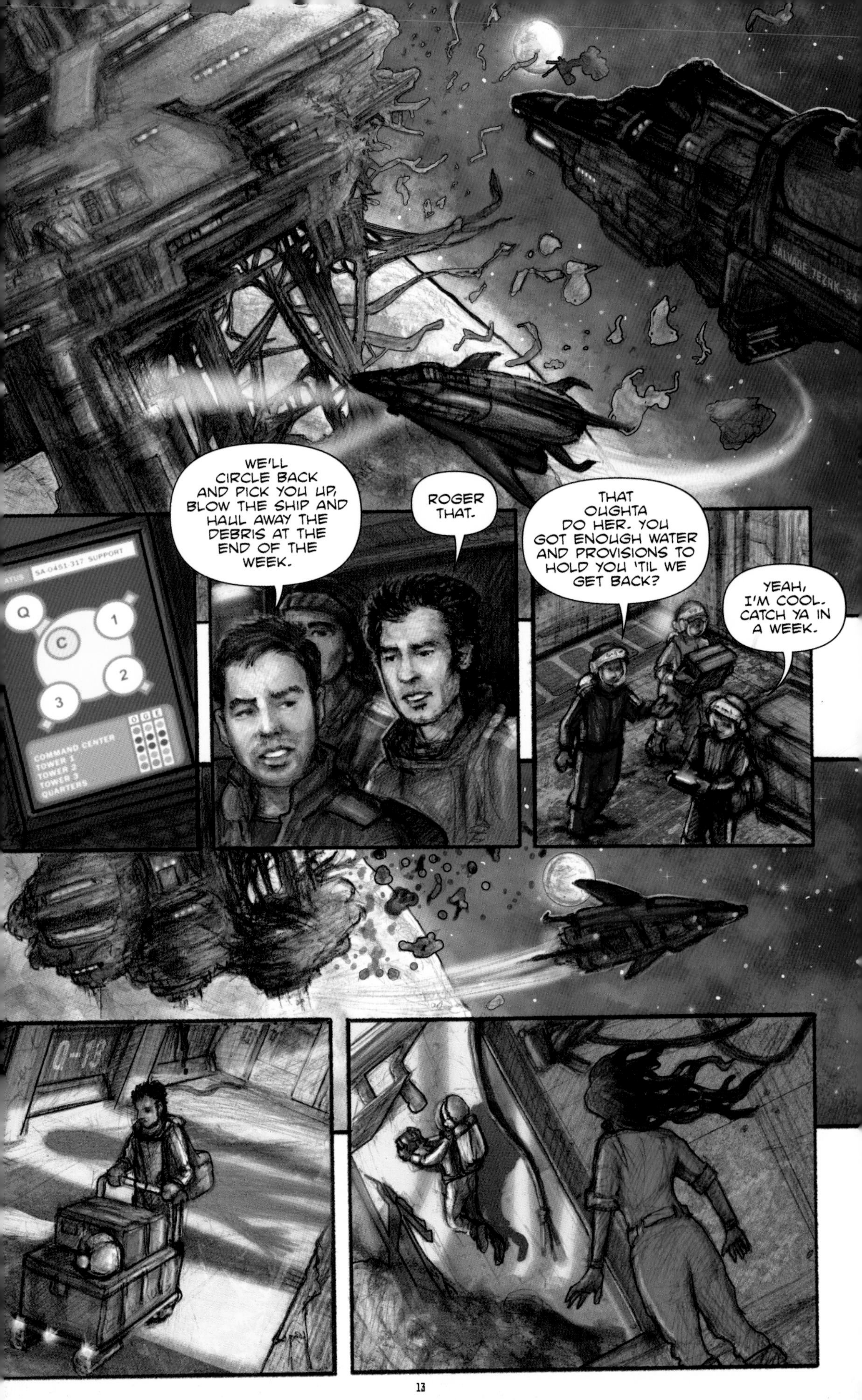
SALVAGE TEZRK-34
WE'LL CIRCLE BACK AND PICK YOU UP, BLOW THE SHIP AND HAUL AWAY THE DEBRIS AT THE END OF THE WEEK.
ROGER THAT.
ATUS
SA-0451-317 SUPPORT
Q
C
1
2
3
O G E
COMMAND CENTER
TOWER 1
TOWER 2
TOWER 3
QUARTERS
THAT OUGHTA DO HER. YOU GOT ENOUGH WATER AND PROVISIONS TO HOLD YOU 'TIL WE GET BACK?
YEAH, I'M COOL. CATCH YA IN A WEEK.
0-13

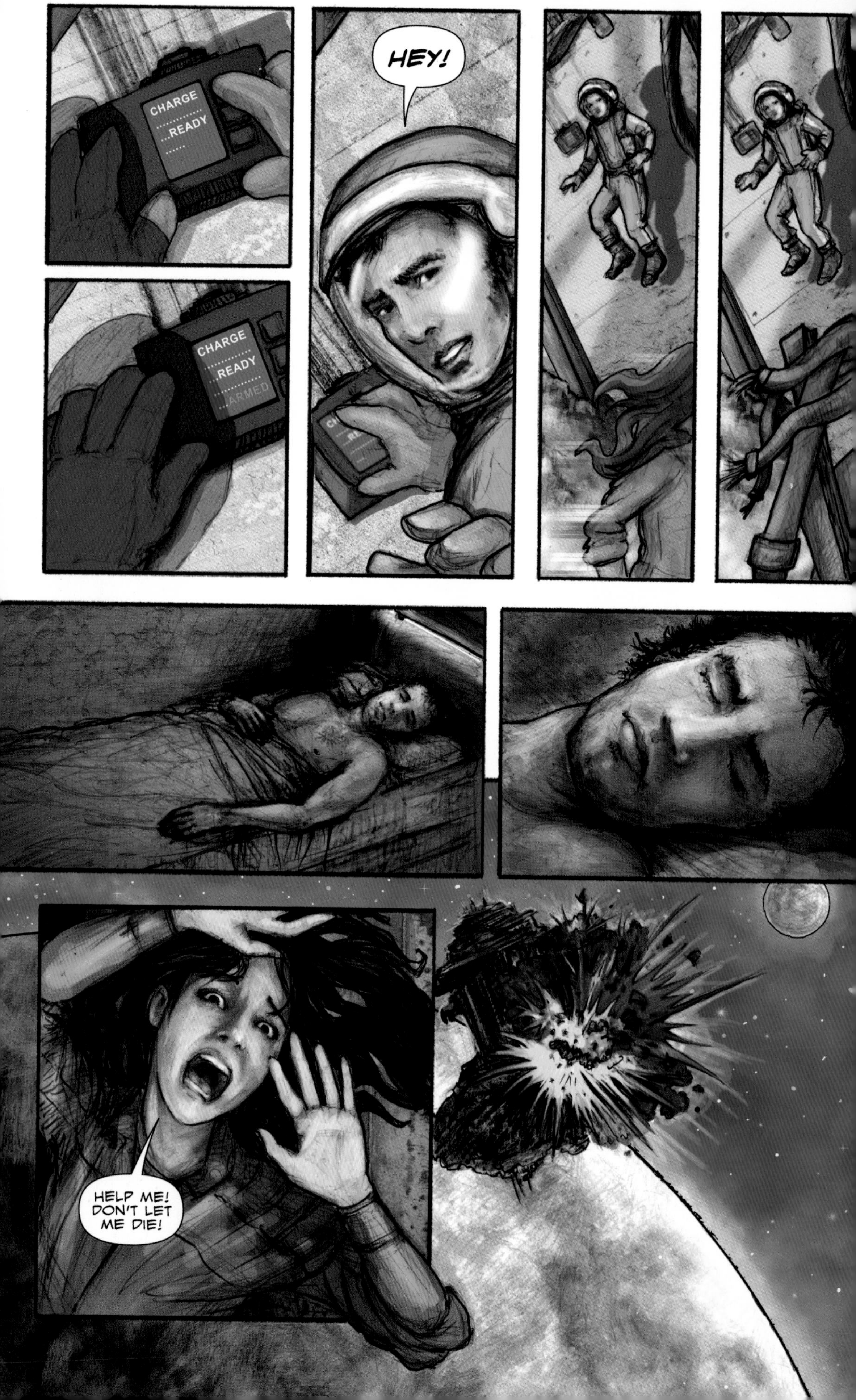
CHARGE
...READY
CHARGE
..READY
ARMED
HEY!
HELP ME! DON'T LET ME DIE!

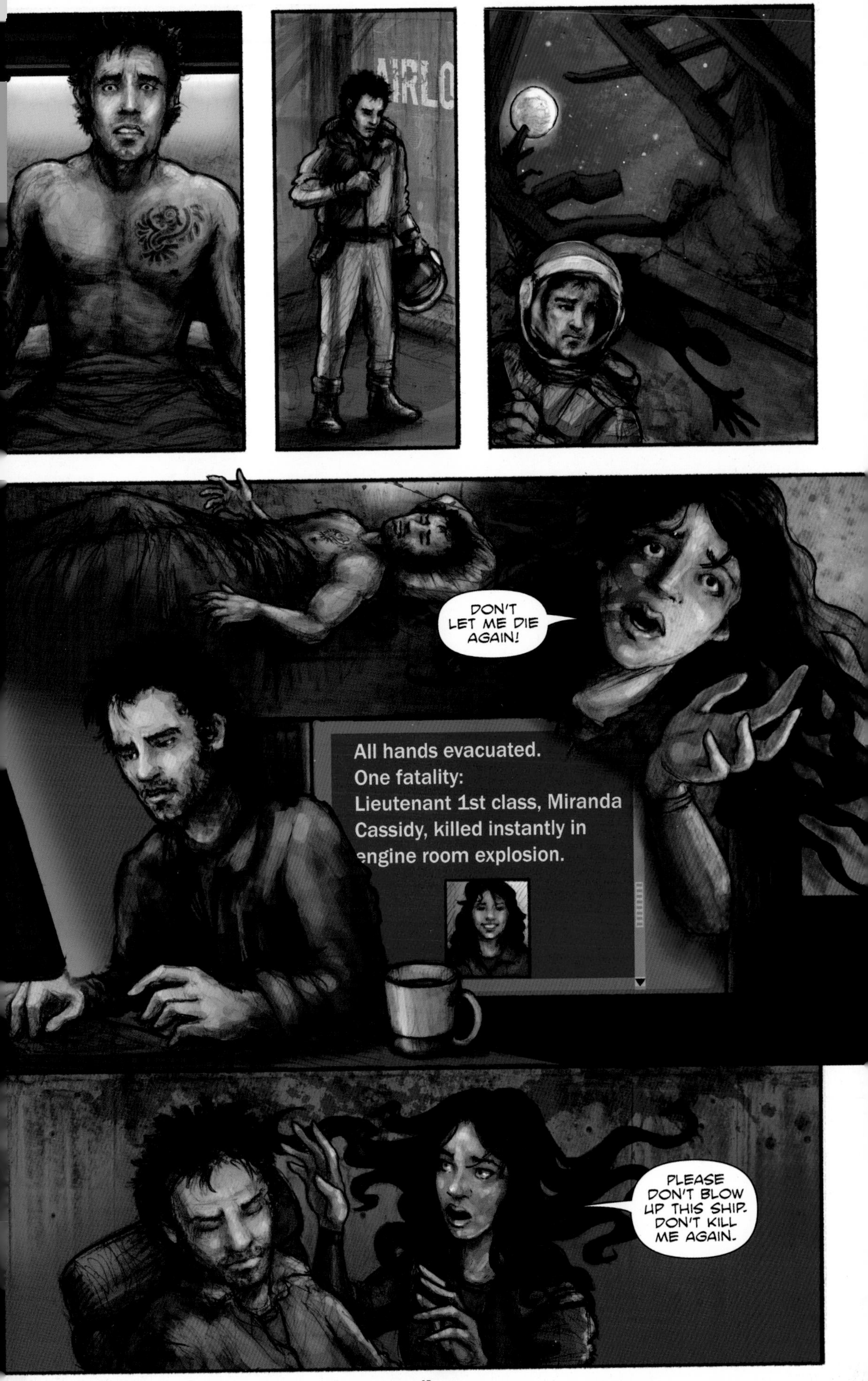
AIRLO
DON'T LET ME DIE AGAIN!
All hands evacuated.
One fatality:
Lieutenant 1st class, Miranda Cassidy, killed instantly in engine room explosion.
PLEASE DON'T BLOW UP THIS SHIP. DON'T KILL ME AGAIN.

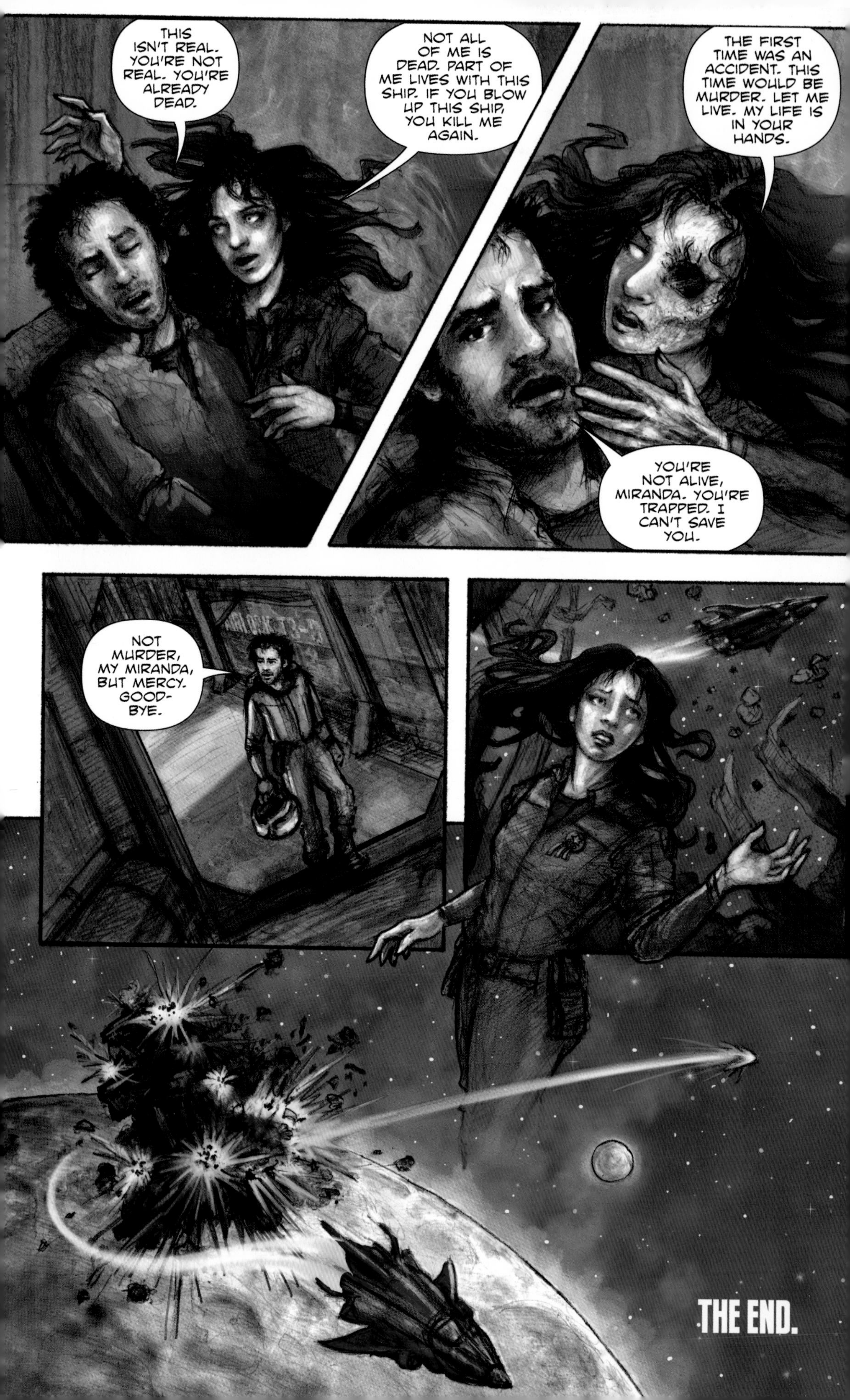
THIS ISN'T REAL. YOU'RE NOT REAL. YOU'RE ALREADY DEAD.
NOT ALL OF ME IS DEAD. PART OF ME LIVES WITH THIS SHIP. IF YOU BLOW UP THIS SHIP, YOU KILL ME AGAIN.
THE FIRST TIME WAS AN ACCIDENT. THIS TIME WOULD BE MURDER. LET ME LIVE. MY LIFE IS IN YOUR HANDS.
YOU'RE NOT ALIVE, MIRANDA. YOU'RE TRAPPED. I CAN'T SAVE YOU.
NOT MURDER, MY MIRANDA, BUT MERCY. GOOD-BYE.
THE END.

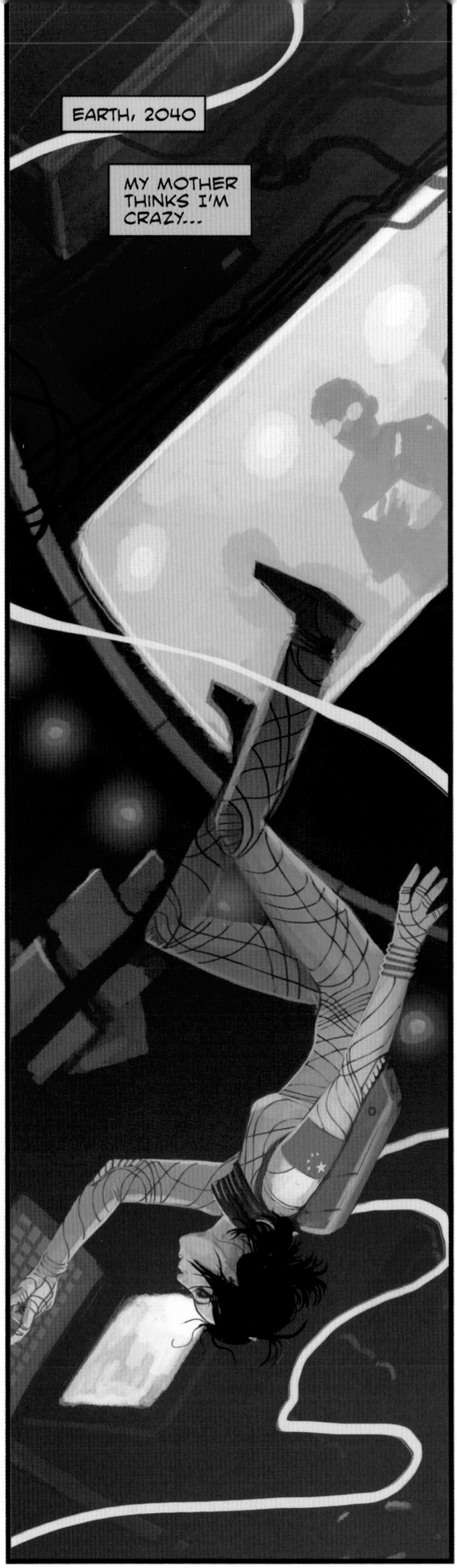
EARTH, 2040
MY MOTHER THINKS I'M CRAZY...

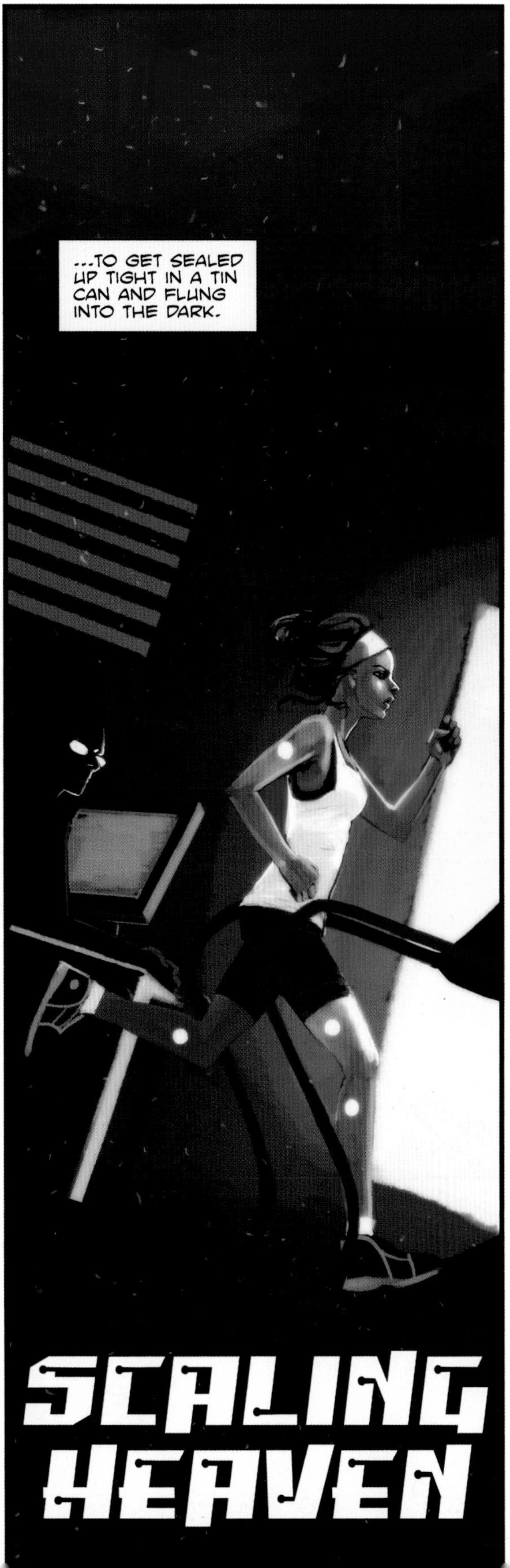
...TO GET SEALED UP TIGHT IN A TIN CAN AND FLUNG INTO THE DARK.
SCALING HEAVEN

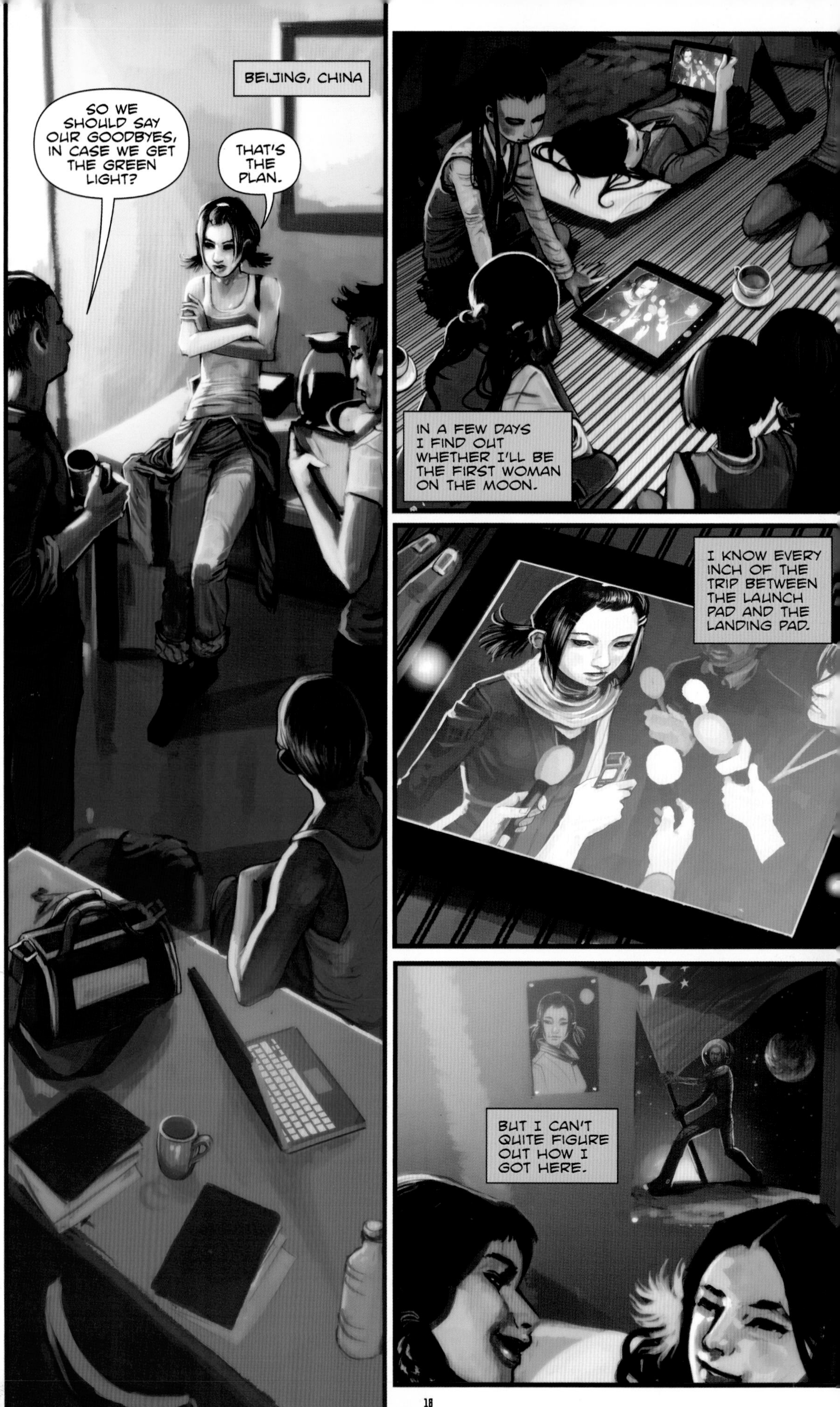

BEIJING, CHINA
SO WE SHOULD SAY OUR GOODBYES, IN CASE WE GET THE GREEN LIGHT?
THAT'S THE PLAN.
IN A FEW DAYS I FIND OUT WHETHER I'LL BE THE FIRST WOMAN ON THE MOON.
I KNOW EVERY INCH OF THE TRIP BETWEEN THE LAUNCH PAD AND THE LANDING PAD.
BUT I CAN'T QUITE FIGURE OUT HOW I GOT HERE.

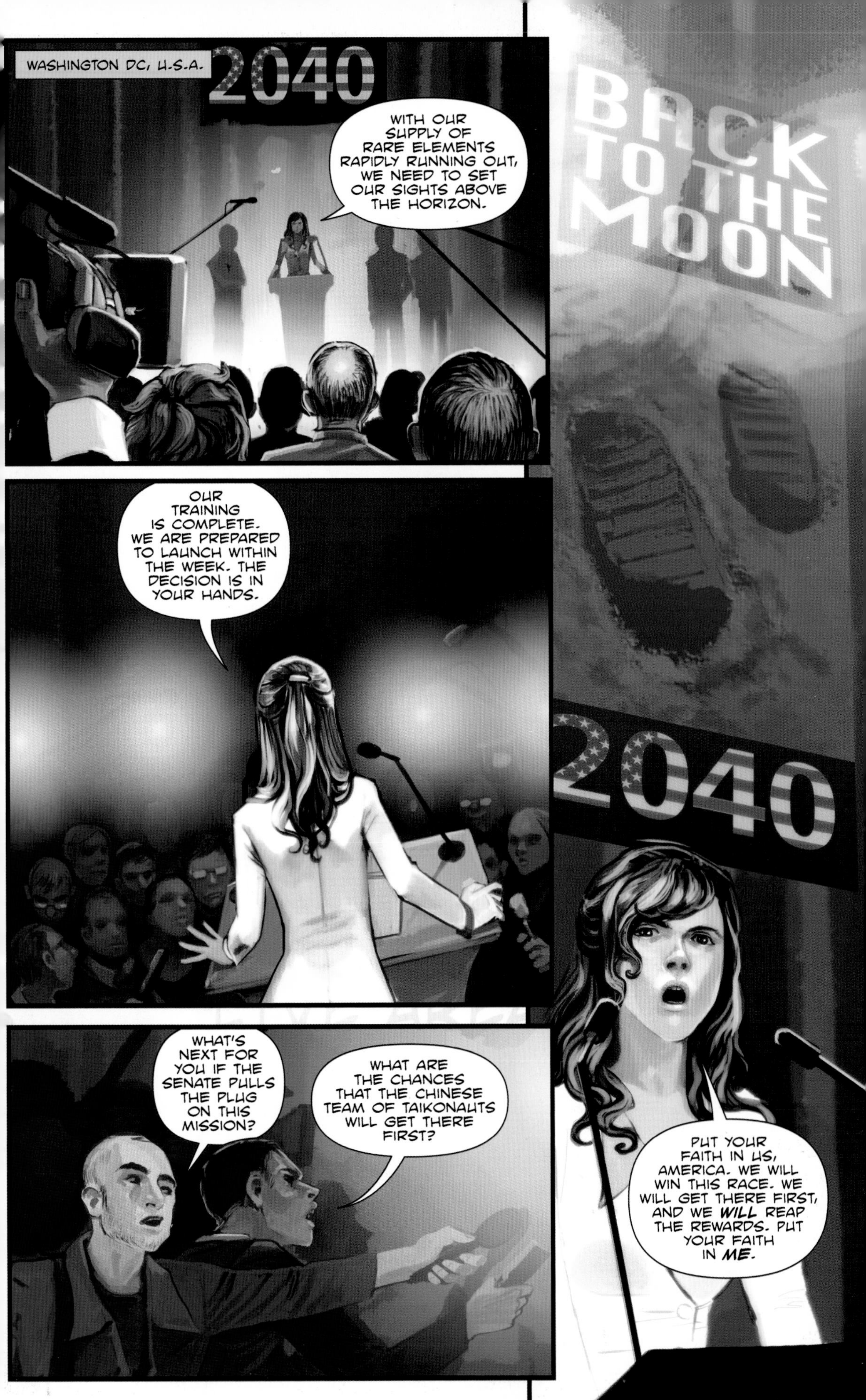
WASHINGTON DC, U.S.A.
2040
WITH OUR SUPPLY OF RARE ELEMENTS RAPIDLY RUNNING OUT, WE NEED TO SET OUR SIGHTS ABOVE THE HORIZON.
BACK TO THE MOON
OUR TRAINING IS COMPLETE. WE ARE PREPARED TO LAUNCH WITHIN THE WEEK. THE DECISION IS IN YOUR HANDS.
2040
WHAT'S NEXT FOR YOU IF THE SENATE PULLS THE PLUG ON THIS MISSION?
WHAT ARE THE CHANCES THAT THE CHINESE TEAM OF TAIKONAUTS WILL GET THERE FIRST?
PUT YOUR FAITH IN US, AMERICA. WE WILL WIN THIS RACE. WE WILL GET THERE FIRST, AND WE WILL REAP THE REWARDS. PUT YOUR FAITH IN ME.

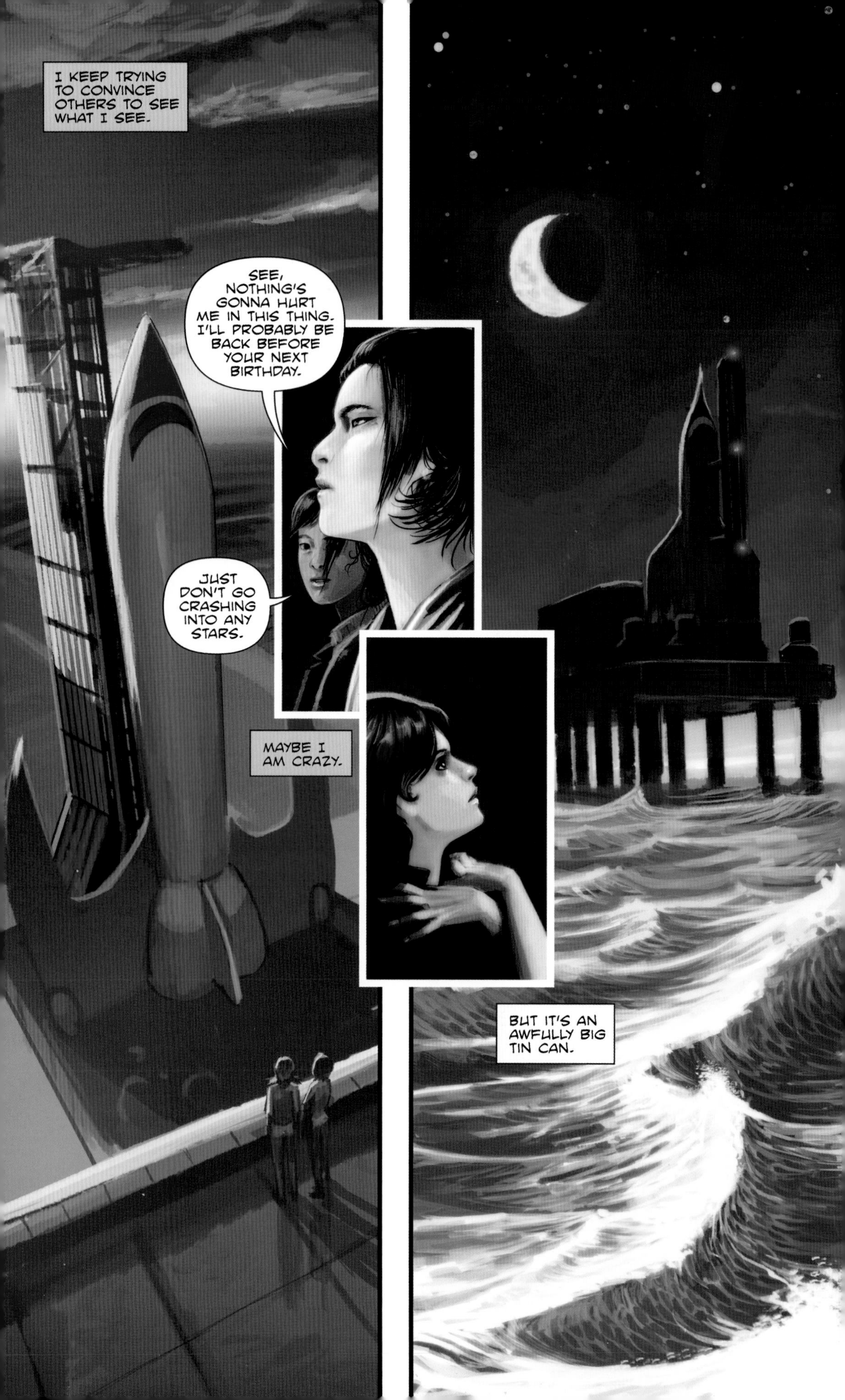
I KEEP TRYING TO CONVINCE OTHERS TO SEE WHAT I SEE.
SEE, NOTHING'S GONNA HURT ME IN THIS THING. I'LL PROBABLY BE BACK BEFORE YOUR NEXT BIRTHDAY.
JUST DON'T GO CRASHING INTO ANY STARS.
MAYBE I AM CRAZY.
BUT IT'S AN AWFULLY BIG TIN CAN.

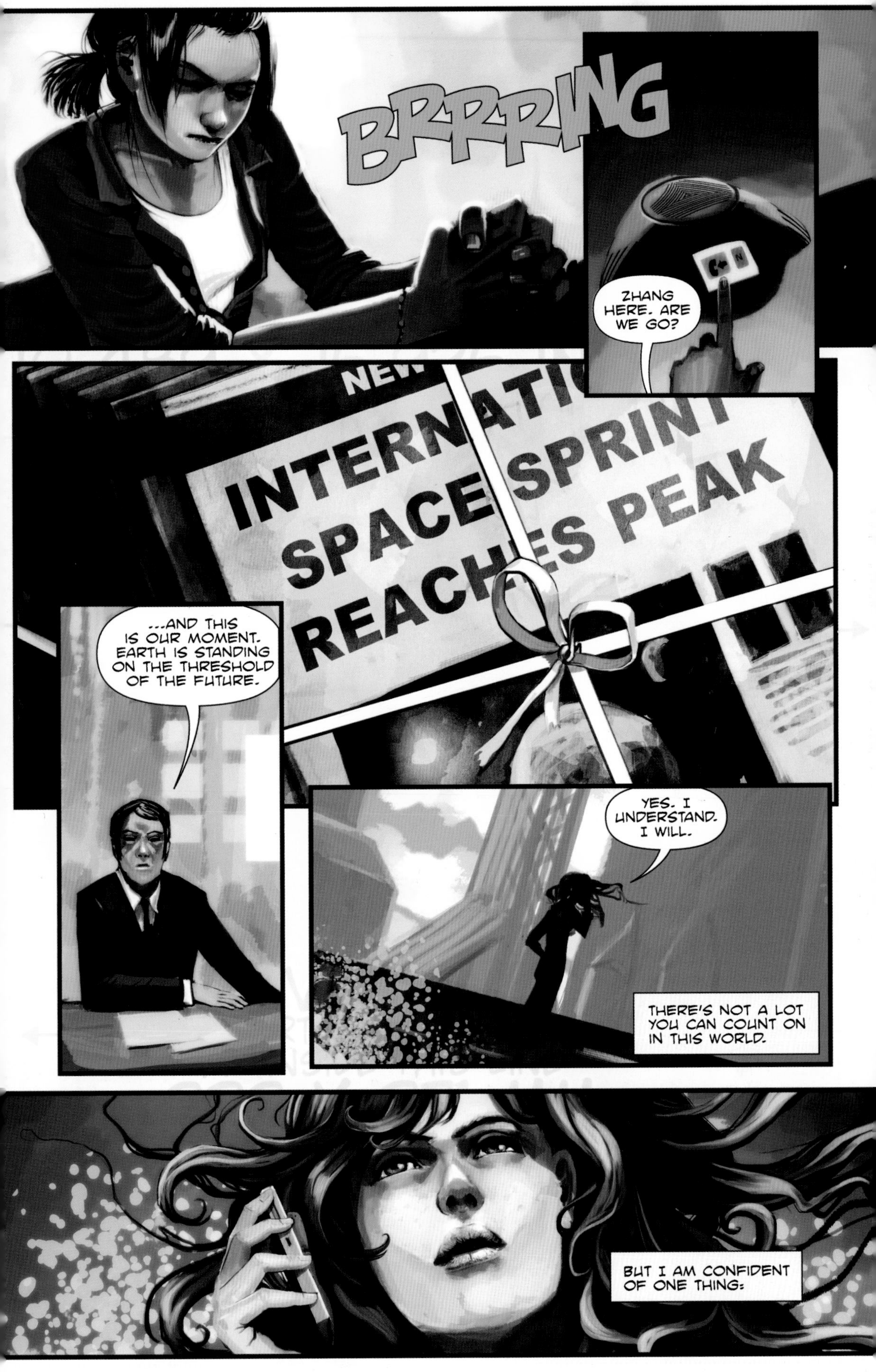
BRRRING
ZHANG HERE. ARE WE GO?
NEW
INTERNATI
SPACE SPRINT
REACHES PEAK
...AND THIS IS OUR MOMENT. EARTH IS STANDING ON THE THRESHOLD OF THE FUTURE.
YES. I UNDERSTAND. I WILL.
THERE'S NOT A LOT YOU CAN COUNT ON IN THIS WORLD.
BUT I AM CONFIDENT OF ONE THING:

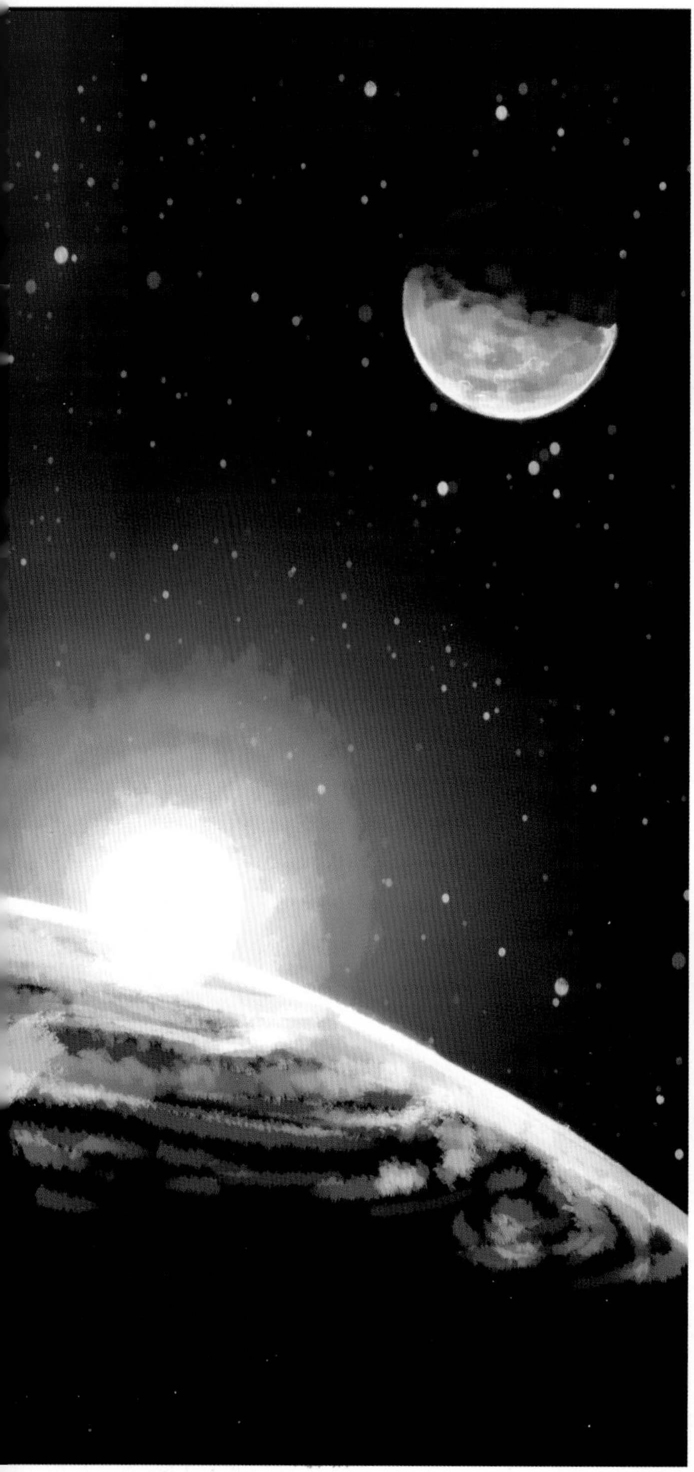

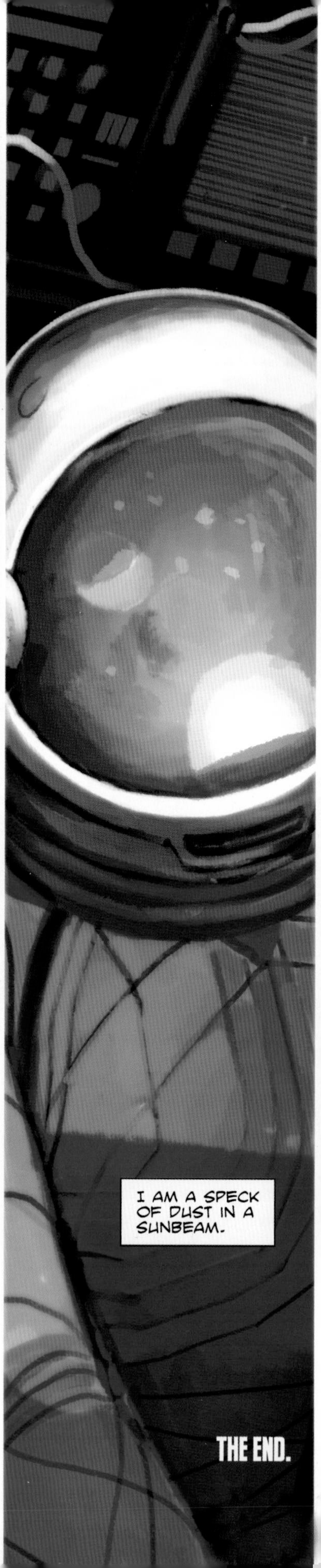
I AM A SPECK OF DUST IN A SUNBEAM.
THE END.

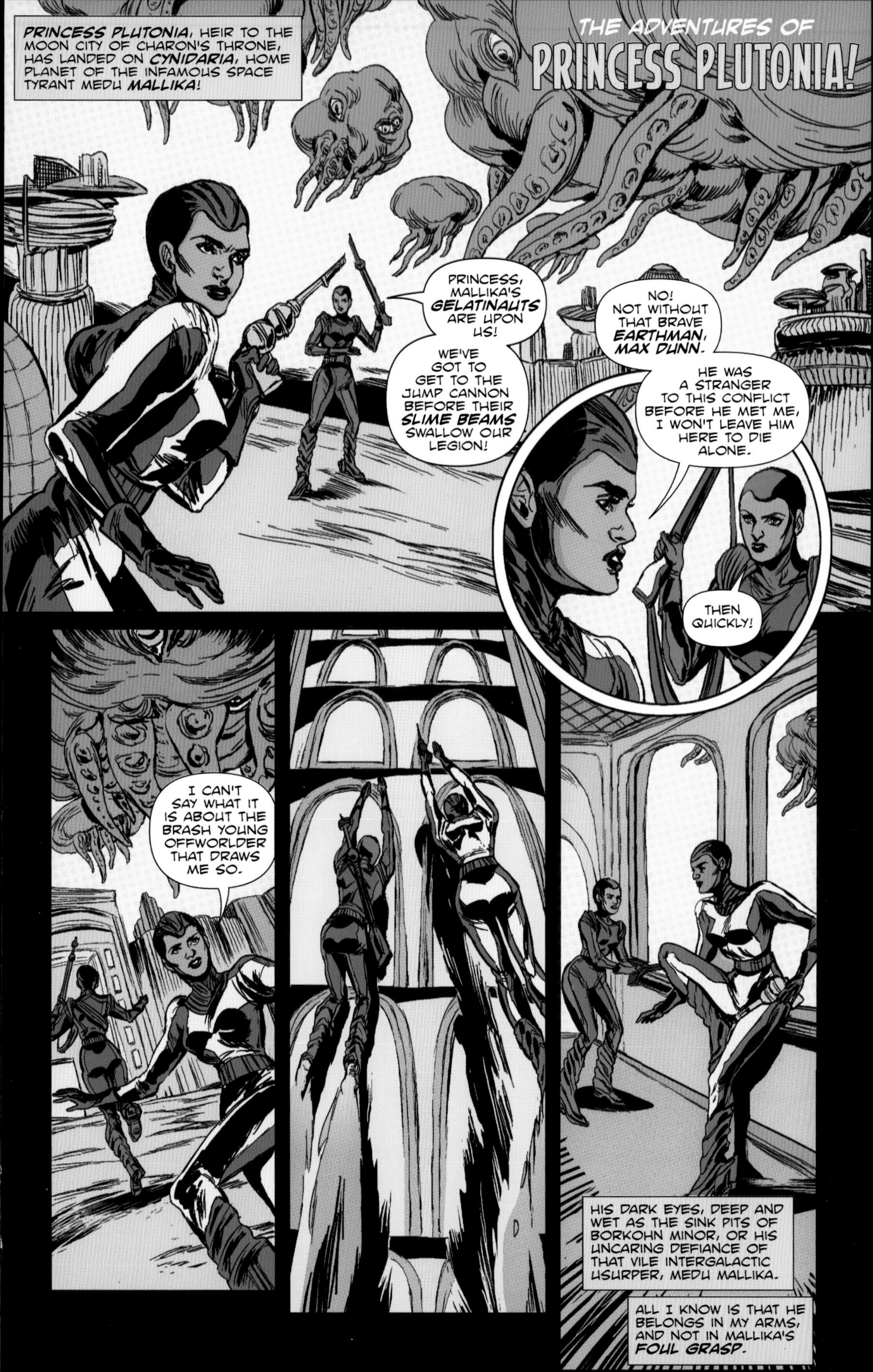
PRINCESS PLUTONIA, HEIR TO THE MOON CITY OF CHARON'S THRONE, HAS LANDED ON CYNIDARIA, HOME PLANET OF THE INFAMOUS SPACE TYRANT MEDU MALLIKA!
THE ADVENTURES OF
PRINCESS PLUTONIA!
PRINCESS, MALLIKA'S GELATINAUTS ARE UPON US!
WE'VE GOT TO GET TO THE JUMP CANNON BEFORE THEIR SLIME BEAMS SWALLOW OUR LEGION!
NO! NOT WITHOUT THAT BRAVE EARTHMAN, MAX DUNN.
HE WAS A STRANGER TO THIS CONFLICT BEFORE HE MET ME, I WON'T LEAVE HIM HERE TO DIE ALONE.
THEN QUICKLY!
I CAN'T SAY WHAT IT IS ABOUT THE BRASH YOUNG OFFWORLDER THAT DRAWS ME SO.
HIS DARK EYES, DEEP AND WET AS THE SINK PITS OF BORKOHN MINOR, OR HIS UNCARING DEFIANCE OF THAT VILE INTERGALACTIC USURPER, MEDU MALLIKA.
ALL I KNOW IS THAT HE BELONGS IN MY ARMS, AND NOT IN MALLIKA'S FOUL GRASP.

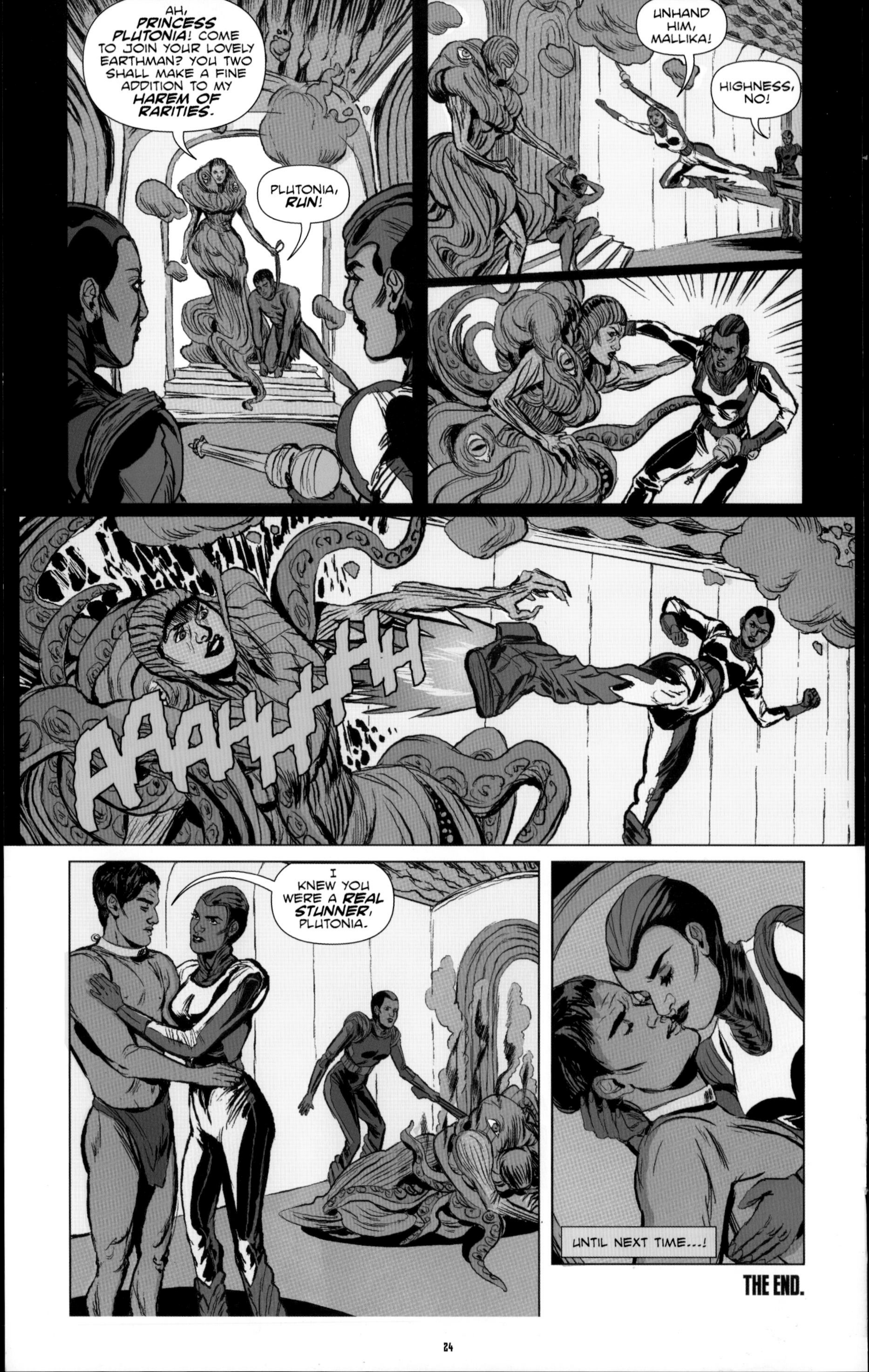
AH, PRINCESS PLUTONIA! COME TO JOIN YOUR LOVELY EARTHMAN? YOU TWO SHALL MAKE A FINE ADDITION TO MY HAREM OF RARITIES.
PLUTONIA, RUN!
UNHAND HIM, MALLIKA!
HIGHNESS, NO!
AAAHHHHH
I KNEW YOU WERE A REAL STUNNER, PLUTONIA.
UNTIL NEXT TIME...!

THE END.

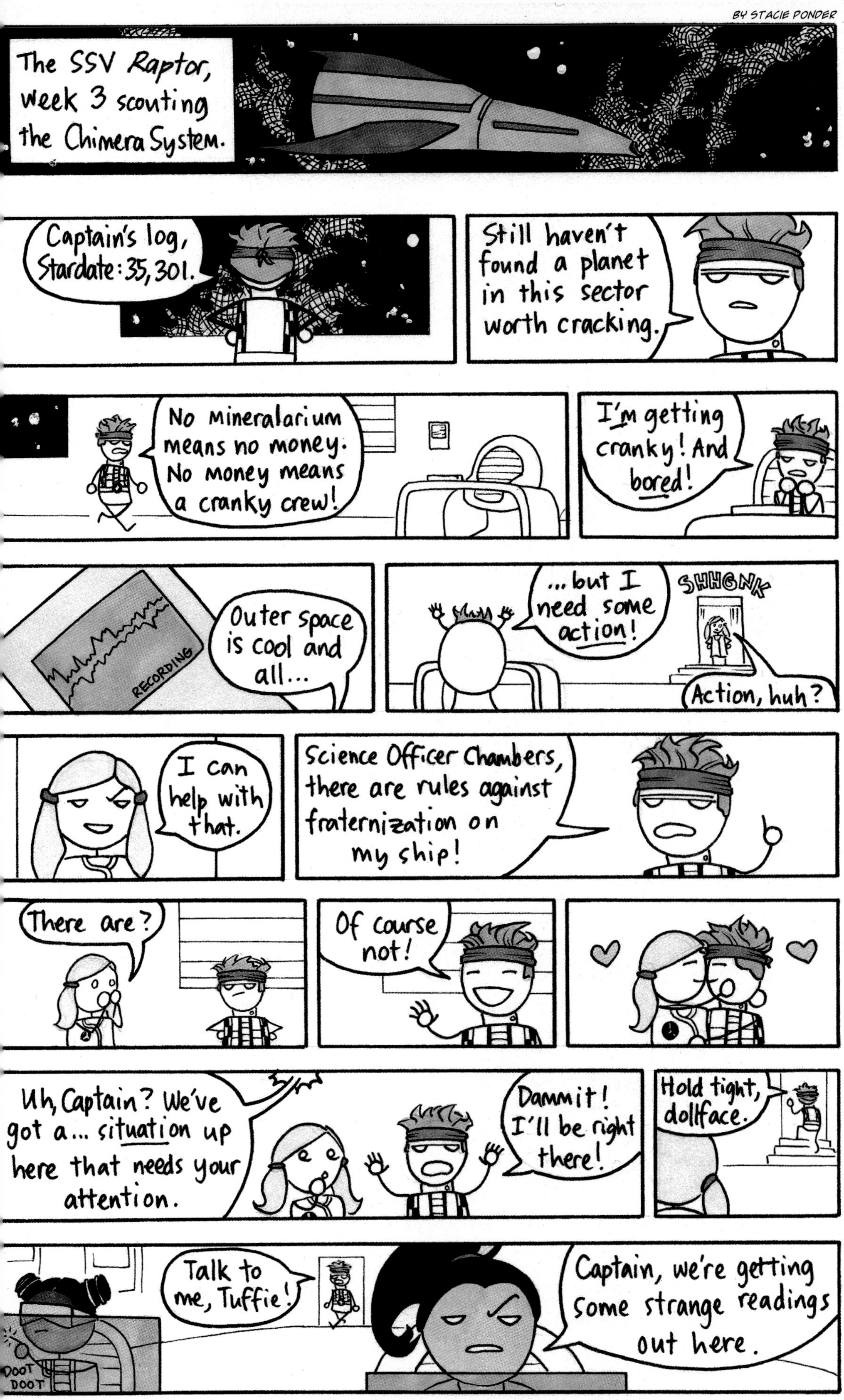
BY STACIE PONDER
The SSV Raptor, week 3 scouting the Chimera System.
Captain's log, Stardate: 35,301.
Still haven't found a planet in this sector worth cracking.
No Mineralarium means no money. No money means a cranky crew!
I'm getting cranky! And bored!
RECORDING
Outer space is cool and all...
...but I need some action!
SHHGNK
Action, huh?
I can help with that.
Science Officer Chambers, there are rules against fraternization on my ship!
There are?
Of course not!
Uh, Captain? We've got a... situation up here that needs your attention.
Dammit! I'll be right there!
Hold tight, dollface.
DOOT DOOT
Talk to me, Tuffie!
Captain, we're getting some strange readings out here.

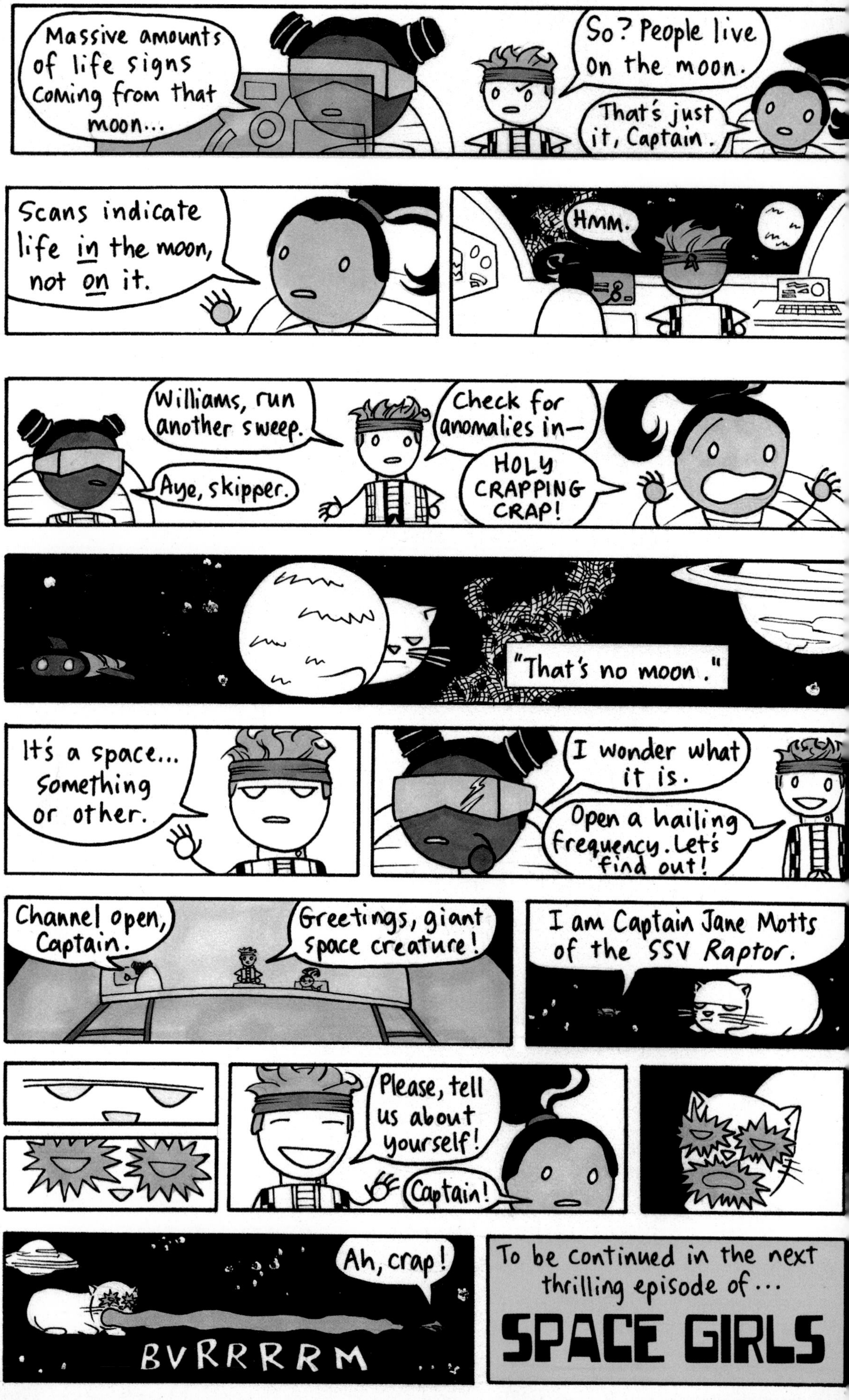
Massive amounts of life signs coming from that moon...
So? People live on the moon.
That's just it, Captain.
Scans indicate life in the moon, not on it.
Hmm.
Williams, run another sweep.
Aye, skipper.
Check for anomalies in—
HOLY CRAPPING CRAP!
"That's no moon."
It's a space... something or other.
I wonder what it is.
Open a hailing frequency. Let's find out!
Channel open, Captain.
Greetings, giant space creature!
I am Captain Jane Motts of the SSV Raptor.
Please, tell us about yourself!
Captain!
Ah, crap!
BVRRRRRM
To be continued in the next thrilling episode of...
SPACE GIRLS

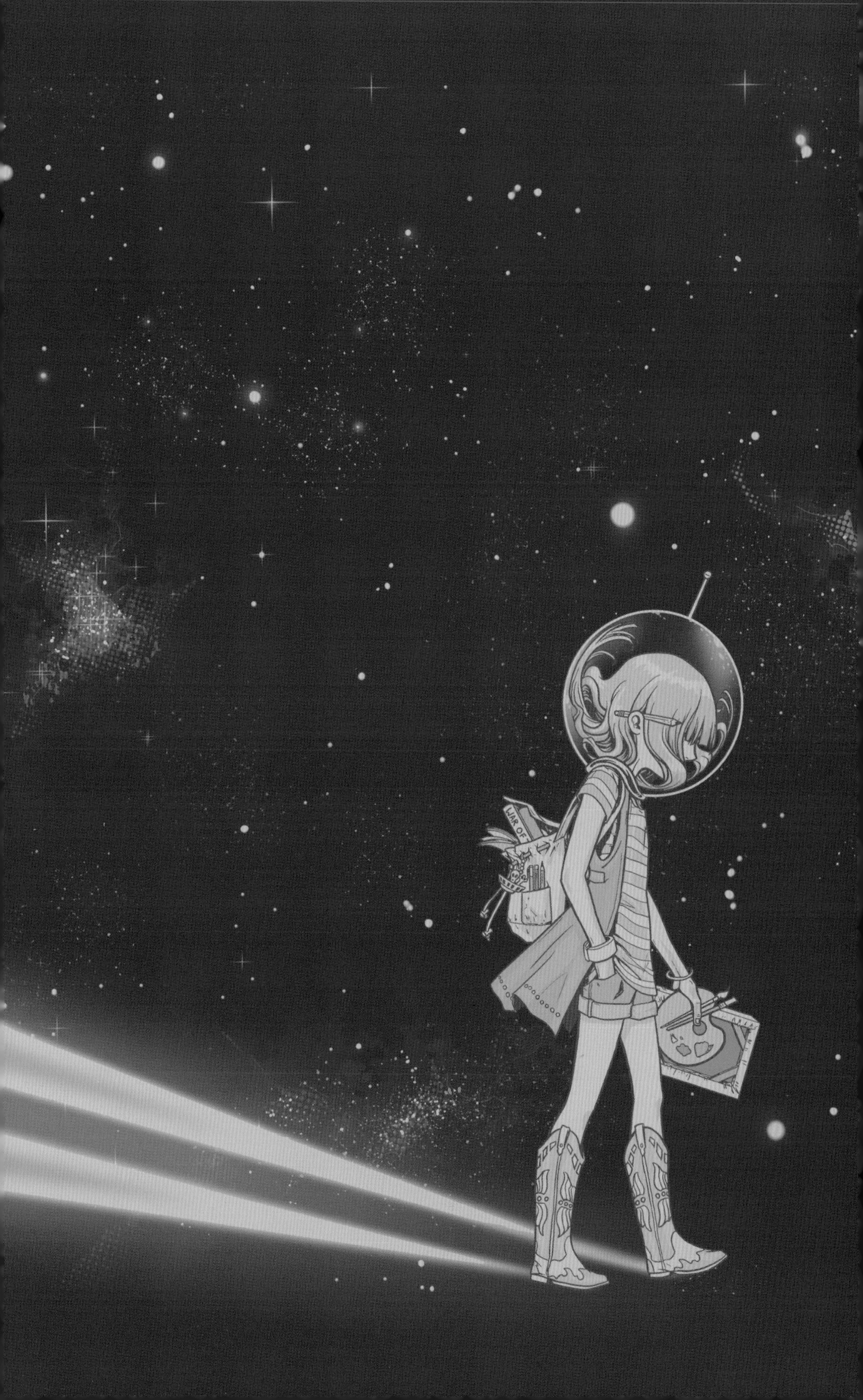
WAR OF

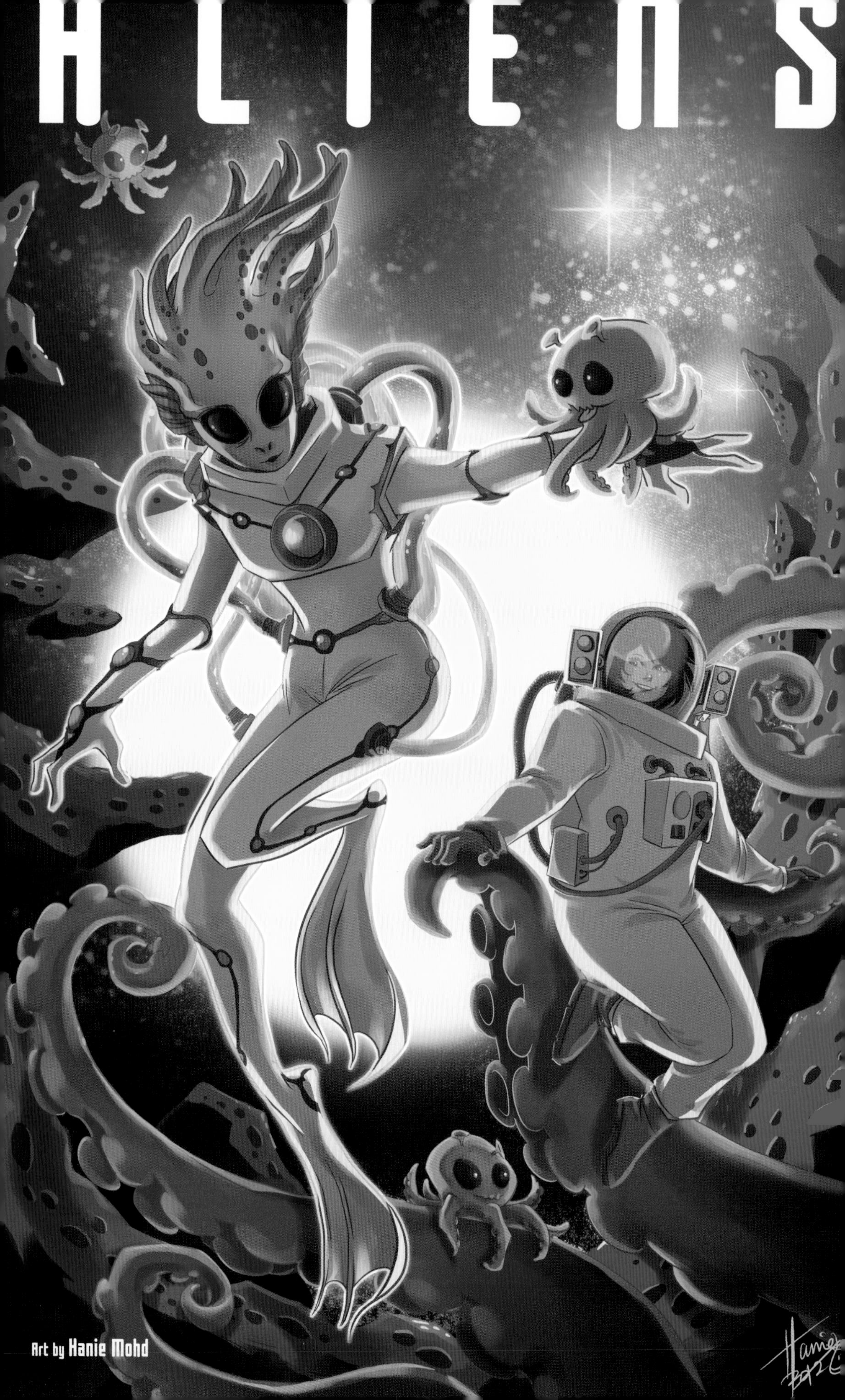
ALIENS
Art by Hanie Mohd

Чайка

IT IS *JUNE 16TH, 1963.*

VALENTINA TERESHKOVA, A FORMER TEXTILE-FACTORY WORKER, HAS JUST BECOME THE FIRST WOMAN IN SPACE.

HER SHIP, *VOSTOK-6,* WILL ORBIT THE EARTH FOR *2 DAYS, 22 HOURS, AND 50 MINUTES.*

SHE IS *26 YEARS OLD.*

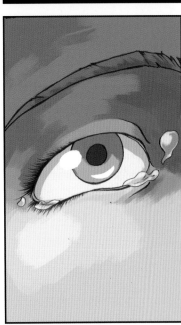

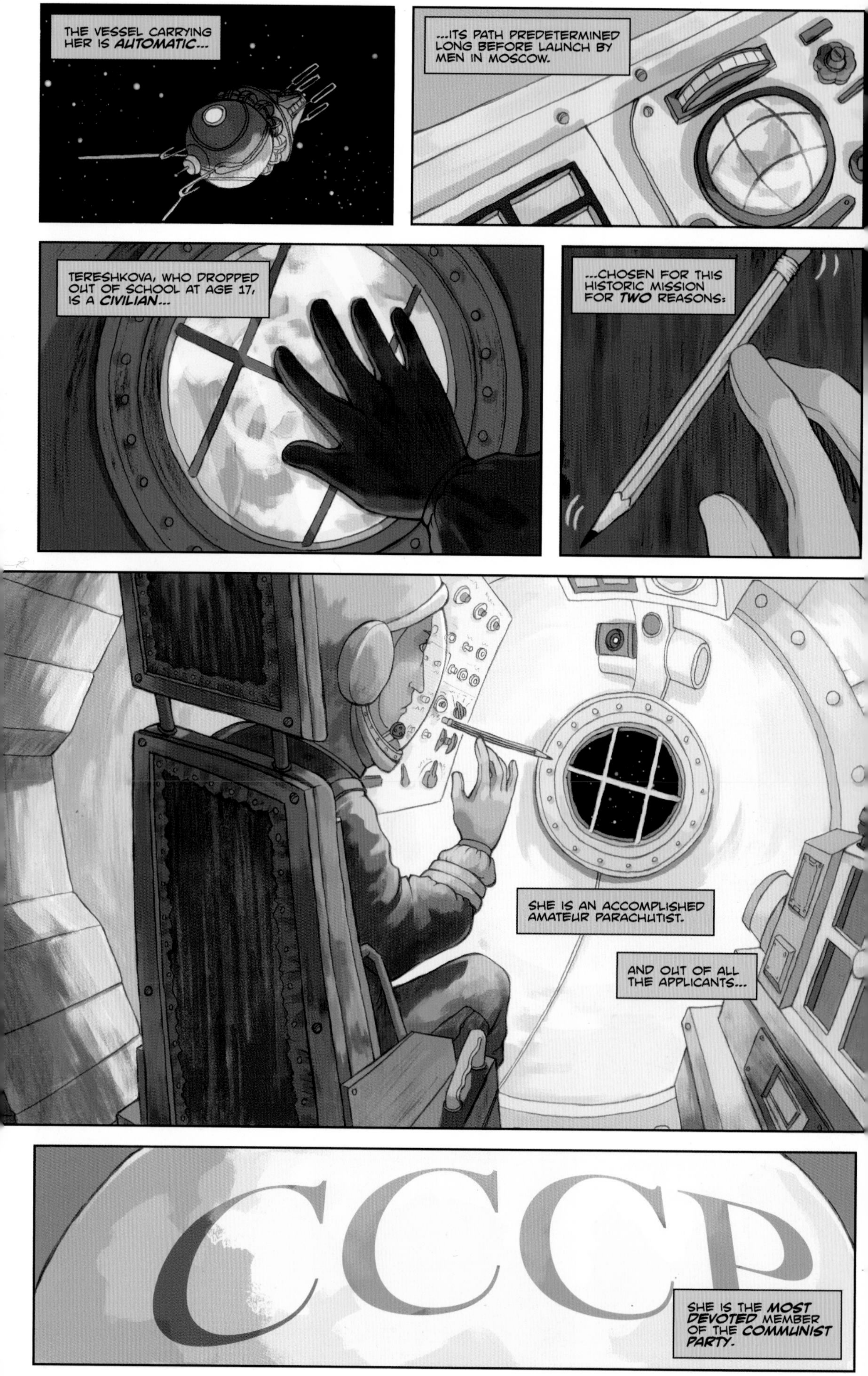
THE VESSEL CARRYING HER IS AUTOMATIC...
...ITS PATH PREDETERMINED LONG BEFORE LAUNCH BY MEN IN MOSCOW.
TERESHKOVA, WHO DROPPED OUT OF SCHOOL AT AGE 17, IS A CIVILIAN...
...CHOSEN FOR THIS HISTORIC MISSION FOR TWO REASONS:
SHE IS AN ACCOMPLISHED AMATEUR PARACHUTIST.
AND OUT OF ALL THE APPLICANTS...
CCCP
SHE IS THE MOST DEVOTED MEMBER OF THE COMMUNIST PARTY.

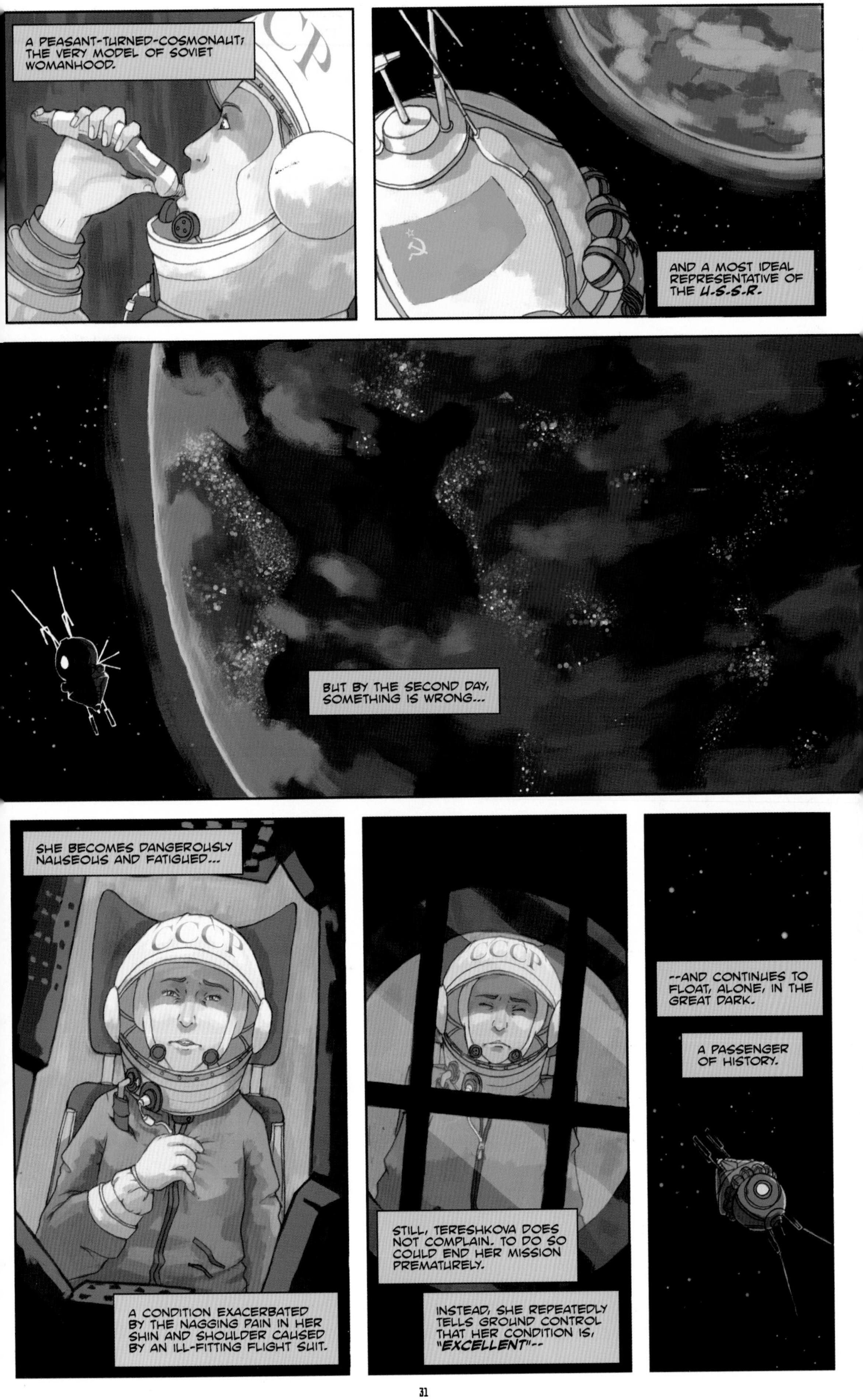
A PEASANT-TURNED-COSMONAUT; THE VERY MODEL OF SOVIET WOMANHOOD.
CCCP
AND A MOST IDEAL REPRESENTATIVE OF THE *U.S.S.R.*
BUT BY THE SECOND DAY, SOMETHING IS WRONG...
SHE BECOMES DANGEROUSLY NAUSEOUS AND FATIGUED...
CCCP
A CONDITION EXACERBATED BY THE NAGGING PAIN IN HER SHIN AND SHOULDER CAUSED BY AN ILL-FITTING FLIGHT SUIT.
CCCP
STILL, TERESHKOVA DOES NOT COMPLAIN. TO DO SO COULD END HER MISSION PREMATURELY.
INSTEAD, SHE REPEATEDLY TELLS GROUND CONTROL THAT HER CONDITION IS, "*EXCELLENT*"--
--AND CONTINUES TO FLOAT, ALONE, IN THE GREAT DARK.
A PASSENGER OF HISTORY.

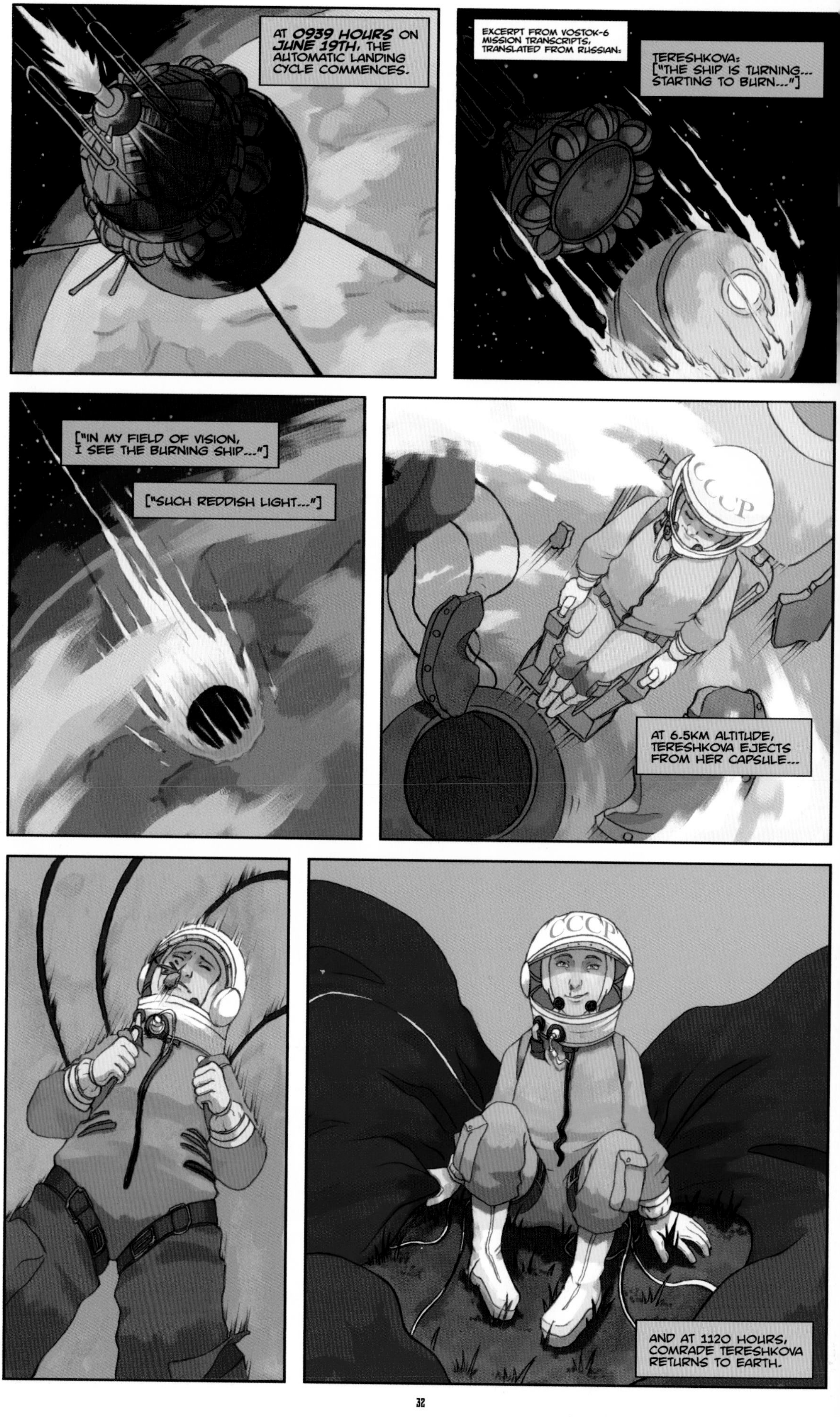
AT 0939 HOURS ON JUNE 19TH, THE AUTOMATIC LANDING CYCLE COMMENCES.
EXCERPT FROM VOSTOK-6 MISSION TRANSCRIPTS, TRANSLATED FROM RUSSIAN:
TERESHKOVA: ["THE SHIP IS TURNING... STARTING TO BURN..."]
["IN MY FIELD OF VISION, I SEE THE BURNING SHIP..."]
["SUCH REDDISH LIGHT..."]
CCCP
AT 6.5KM ALTITUDE, TERESHKOVA EJECTS FROM HER CAPSULE...
CCCP
AND AT 1120 HOURS, COMRADE TERESHKOVA RETURNS TO EARTH.

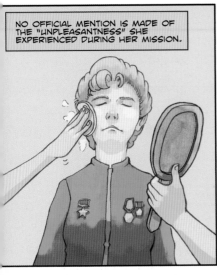

NO OFFICIAL MENTION IS MADE OF THE "UNPLEASANTNESS" SHE EXPERIENCED DURING HER MISSION.

VOSTOK-6 IS HAILED AS AN UNMITIGATED TRIUMPH...

...AND TERESHKOVA IS AWARDED THE TITLE, *"HERO OF THE SOVIET UNION."*

SIX MONTHS LATER, SHE MARRIES FELLOW COSMONAUT *ANDRIYAN NIKOLAYEV* AT A WEDDING CEREMONY PRESIDED OVER BY *NIKITA KHRUSHCHEV* HIMSELF.

RUMORS PERSIST THAT THEIR UNION HAS BEEN *ARRANGED;* A MASTERSTROKE OF SOVIET PROPAGANDA.

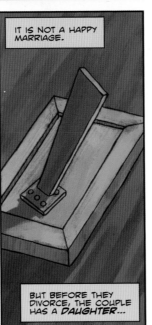

IT IS NOT A HAPPY MARRIAGE.

BUT BEFORE THEY DIVORCE, THE COUPLE HAS A *DAUGHTER*...

THE FIRST PERSON IN THE WORLD CONCEIVED BY TWO PEOPLE--

--WHO HAVE *BOTH* BEEN TO SPACE.

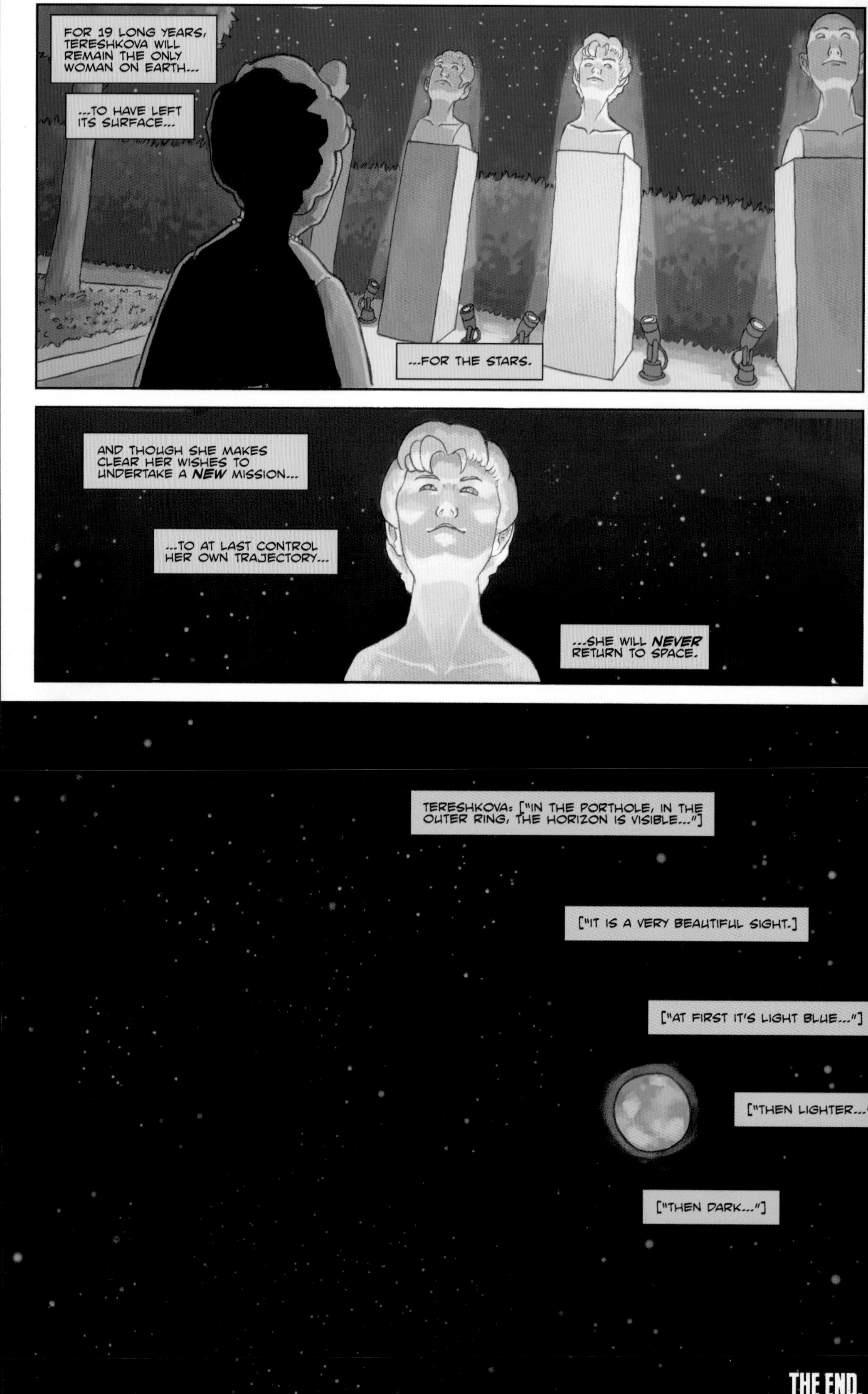
FOR 19 LONG YEARS, TERESHKOVA WILL REMAIN THE ONLY WOMAN ON EARTH...
...TO HAVE LEFT ITS SURFACE...
...FOR THE STARS.
AND THOUGH SHE MAKES CLEAR HER WISHES TO UNDERTAKE A NEW MISSION...
...TO AT LAST CONTROL HER OWN TRAJECTORY...
...SHE WILL NEVER RETURN TO SPACE.
TERESHKOVA: ["IN THE PORTHOLE, IN THE OUTER RING, THE HORIZON IS VISIBLE..."]
["IT IS A VERY BEAUTIFUL SIGHT.]
["AT FIRST IT'S LIGHT BLUE..."]
["THEN LIGHTER...
["THEN DARK..."]
THE END.

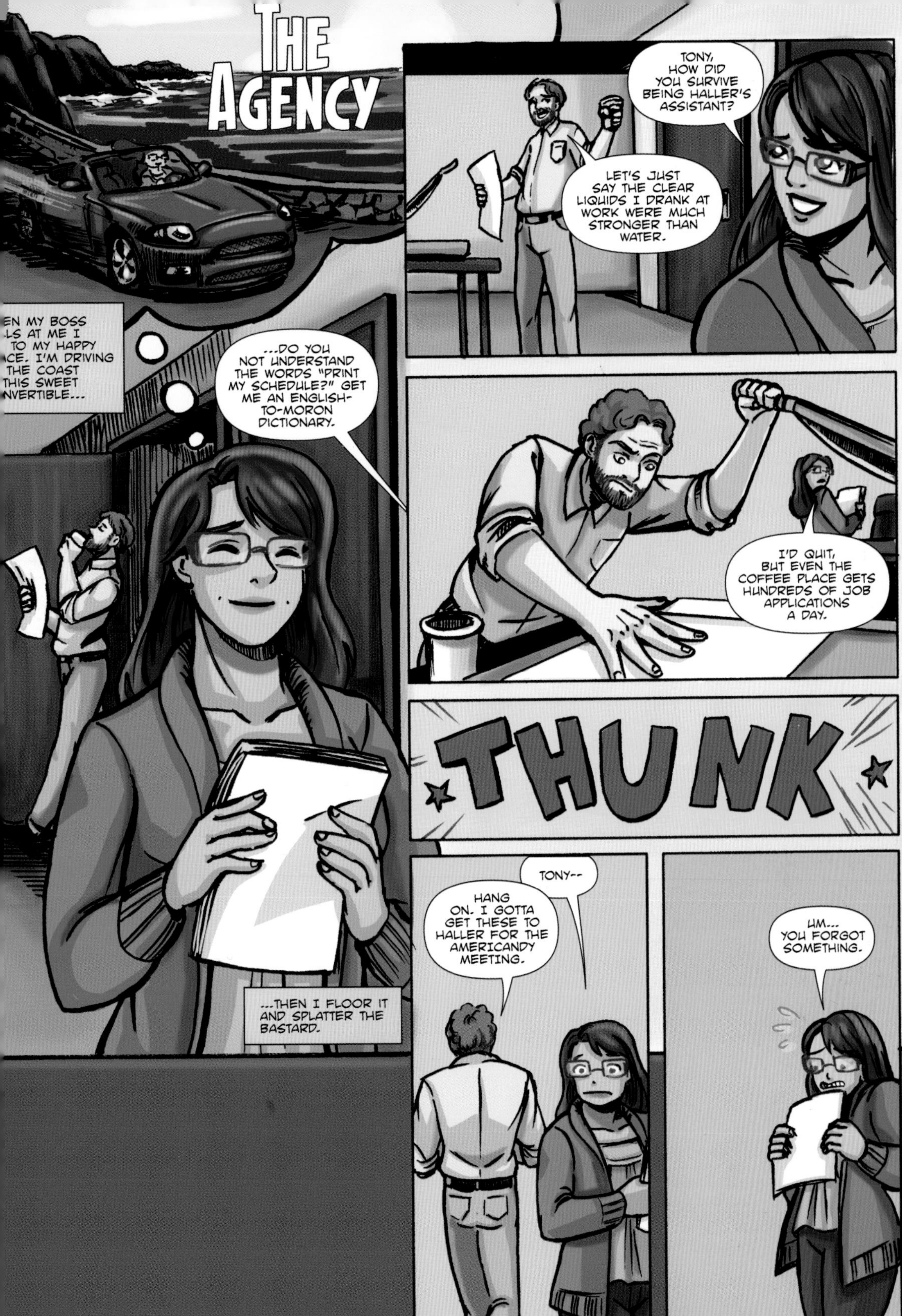
THE AGENCY
EN MY BOSS LS AT ME I TO MY HAPPY ACE. I'M DRIVING THE COAST THIS SWEET NVERTIBLE...
...DO YOU NOT UNDERSTAND THE WORDS "PRINT MY SCHEDULE?" GET ME AN ENGLISH-TO-MORON DICTIONARY.
...THEN I FLOOR IT AND SPLATTER THE BASTARD.
TONY, HOW DID YOU SURVIVE BEING HALLER'S ASSISTANT?
LET'S JUST SAY THE CLEAR LIQUIDS I DRANK AT WORK WERE MUCH STRONGER THAN WATER.
I'D QUIT, BUT EVEN THE COFFEE PLACE GETS HUNDREDS OF JOB APPLICATIONS A DAY.
THUNK
TONY--
HANG ON. I GOTTA GET THESE TO HALLER FOR THE AMERICANDY MEETING.
UM... YOU FORGOT SOMETHING.

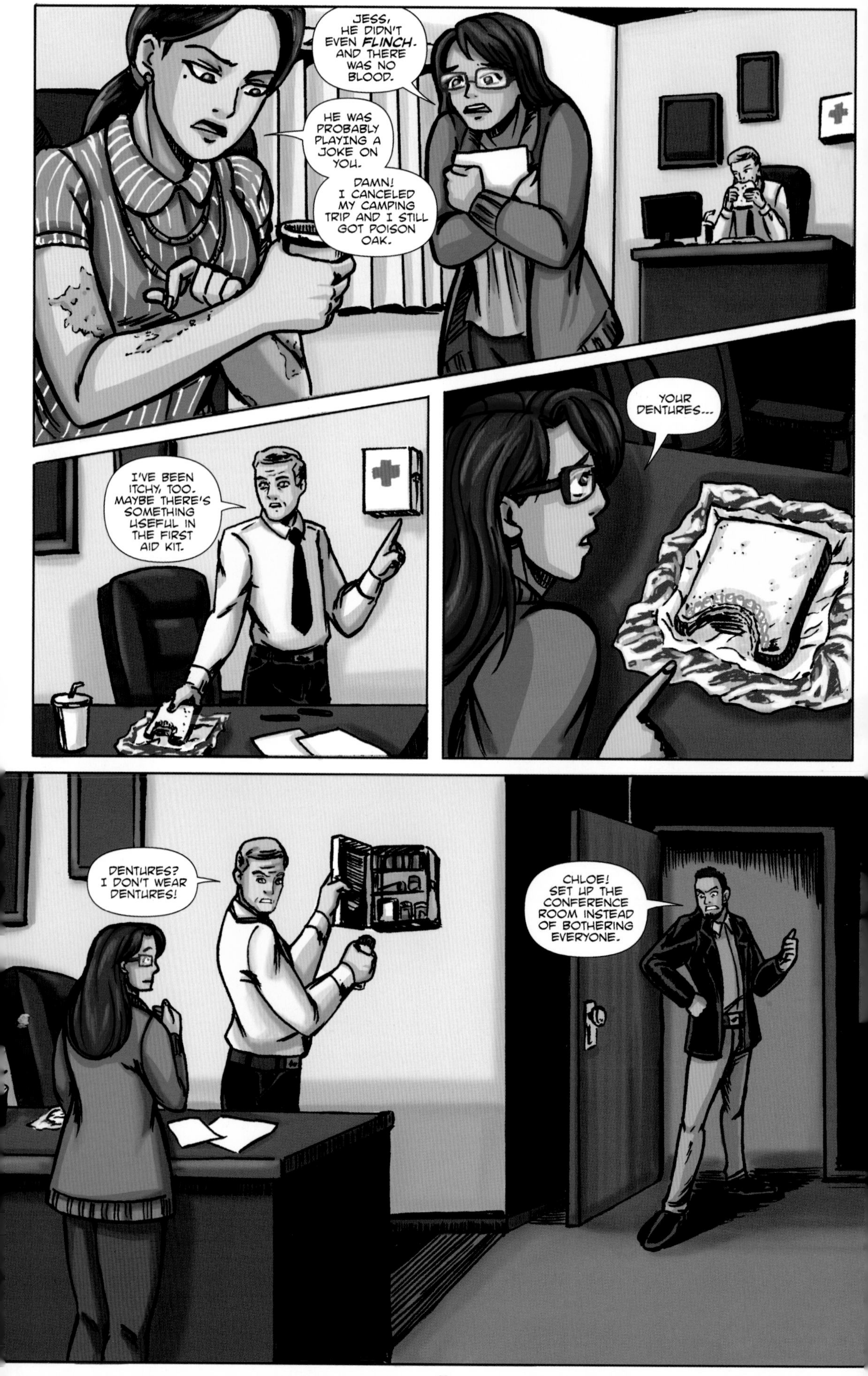
JESS, HE DIDN'T EVEN FLINCH. AND THERE WAS NO BLOOD.
HE WAS PROBABLY PLAYING A JOKE ON YOU.
DAMN! I CANCELED MY CAMPING TRIP AND I STILL GOT POISON OAK.
I'VE BEEN ITCHY, TOO. MAYBE THERE'S SOMETHING USEFUL IN THE FIRST AID KIT.
YOUR DENTURES...
DENTURES? I DON'T WEAR DENTURES!
CHLOE! SET UP THE CONFERENCE ROOM INSTEAD OF BOTHERING EVERYONE.

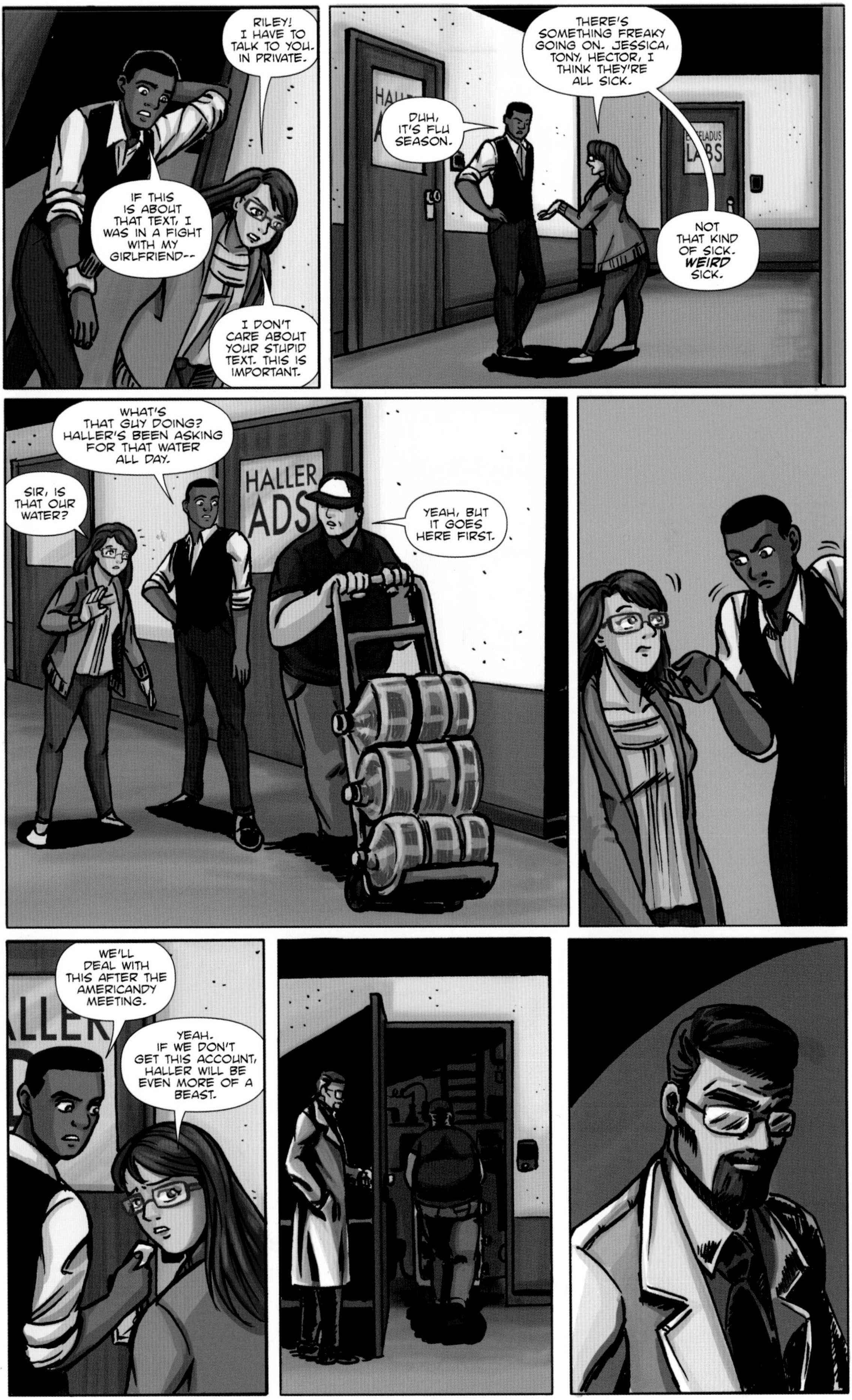
RILEY! I HAVE TO TALK TO YOU. IN PRIVATE.
IF THIS IS ABOUT THAT TEXT, I WAS IN A FIGHT WITH MY GIRLFRIEND--
I DON'T CARE ABOUT YOUR STUPID TEXT. THIS IS IMPORTANT.
THERE'S SOMETHING FREAKY GOING ON. JESSICA, TONY, HECTOR, I THINK THEY'RE ALL SICK.
DUH, IT'S FLU SEASON.
NOT THAT KIND OF SICK. **WEIRD** SICK.
WHAT'S THAT GUY DOING? HALLER'S BEEN ASKING FOR THAT WATER ALL DAY.
SIR, IS THAT OUR WATER?
HALLER ADS
YEAH, BUT IT GOES HERE FIRST.
WE'LL DEAL WITH THIS AFTER THE AMERICANDY MEETING.
YEAH. IF WE DON'T GET THIS ACCOUNT, HALLER WILL BE EVEN MORE OF A BEAST.

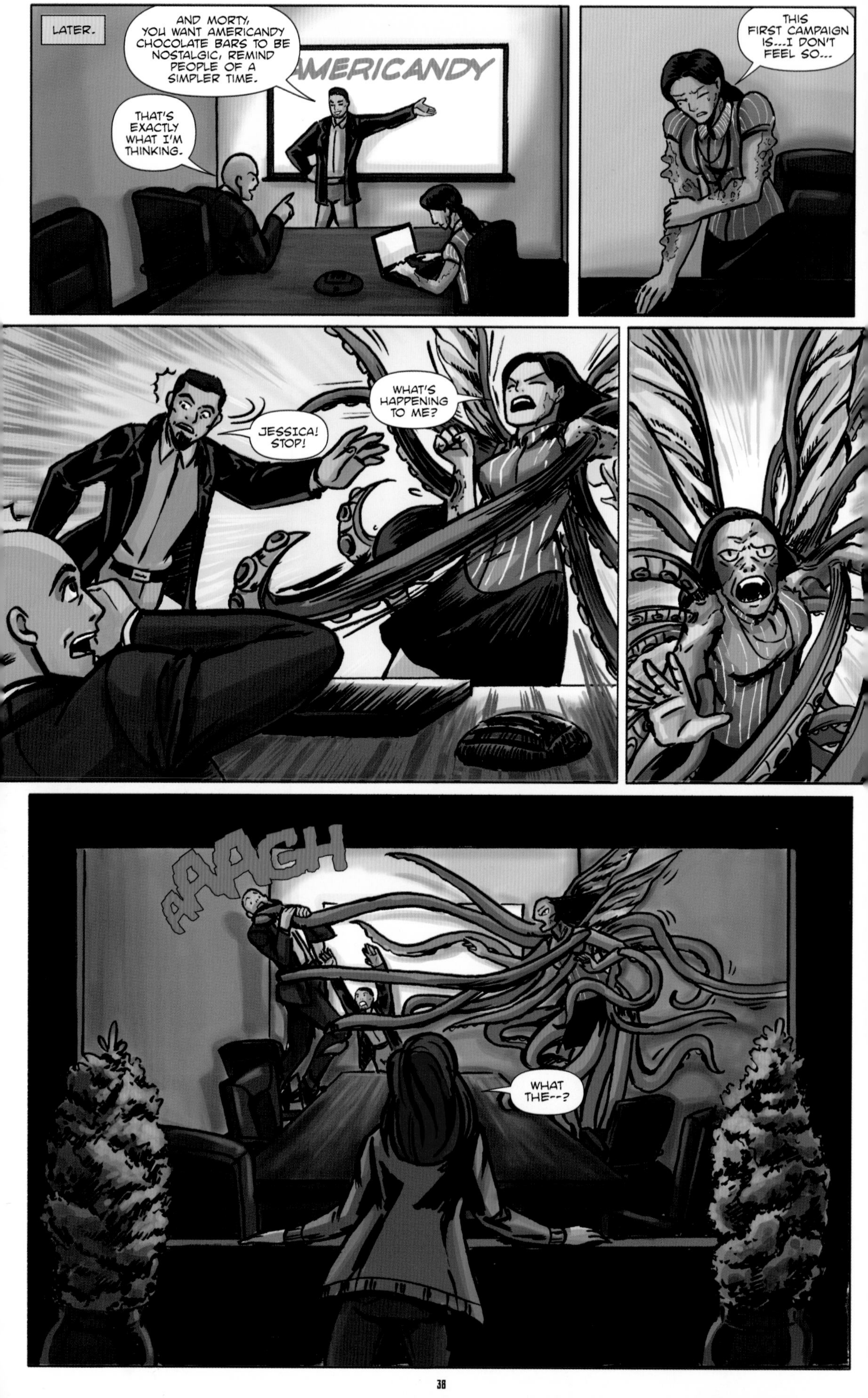
LATER.
AND MORTY, YOU WANT AMERICANDY CHOCOLATE BARS TO BE NOSTALGIC, REMIND PEOPLE OF A SIMPLER TIME.
AMERICANDY
THAT'S EXACTLY WHAT I'M THINKING.
THIS FIRST CAMPAIGN IS...I DON'T FEEL SO...
WHAT'S HAPPENING TO ME?
JESSICA! STOP!
RRAGH
WHAT THE--?

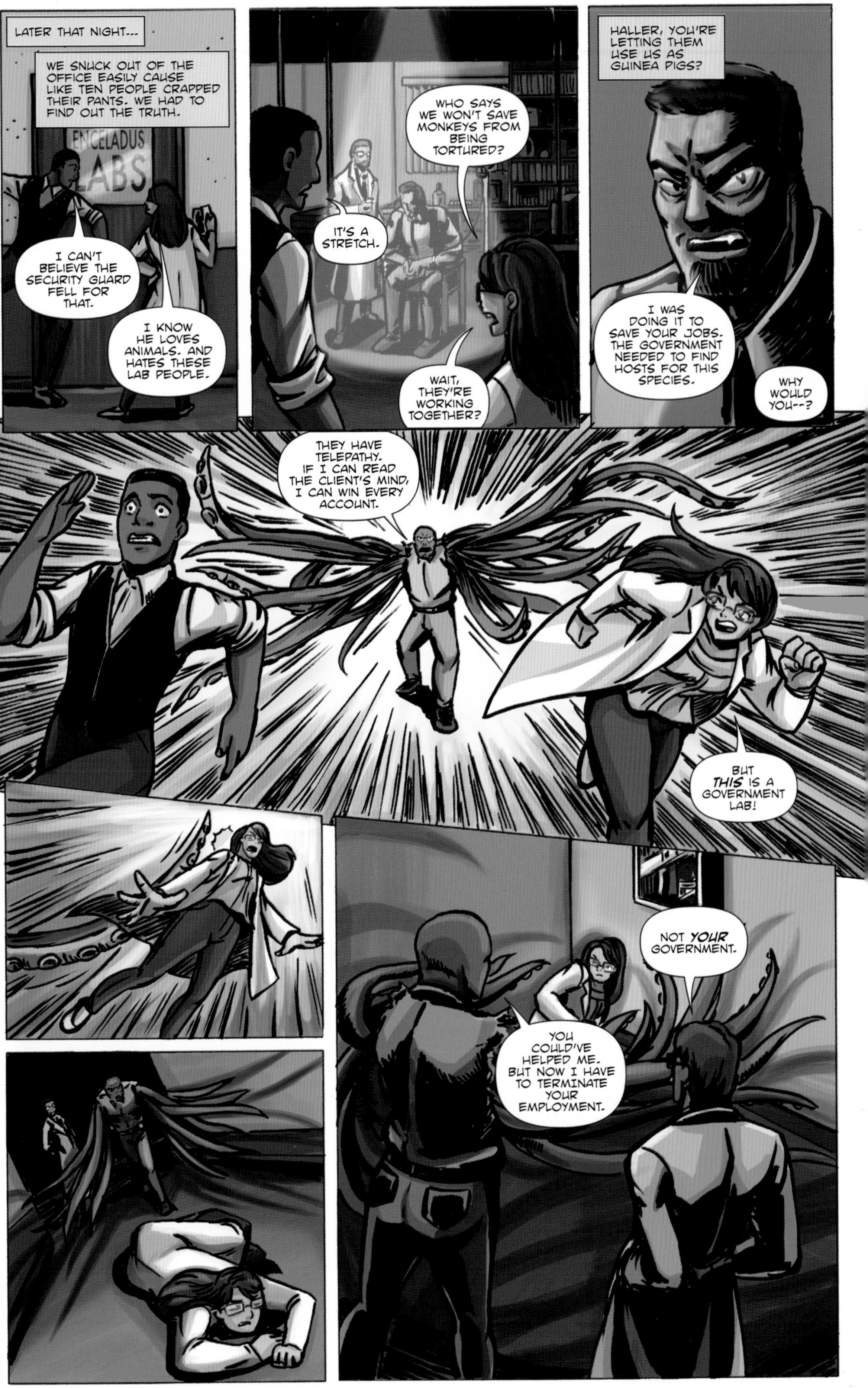
LATER THAT NIGHT...
WE SNUCK OUT OF THE OFFICE EASILY CAUSE LIKE TEN PEOPLE CRAPPED THEIR PANTS. WE HAD TO FIND OUT THE TRUTH.
ENCELADUS LABS
I CAN'T BELIEVE THE SECURITY GUARD FELL FOR THAT.
I KNOW HE LOVES ANIMALS. AND HATES THESE LAB PEOPLE.
WHO SAYS WE WON'T SAVE MONKEYS FROM BEING TORTURED?
IT'S A STRETCH.
WAIT, THEY'RE WORKING TOGETHER?
HALLER, YOU'RE LETTING THEM USE US AS GUINEA PIGS?
I WAS DOING IT TO SAVE YOUR JOBS. THE GOVERNMENT NEEDED TO FIND HOSTS FOR THIS SPECIES.
WHY WOULD YOU--?
THEY HAVE TELEPATHY. IF I CAN READ THE CLIENT'S MIND, I CAN WIN EVERY ACCOUNT.
BUT THIS IS A GOVERNMENT LAB!
NOT YOUR GOVERNMENT.
YOU COULD'VE HELPED ME. BUT NOW I HAVE TO TERMINATE YOUR EMPLOYMENT.

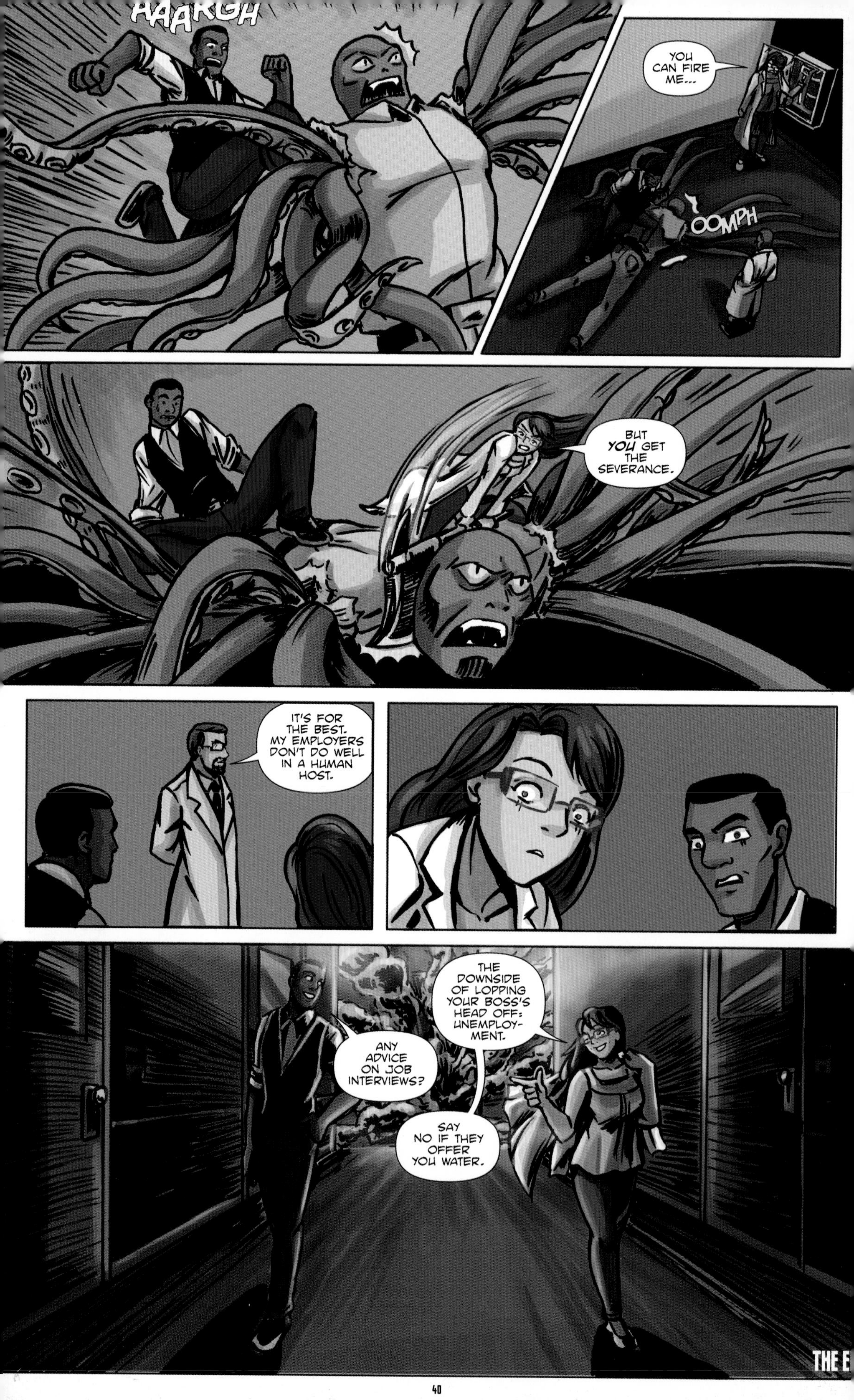
HAAARGH
YOU CAN FIRE ME...
OOMPH
BUT YOU GET THE SEVERANCE.
IT'S FOR THE BEST. MY EMPLOYERS DON'T DO WELL IN A HUMAN HOST.
THE DOWNSIDE OF LOPPING YOUR BOSS'S HEAD OFF: UNEMPLOYMENT.
ANY ADVICE ON JOB INTERVIEWS?
SAY NO IF THEY OFFER YOU WATER.
THE E

ALL CATS ARE QUANTUM

AFTER TOO MANY QUIET CYCLES OF NEGATIVE COMMUNICATION...

GZZZUUURRUUZZUURR

GNYAR! SSSST!

AWAY FROM THAT, THAT'S DELICATE EQUIPMENT! I'LL BE HERE FOREVER IF SOMETHING HAPPENS TO IT!

GZZZUUURRUUZ ZUURRRRRR

...EVERY SIGNAL WAS WORTHY OF REPORT, NO MATTER HOW WEAK.

"WE HAVE RECIEVED AN ANSWERING WAVE. I HAVE SENT MY FINDINGS TO THE CENTRAL TOWER AND WILL AWAIT FURTHER INSTRUCTIONS..."

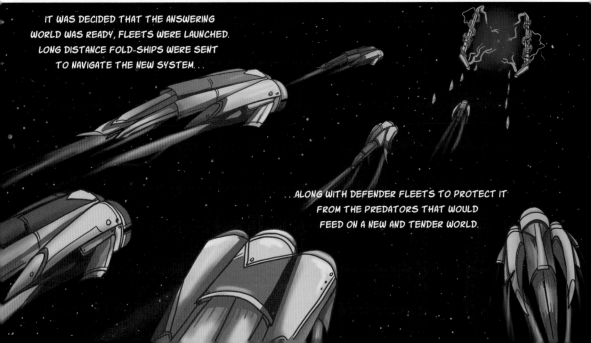

IT WAS DECIDED THAT THE ANSWERING WORLD WAS READY, FLEETS WERE LAUNCHED. LONG DISTANCE FOLD-SHIPS WERE SENT TO NAVIGATE THE NEW SYSTEM...

...ALONG WITH DEFENDER FLEETS TO PROTECT IT FROM THE PREDATORS THAT WOULD FEED ON A NEW AND TENDER WORLD.

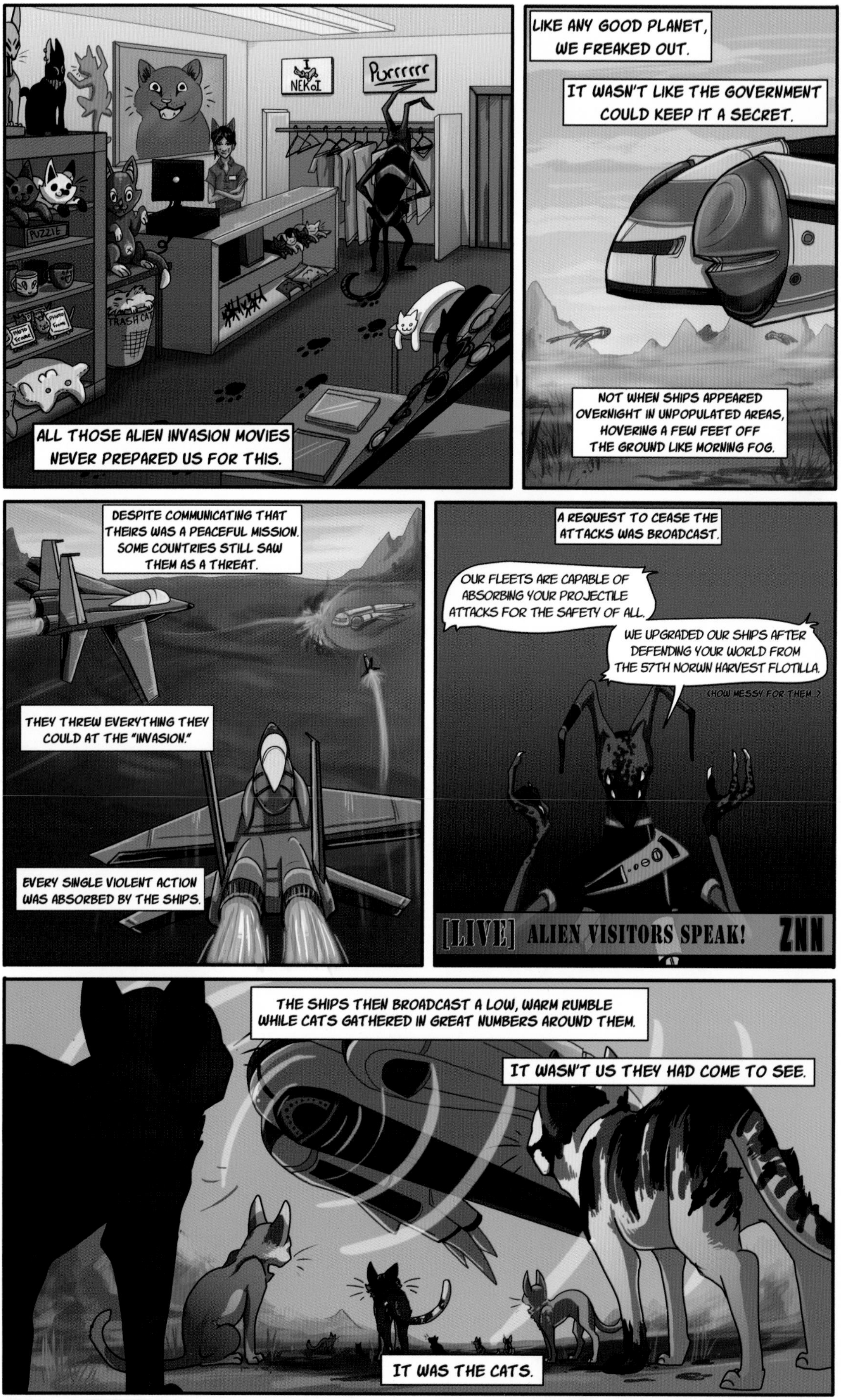
ALL THOSE ALIEN INVASION MOVIES NEVER PREPARED US FOR THIS.
LIKE ANY GOOD PLANET, WE FREAKED OUT.
IT WASN'T LIKE THE GOVERNMENT COULD KEEP IT A SECRET.
NOT WHEN SHIPS APPEARED OVERNIGHT IN UNPOPULATED AREAS, HOVERING A FEW FEET OFF THE GROUND LIKE MORNING FOG.
DESPITE COMMUNICATING THAT THEIRS WAS A PEACEFUL MISSION. SOME COUNTRIES STILL SAW THEM AS A THREAT.
THEY THREW EVERYTHING THEY COULD AT THE "INVASION."
EVERY SINGLE VIOLENT ACTION WAS ABSORBED BY THE SHIPS.
A REQUEST TO CEASE THE ATTACKS WAS BROADCAST.
OUR FLEETS ARE CAPABLE OF ABSORBING YOUR PROJECTILE ATTACKS FOR THE SAFETY OF ALL.
WE UPGRADED OUR SHIPS AFTER DEFENDING YOUR WORLD FROM THE 57TH NORWN HARVEST FLOTILLA.
(HOW MESSY FOR THEM...)
[LIVE] ALIEN VISITORS SPEAK! ZNN
THE SHIPS THEN BROADCAST A LOW, WARM RUMBLE WHILE CATS GATHERED IN GREAT NUMBERS AROUND THEM.
IT WASN'T US THEY HAD COME TO SEE.
IT WAS THE CATS.

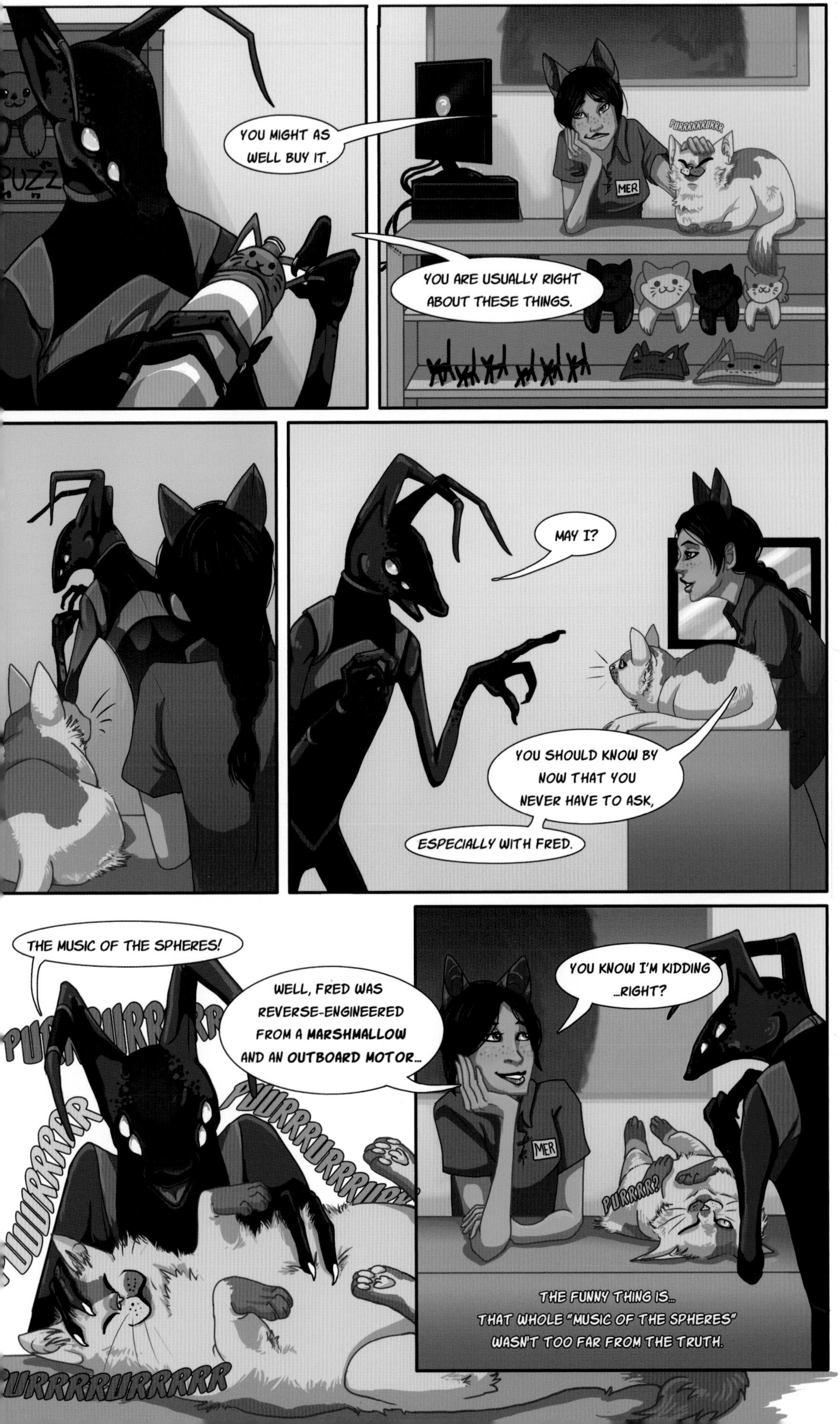

YOU MIGHT AS WELL BUY IT.
PURRRRRRRURRR
YOU ARE USUALLY RIGHT ABOUT THESE THINGS.
MAY I?
YOU SHOULD KNOW BY NOW THAT YOU NEVER HAVE TO ASK,
ESPECIALLY WITH FRED.
THE MUSIC OF THE SPHERES!
WELL, FRED WAS REVERSE-ENGINEERED FROM A MARSHMALLOW AND AN OUTBOARD MOTOR...
URRRRRURRRRRR
YOU KNOW I'M KIDDING ...RIGHT?
PURRRR?
THE FUNNY THING IS... THAT WHOLE "MUSIC OF THE SPHERES" WASN'T TOO FAR FROM THE TRUTH.

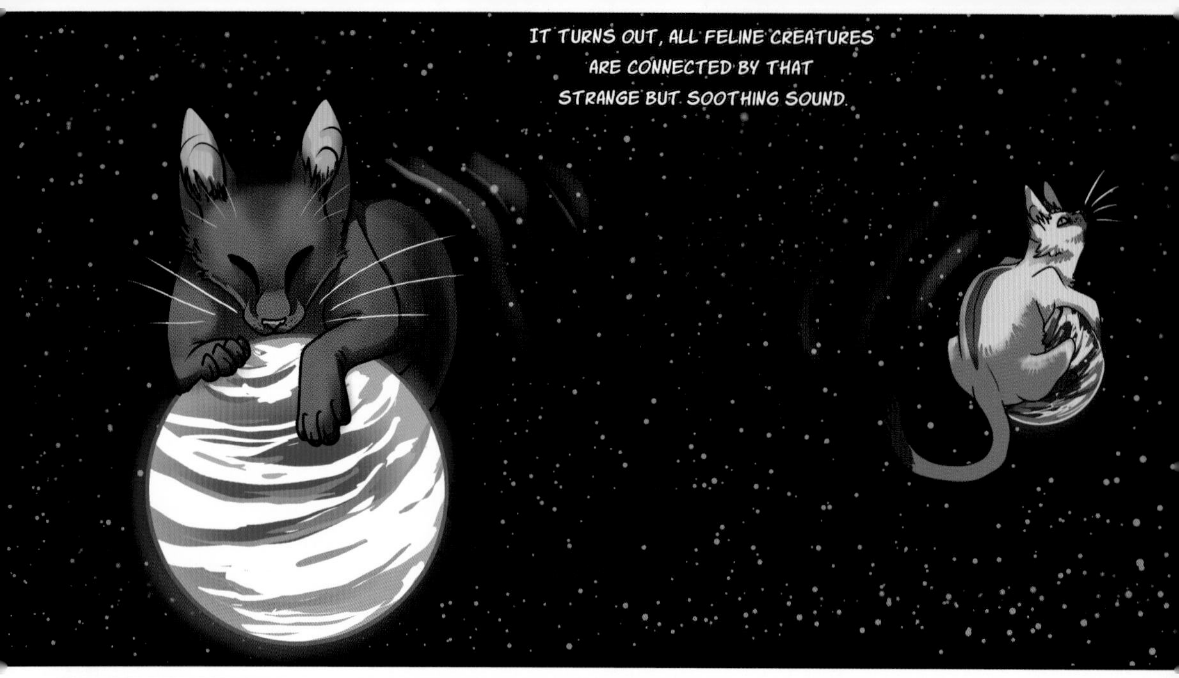
IT TURNS OUT, ALL FELINE CREATURES ARE CONNECTED BY THAT STRANGE BUT SOOTHING SOUND.

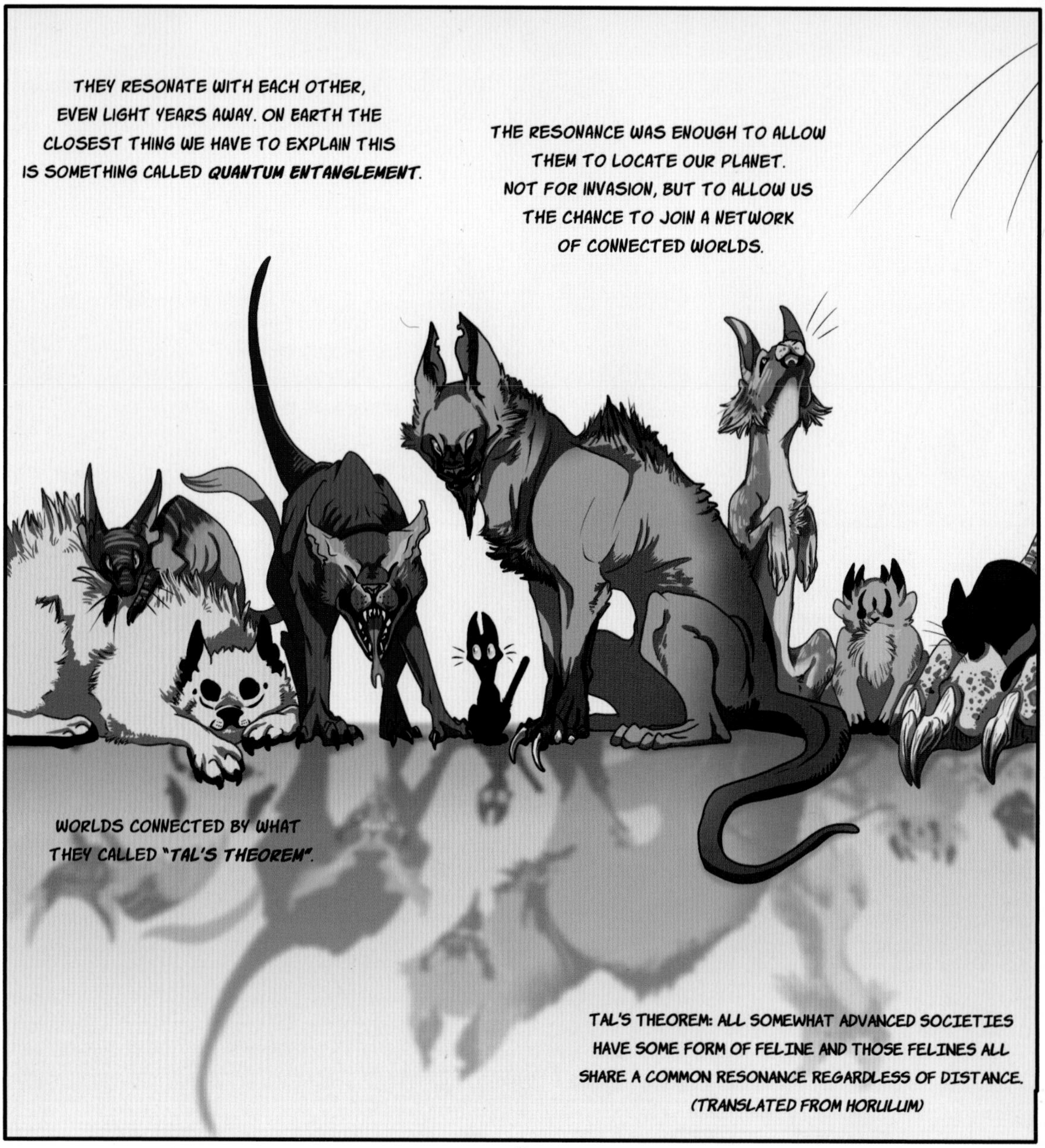
THEY RESONATE WITH EACH OTHER, EVEN LIGHT YEARS AWAY. ON EARTH THE CLOSEST THING WE HAVE TO EXPLAIN THIS IS SOMETHING CALLED QUANTUM ENTANGLEMENT.
THE RESONANCE WAS ENOUGH TO ALLOW THEM TO LOCATE OUR PLANET. NOT FOR INVASION, BUT TO ALLOW US THE CHANCE TO JOIN A NETWORK OF CONNECTED WORLDS.
WORLDS CONNECTED BY WHAT THEY CALLED "TAL'S THEOREM".
TAL'S THEOREM: ALL SOMEWHAT ADVANCED SOCIETIES HAVE SOME FORM OF FELINE AND THOSE FELINES ALL SHARE A COMMON RESONANCE REGARDLESS OF DISTANCE.
(TRANSLATED FROM HORULUM)

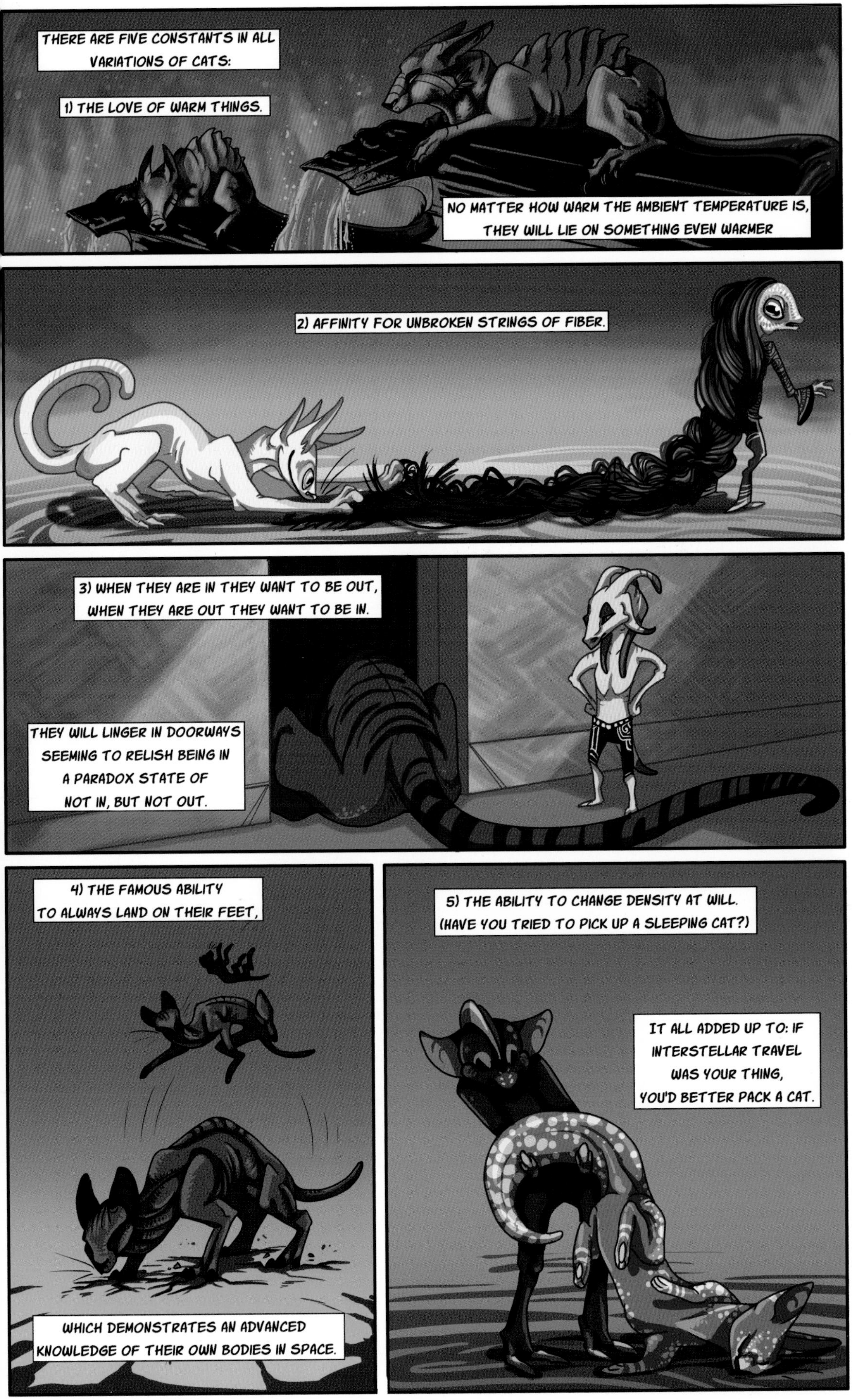
THERE ARE FIVE CONSTANTS IN ALL VARIATIONS OF CATS:
1) THE LOVE OF WARM THINGS.
NO MATTER HOW WARM THE AMBIENT TEMPERATURE IS, THEY WILL LIE ON SOMETHING EVEN WARMER
2) AFFINITY FOR UNBROKEN STRINGS OF FIBER.
3) WHEN THEY ARE IN THEY WANT TO BE OUT, WHEN THEY ARE OUT THEY WANT TO BE IN.
THEY WILL LINGER IN DOORWAYS SEEMING TO RELISH BEING IN A PARADOX STATE OF NOT IN, BUT NOT OUT.
4) THE FAMOUS ABILITY TO ALWAYS LAND ON THEIR FEET,
WHICH DEMONSTRATES AN ADVANCED KNOWLEDGE OF THEIR OWN BODIES IN SPACE.
5) THE ABILITY TO CHANGE DENSITY AT WILL. (HAVE YOU TRIED TO PICK UP A SLEEPING CAT?)
IT ALL ADDED UP TO: IF INTERSTELLAR TRAVEL WAS YOUR THING, YOU'D BETTER PACK A CAT.

I ENDED UP TAKING THE TESTS TO JOIN THE CREW OF THE SEKHMET...

...THE FIRST SHIP TO TRANSPORT EARTH CATS TO OTHER WORLDS SO WE COULD BEGIN TRADE AND EXPLORATION OF CONNECTED WORLDS.

I PASSED.

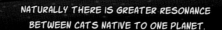

NATURALLY THERE IS GREATER RESONANCE BETWEEN CATS NATIVE TO ONE PLANET.

ONCE WE HAVE ENOUGH ON H-12 THE SIGNAL WILL BE STRONG ENOUGH FOR STABLE TRAVEL BETWEEN IT AND EARTH.

IT'S WHY EARTH IS NOW HOST TO AT LEAST 3 NEW BREEDS AND WHY I'M ON A SHIP CARRYING EARTH-RESONANT FELINES TO A PLANET ON THE OTHER SIDE OF THE NEAREST FOLD-PORT.

REMEMBER THAT 4TH CONSTANT?

TURNS OUT THEY'RE THE BEST THING TO HAVE AROUND WHEN FOLDING SPACE TO GET FROM ONE GALAXY TO THE NEXT.

THEY JUST KNOW.

THE END.

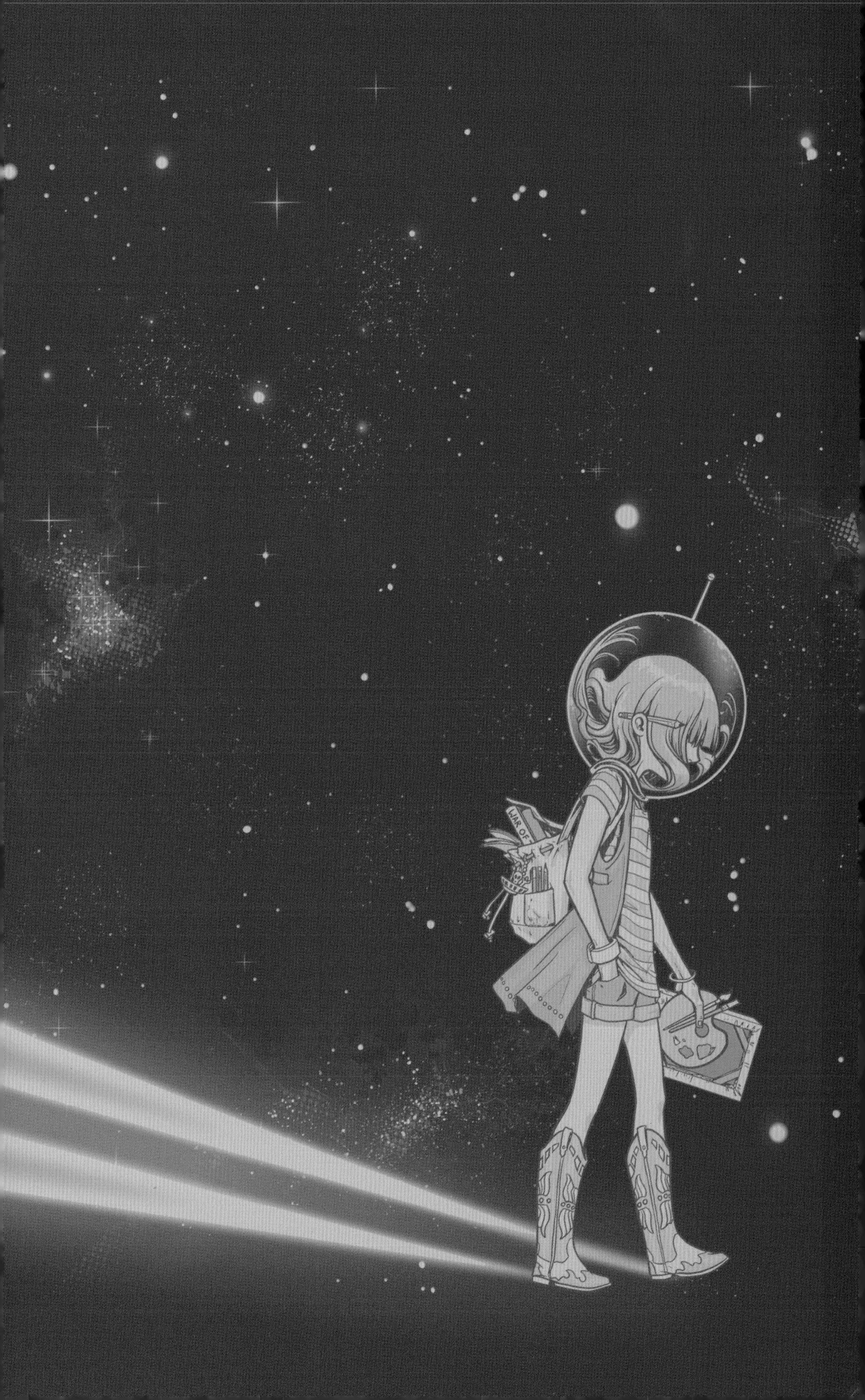
WAR OF

S H I P

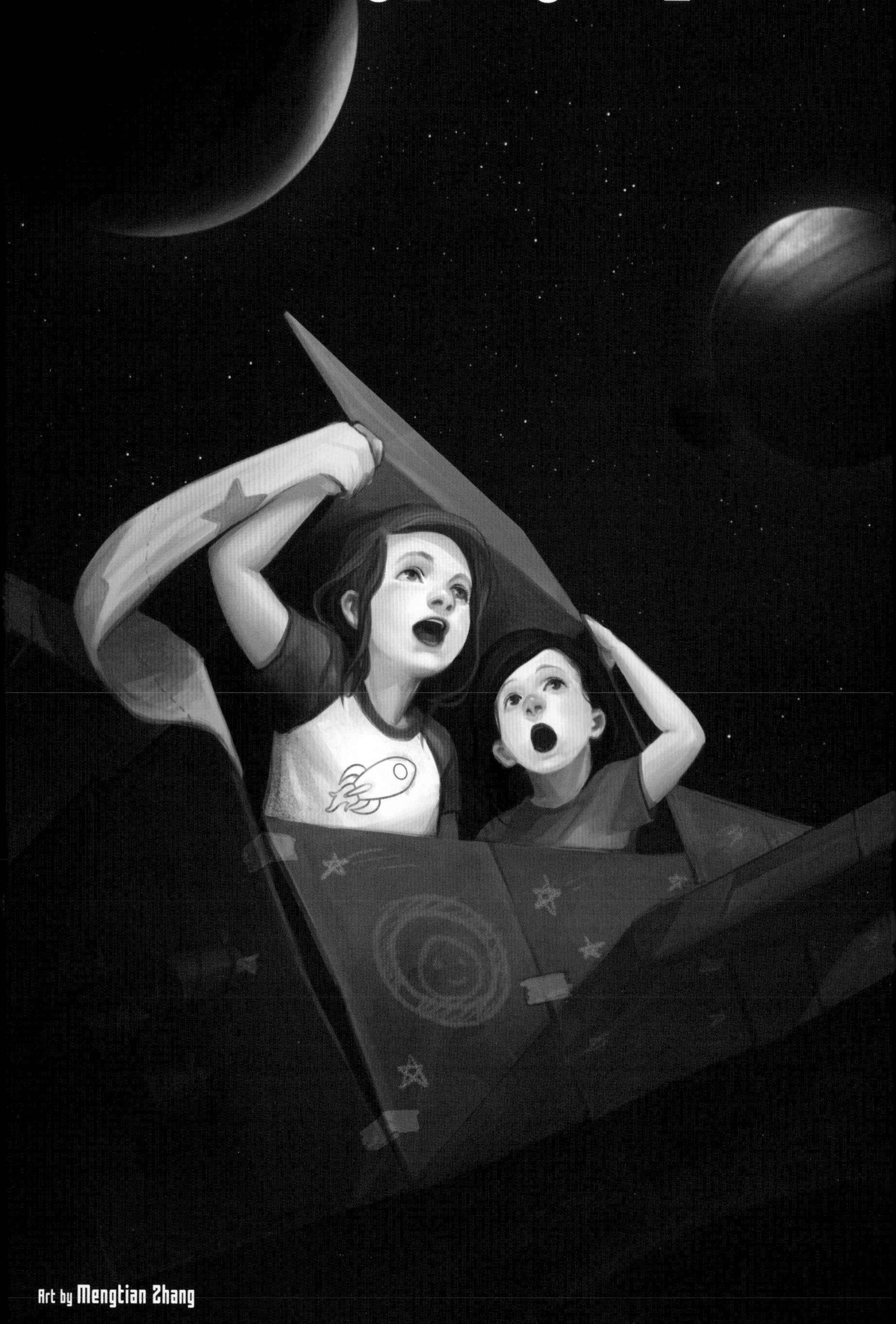

Art by Mengtian Zhang

CENTIPEDE

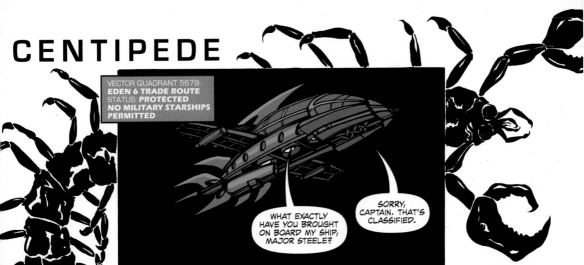

VECTOR QUADRANT 5679:
EDEN 6 TRADE ROUTE
STATUS: **PROTECTED**
NO MILITARY STARSHIPS PERMITTED

WHAT EXACTLY HAVE YOU BROUGHT ON BOARD MY SHIP, MAJOR STEELE?

SORRY, CAPTAIN. THAT'S CLASSIFIED.

CLASSIFIED MIGHT WORK ON AN ARMY VESSEL, MAJOR, BUT THIS IS A CIVILIAN CARGO SHIP. THE ONLY THING I'M CONTRACTED TO TRANSPORT IS ORGANIC MATTER FROM EDEN 6.

SO WHO SAYS YOUR CONTRACT HAS BEEN BROKEN?

I HAVE MY SOURCES.

IF YOU'RE SO INTERESTED, GO OPEN THE STORAGE VESSELS.

YOU'LL GIVE ME THE CODE?

I CAN'T STOP YOU FROM BUSTING THE LOCKS. BUT I WILL TELL YOU THIS—

—INTERFERE AND YOU WILL BE ARRESTED WHEN WE DOCK AT EARTH PORT 23.

ON WHAT GROUNDS?

SMUGGLING.

I HAVE ENOUGH EVIDENCE TO IMPRISON YOU AND YOUR CREW ON PLANET GULAG FOR LIFE.

I WON'T LET YOU THREATEN MY SHIP, MY CREW, OR ME.

LET ME DO MY JOB AND I'LL LET YOU DO YOURS.

THIS ISN'T OVER, MAJOR.

I DIDN'T THINK IT WOULD BE, MY PRETTY CAPTAIN.

SHE CAN'T STOP US, CAN SHE MY FIERCE LITTLE FRIEND?

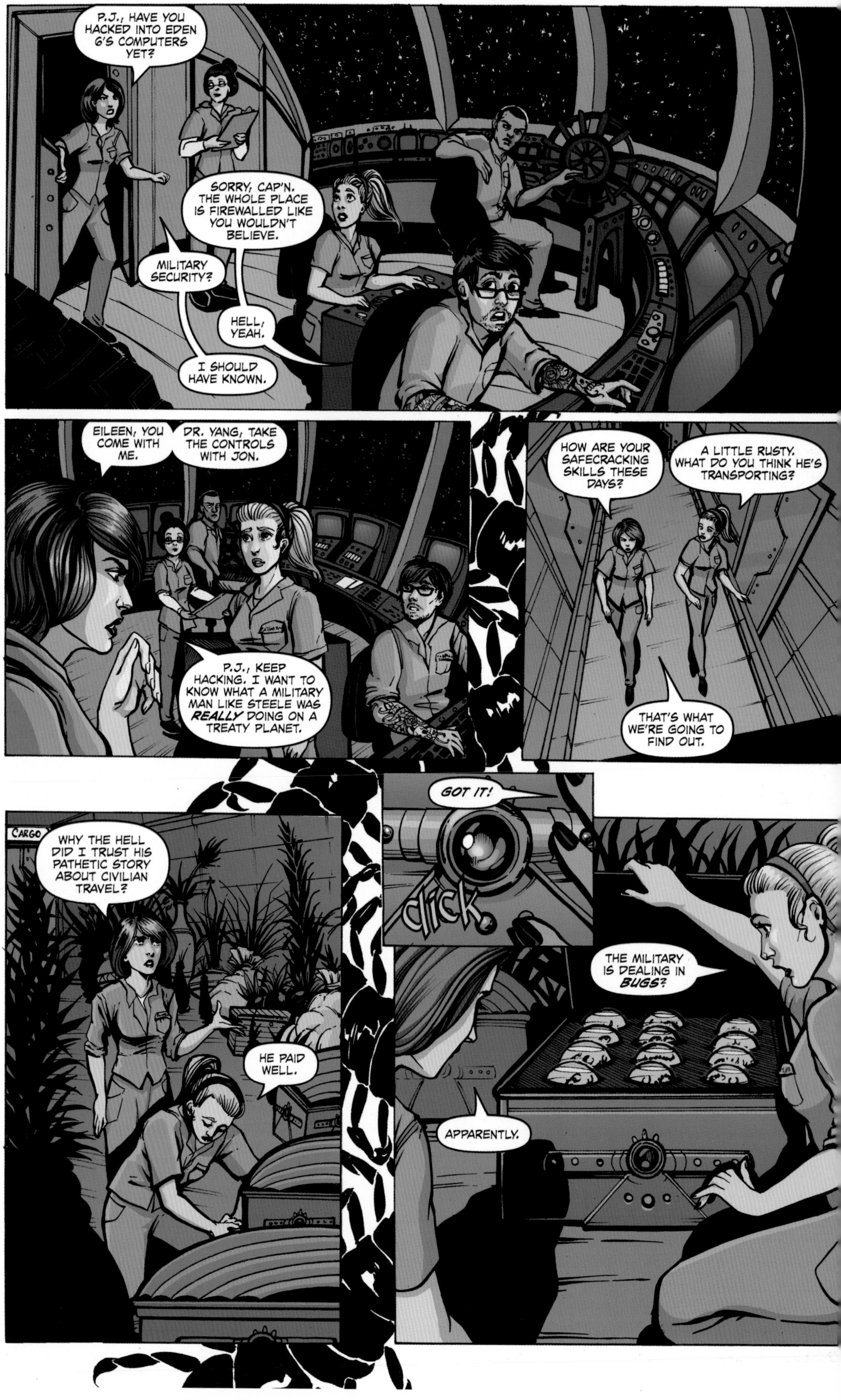
P.J., HAVE YOU HACKED INTO EDEN 6'S COMPUTERS YET?
SORRY, CAP'N. THE WHOLE PLACE IS FIREWALLED LIKE YOU WOULDN'T BELIEVE.
MILITARY SECURITY?
HELL, YEAH.
I SHOULD HAVE KNOWN.
EILEEN, YOU COME WITH ME.
DR. YANG, TAKE THE CONTROLS WITH JON.
P.J., KEEP HACKING. I WANT TO KNOW WHAT A MILITARY MAN LIKE STEELE WAS *REALLY* DOING ON A TREATY PLANET.
HOW ARE YOUR SAFECRACKING SKILLS THESE DAYS?
A LITTLE RUSTY. WHAT DO YOU THINK HE'S TRANSPORTING?
THAT'S WHAT WE'RE GOING TO FIND OUT.
CARGO
WHY THE HELL DID I TRUST HIS PATHETIC STORY ABOUT CIVILIAN TRAVEL?
HE PAID WELL.
GOT IT!
click.
THE MILITARY IS DEALING IN *BUGS*?
APPARENTLY.

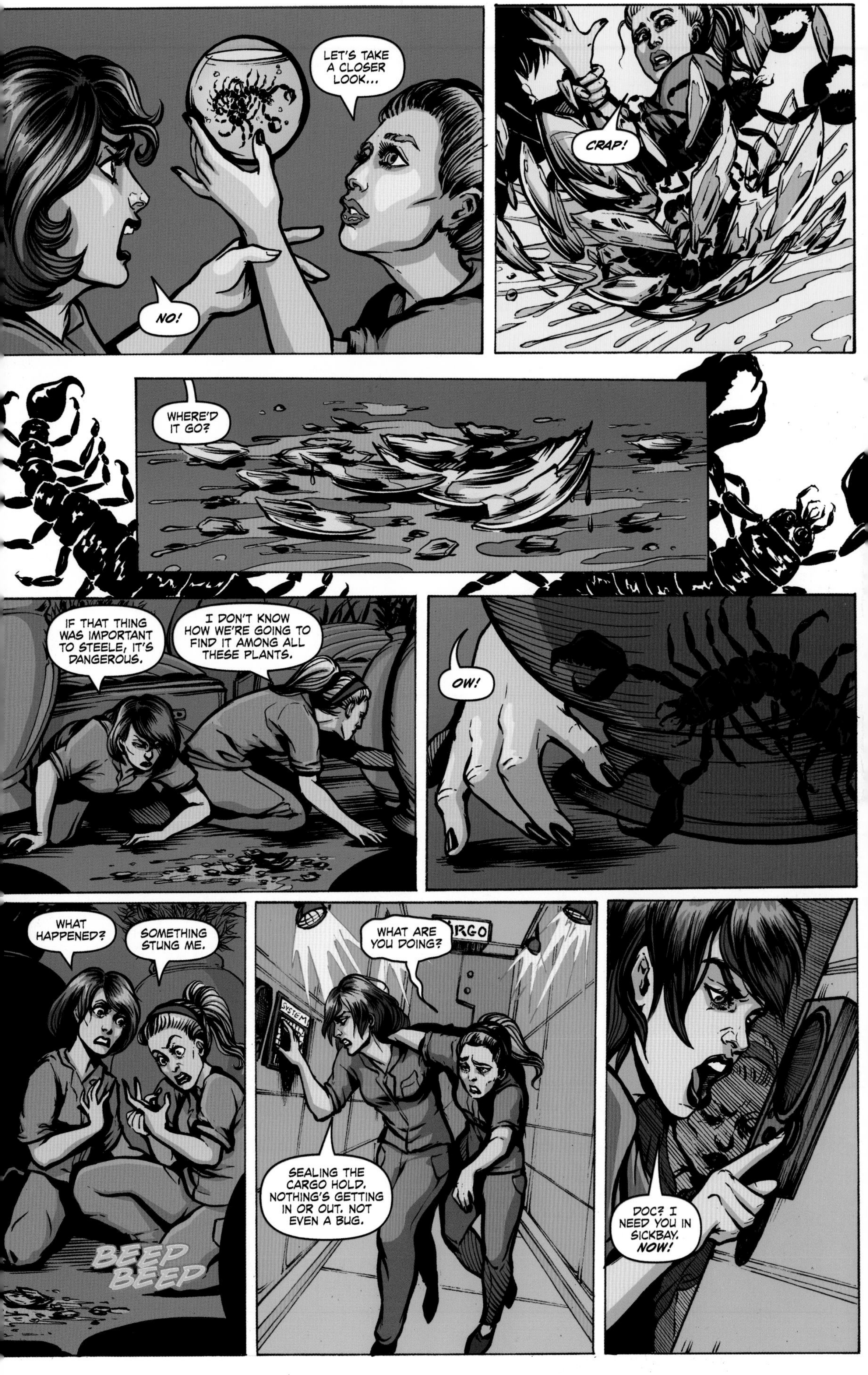

LET'S TAKE A CLOSER LOOK...
NO!
CRAP!
WHERE'D IT GO?
IF THAT THING WAS IMPORTANT TO STEELE, IT'S DANGEROUS.
I DON'T KNOW HOW WE'RE GOING TO FIND IT AMONG ALL THESE PLANTS.
OW!
WHAT HAPPENED?
SOMETHING STUNG ME.
BEEP BEEP
WHAT ARE YOU DOING?
SYSTEM
SEALING THE CARGO HOLD. NOTHING'S GETTING IN OR OUT. NOT EVEN A BUG.
DOC? I NEED YOU IN SICKBAY. NOW!

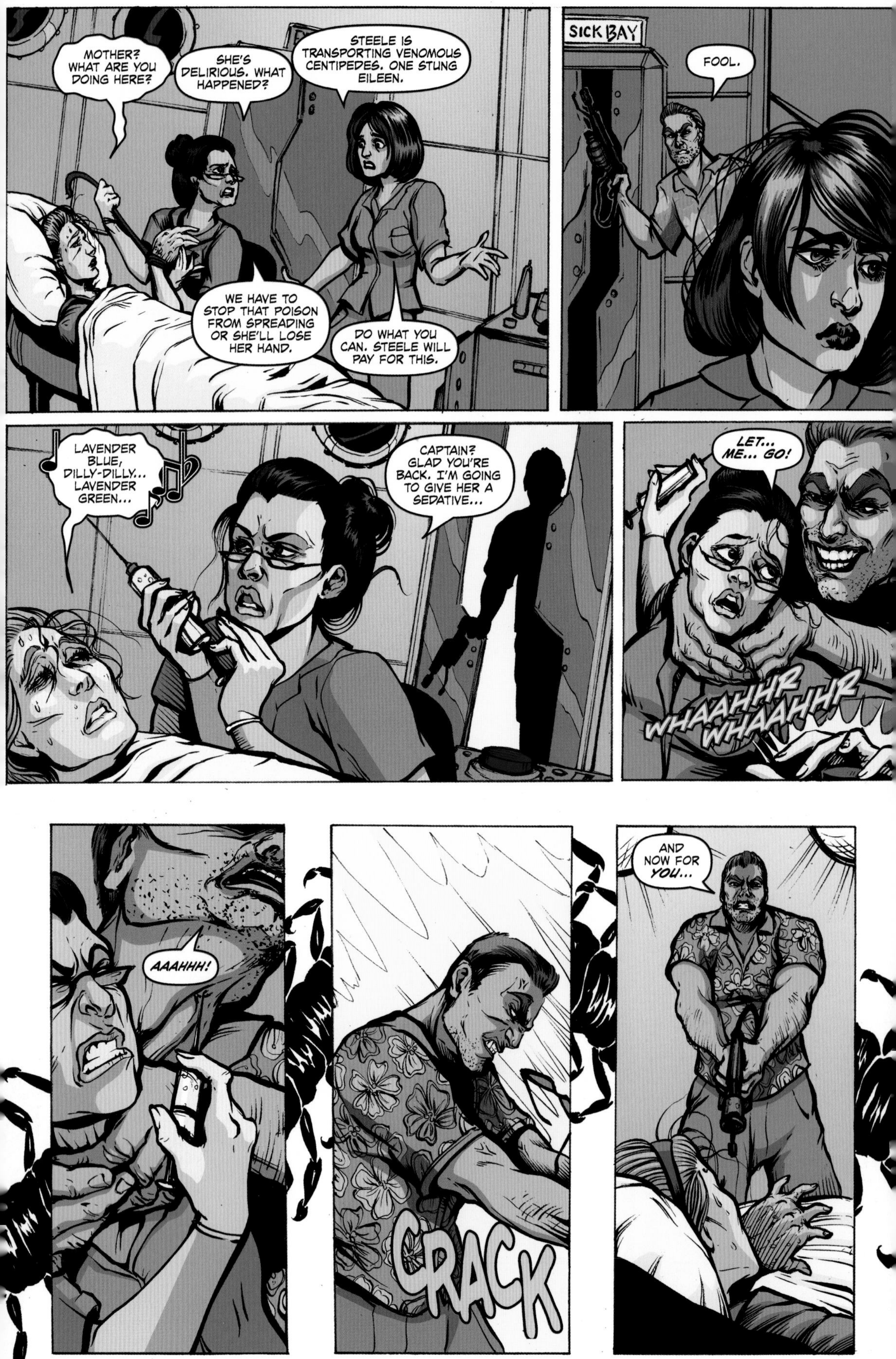
MOTHER? WHAT ARE YOU DOING HERE?
SHE'S DELIRIOUS. WHAT HAPPENED?
STEELE IS TRANSPORTING VENOMOUS CENTIPEDES. ONE STUNG EILEEN.
WE HAVE TO STOP THAT POISON FROM SPREADING OR SHE'LL LOSE HER HAND.
DO WHAT YOU CAN. STEELE WILL PAY FOR THIS.
SICK BAY
FOOL.
LAVENDER BLUE, DILLY-DILLY... LAVENDER GREEN...
CAPTAIN? GLAD YOU'RE BACK. I'M GOING TO GIVE HER A SEDATIVE...
LET... ME... GO!
WHAAAHHR WHAAAHHR
AAAHHH!
CRACK
AND NOW FOR YOU...

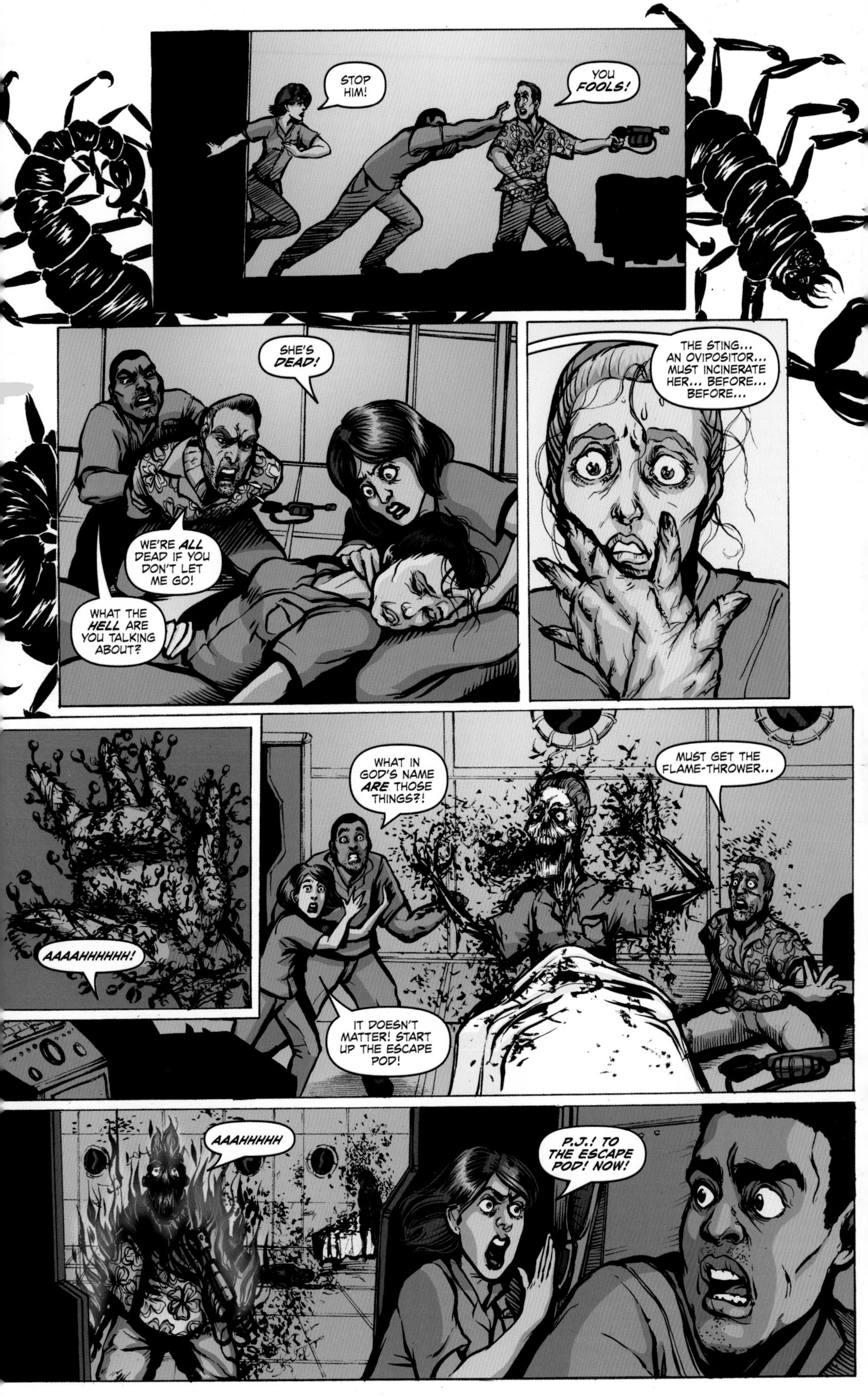
STOP HIM!
YOU FOOLS!
SHE'S DEAD!
WE'RE ALL DEAD IF YOU DON'T LET ME GO!
WHAT THE HELL ARE YOU TALKING ABOUT?
THE STING... AN OVIPOSITOR... MUST INCINERATE HER... BEFORE... BEFORE...
AAAAHHHHHH!
WHAT IN GOD'S NAME ARE THOSE THINGS?!
MUST GET THE FLAME-THROWER...
IT DOESN'T MATTER! START UP THE ESCAPE POD!
AAAHHHHH
P.J.! TO THE ESCAPE POD! NOW!

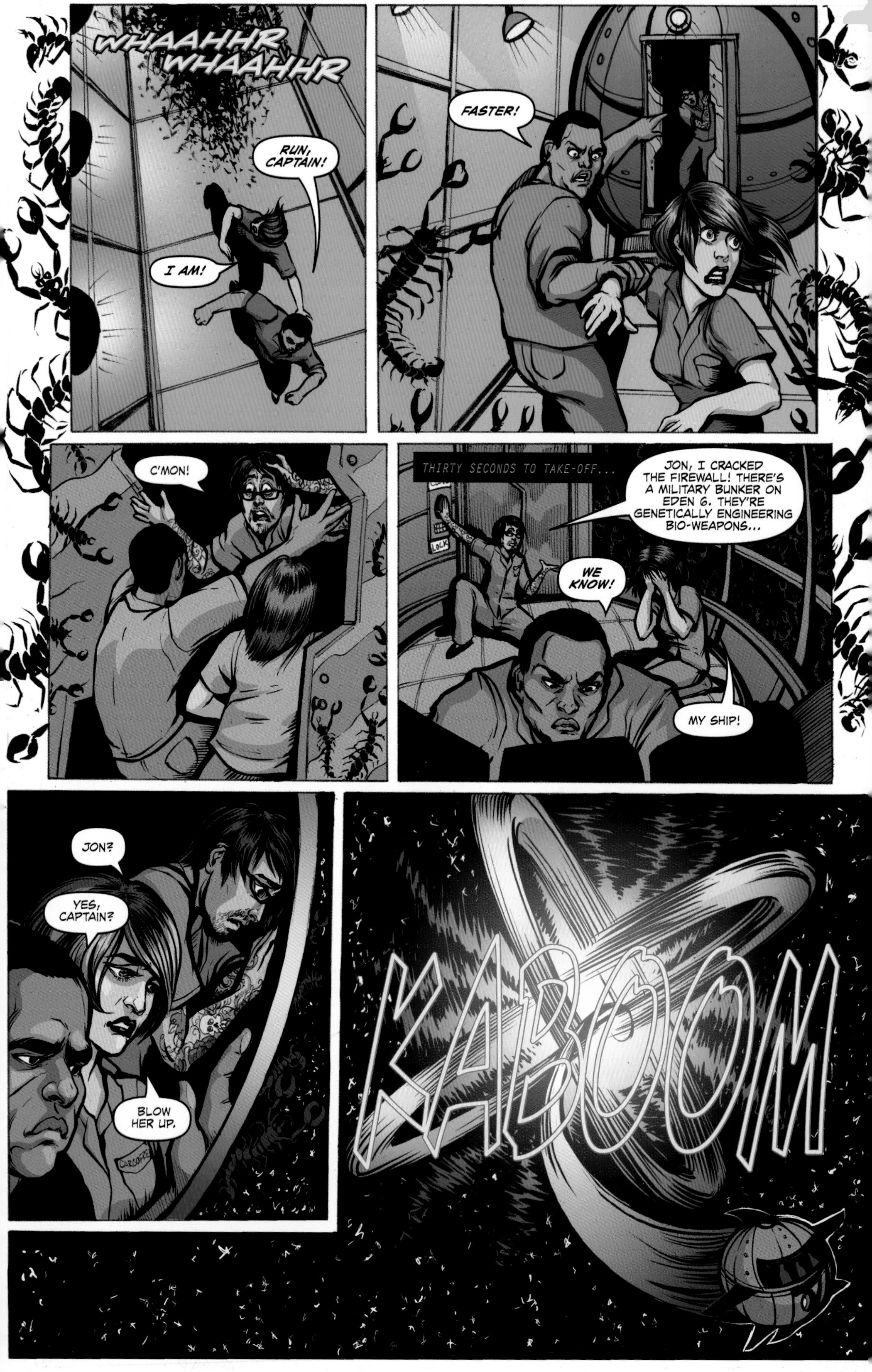
WHAAAHHR WHAAAHHR
RUN, CAPTAIN!
I AM!
FASTER!
C'MON!
THIRTY SECONDS TO TAKE-OFF...
JON, I CRACKED THE FIREWALL! THERE'S A MILITARY BUNKER ON EDEN 6. THEY'RE GENETICALLY ENGINEERING BIO-WEAPONS...
WE KNOW!
MY SHIP!
JON?
YES, CAPTAIN?
BLOW HER UP.
KABOOM

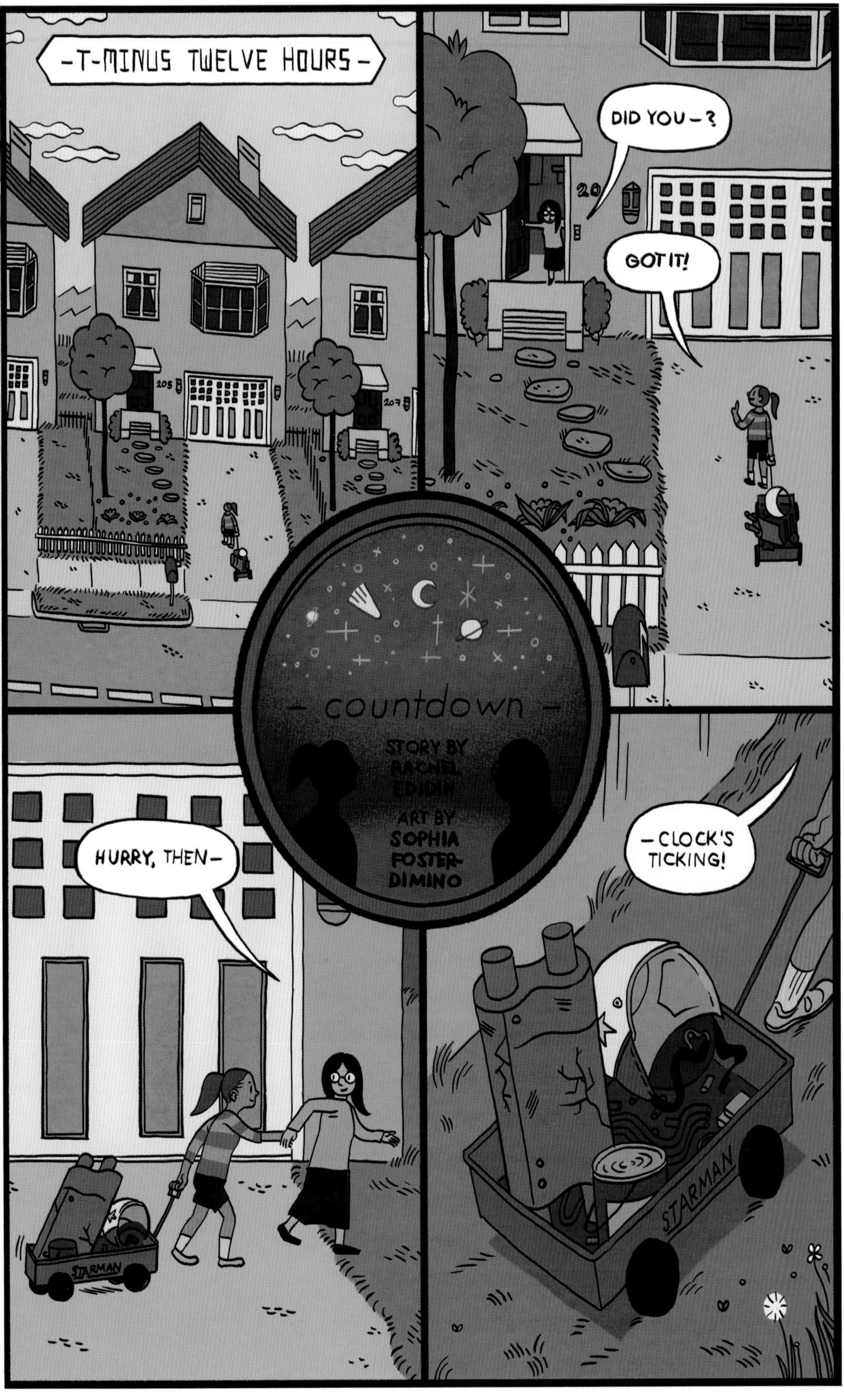

-T-MINUS TWELVE HOURS-
205
207
20
DID YOU—?
GOT IT!
- countdown -
STORY BY RACHEL EDIDIN
ART BY SOPHIA FOSTER-DIMINO
HURRY, THEN—
STARMAN
—CLOCK'S TICKING!
STARMAN

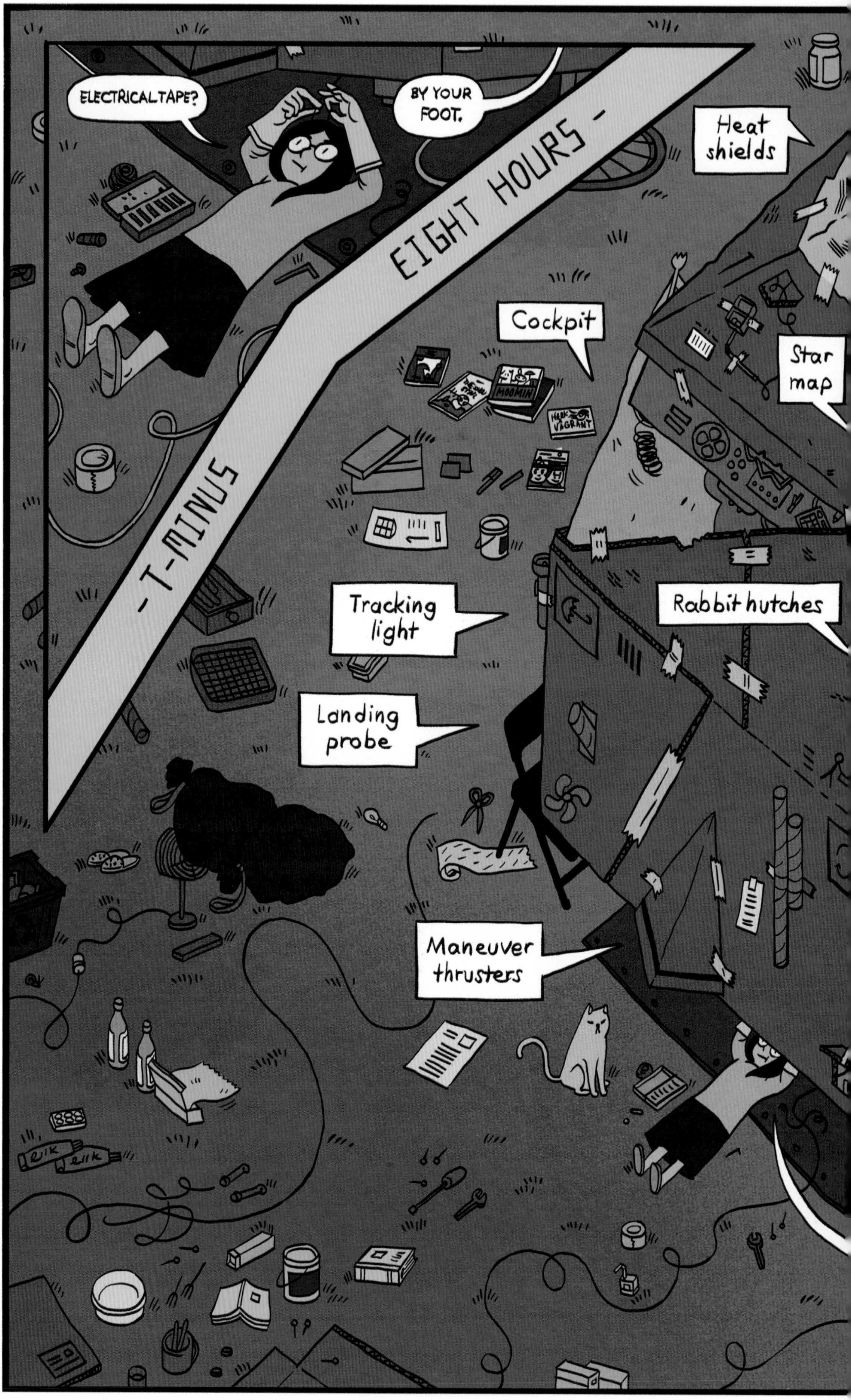
ELECTRICAL TAPE?
BY YOUR FOOT.
-T-MINUS EIGHT HOURS-
Heat shields
Cockpit
Star map
Rabbit hutches
Tracking light
Landing probe
Maneuver thrusters

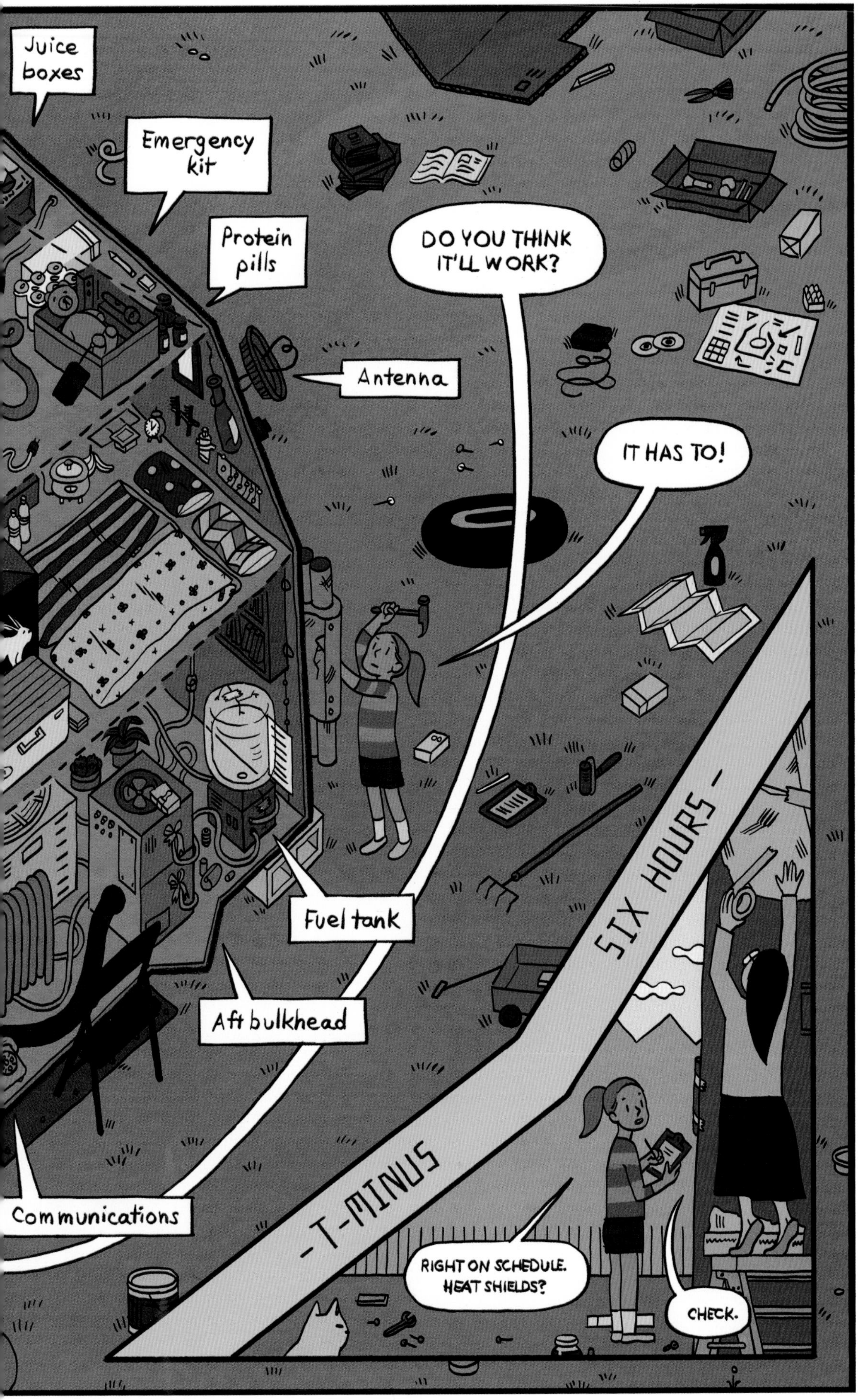
Juice boxes
Emergency kit
Protein pills
DO YOU THINK IT'LL WORK?
Antenna
IT HAS TO!
Fuel tank
Aft bulkhead
Communications
-T-MINUS SIX HOURS-
RIGHT ON SCHEDULE. HEAT SHIELDS?
CHECK.

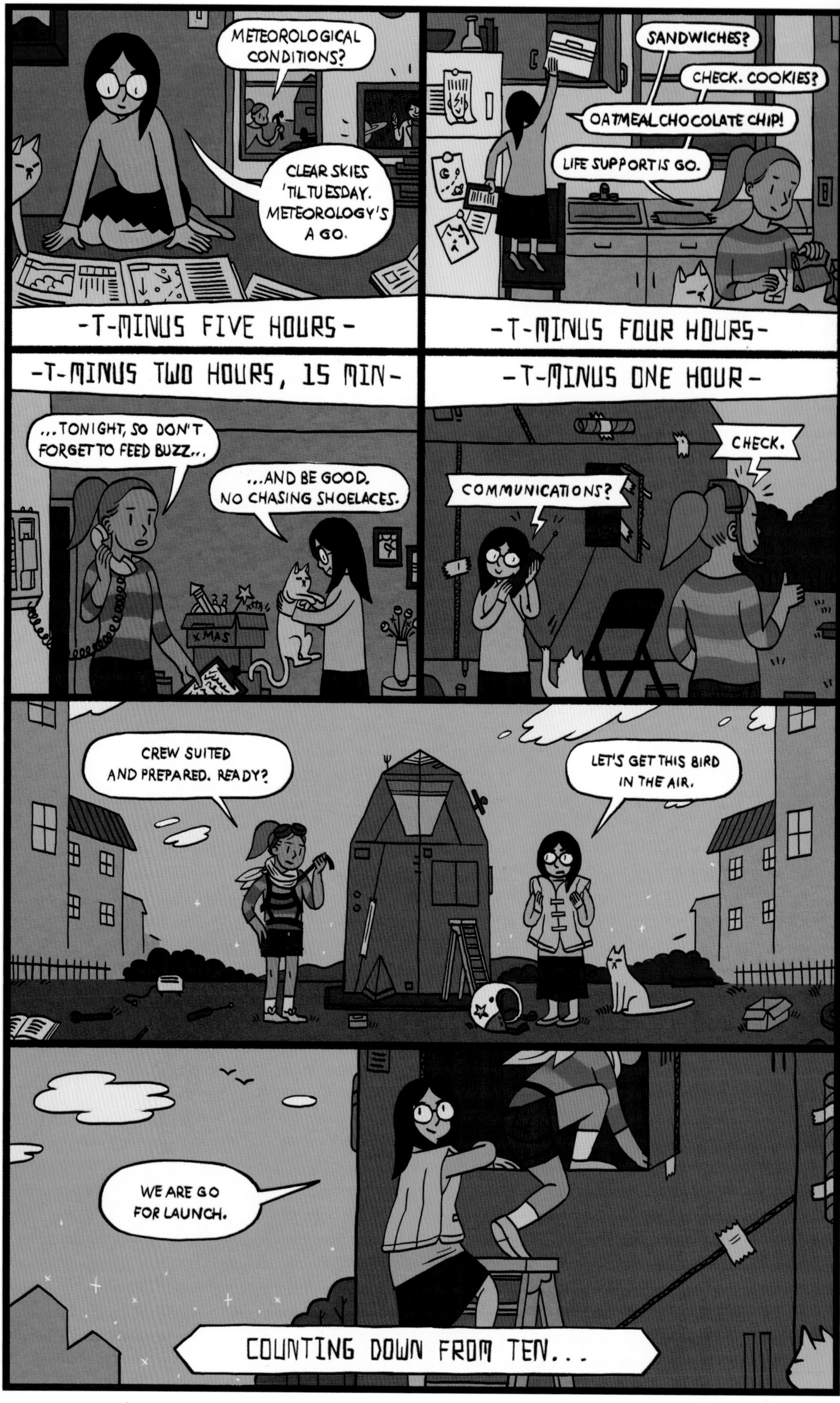
METEOROLOGICAL CONDITIONS?
CLEAR SKIES 'TIL TUESDAY. METEOROLOGY'S A GO.
-T-MINUS FIVE HOURS-
SANDWICHES?
CHECK. COOKIES?
OATMEAL CHOCOLATE CHIP!
LIFE SUPPORT IS GO.
-T-MINUS FOUR HOURS-
-T-MINUS TWO HOURS, 15 MIN-
...TONIGHT, SO DON'T FORGET TO FEED BUZZ...
...AND BE GOOD. NO CHASING SHOELACES.
XMAS
-T-MINUS ONE HOUR-
COMMUNICATIONS?
CHECK.
CREW SUITED AND PREPARED. READY?
LET'S GET THIS BIRD IN THE AIR.
WE ARE GO FOR LAUNCH.
COUNTING DOWN FROM TEN...

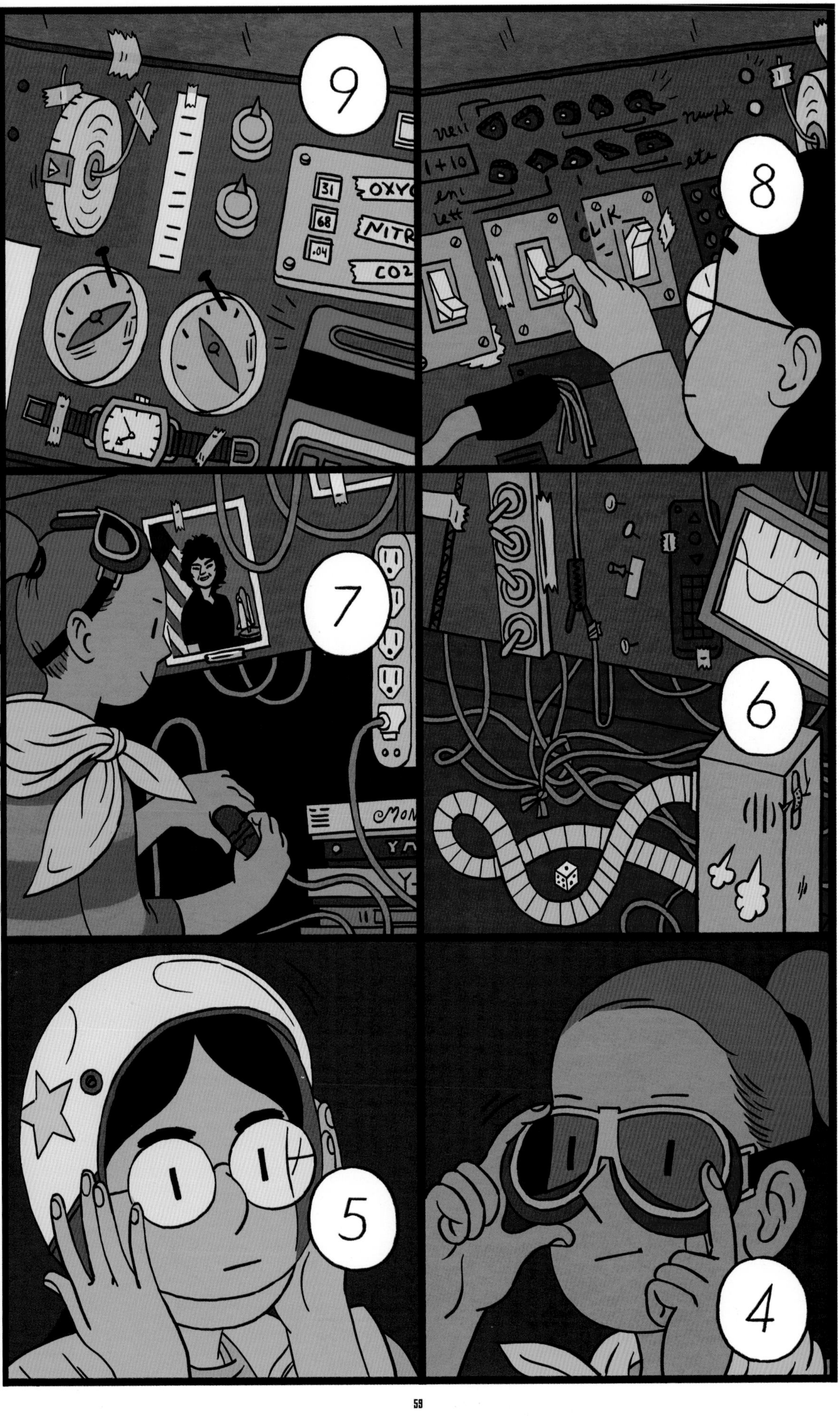
9
31
OXY
68
NITR
.04
CO2
CLIK
8
7
MON
6
5
4

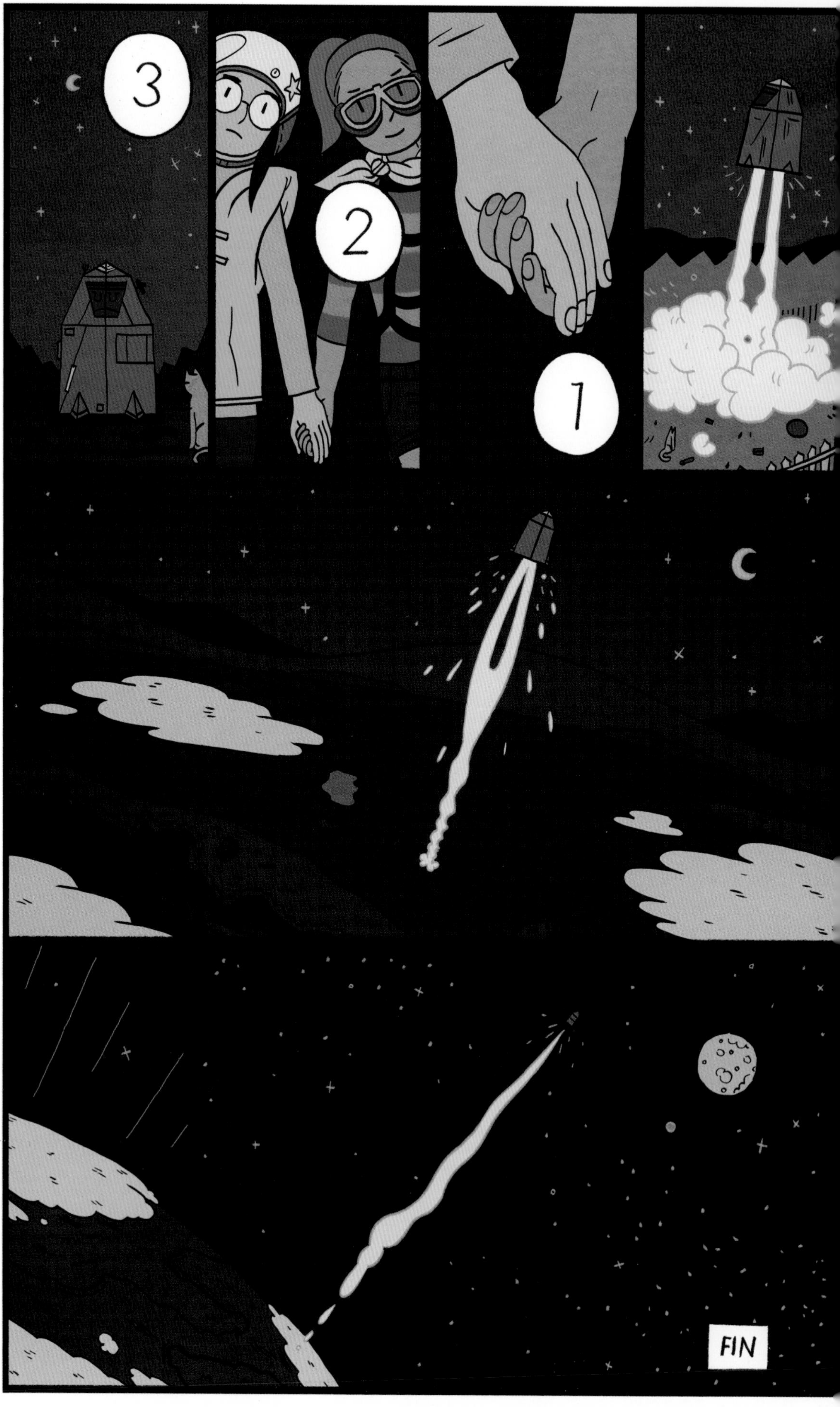
3
2
1
FIN

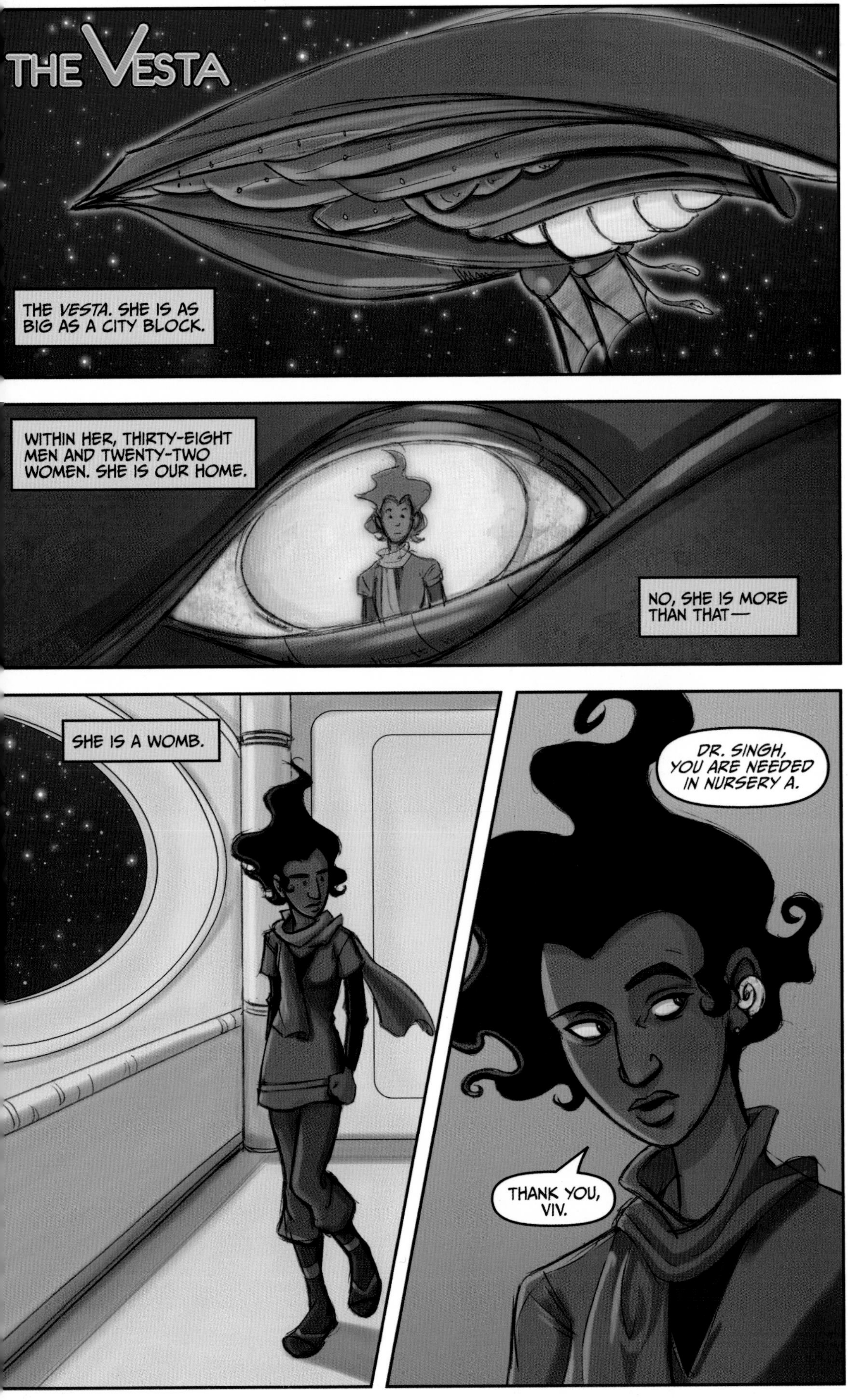
THE VESTA
THE VESTA. SHE IS AS BIG AS A CITY BLOCK.
WITHIN HER, THIRTY-EIGHT MEN AND TWENTY-TWO WOMEN. SHE IS OUR HOME.
NO, SHE IS MORE THAN THAT—
SHE IS A WOMB.
DR. SINGH, YOU ARE NEEDED IN NURSERY A.
THANK YOU, VIV.

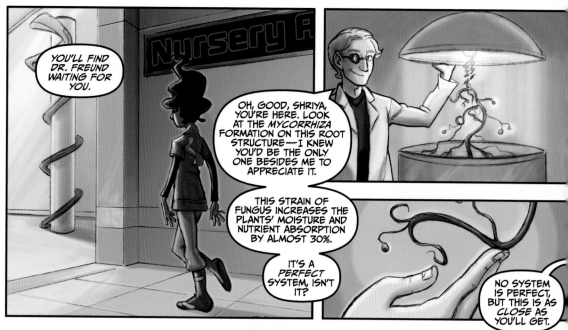

YOU'LL FIND DR. FREUND WAITING FOR YOU.

OH, GOOD, SHRIYA, YOU'RE HERE. LOOK AT THE MYCORRHIZA FORMATION ON THIS ROOT STRUCTURE—I KNEW YOU'D BE THE ONLY ONE BESIDES ME TO APPRECIATE IT.

THIS STRAIN OF FUNGUS INCREASES THE PLANTS' MOISTURE AND NUTRIENT ABSORPTION BY ALMOST 30%.

IT'S A PERFECT SYSTEM, ISN'T IT?

NO SYSTEM IS PERFECT, BUT THIS IS AS CLOSE AS YOU'LL GET.

OUR MISSION HAS NO DESTINATION. IT IS SIMPLY TO LIVE—AS THE VESTA CARRIES US WHERE SHE WILL.

HI, DR. SINGH.

GOOD MORNING, SHRIYA.

HEY, SHRIYA— SEE YOU AT LUNCH?

AND SO WE DO. WE LIVE.

WALK, YOU TWO! YOU ALMOST KNOCKED DOWN DR. SINGH!

I MADE THIS BATCH JUST FOR YOU, SHRIYA— EVERYTHING GROWN IN THAT GARDEN OF YOURS.

IT'S NOT MY GARDEN. THERE'S A WHOLE TEAM OF—

NONSENSE, DEAR, IT'S YOURS. WE WOULDN'T HAVE ALL THIS LOVELY FOOD IF IT WEREN'T FOR YOU. EVERYBODY KNOWS THAT.

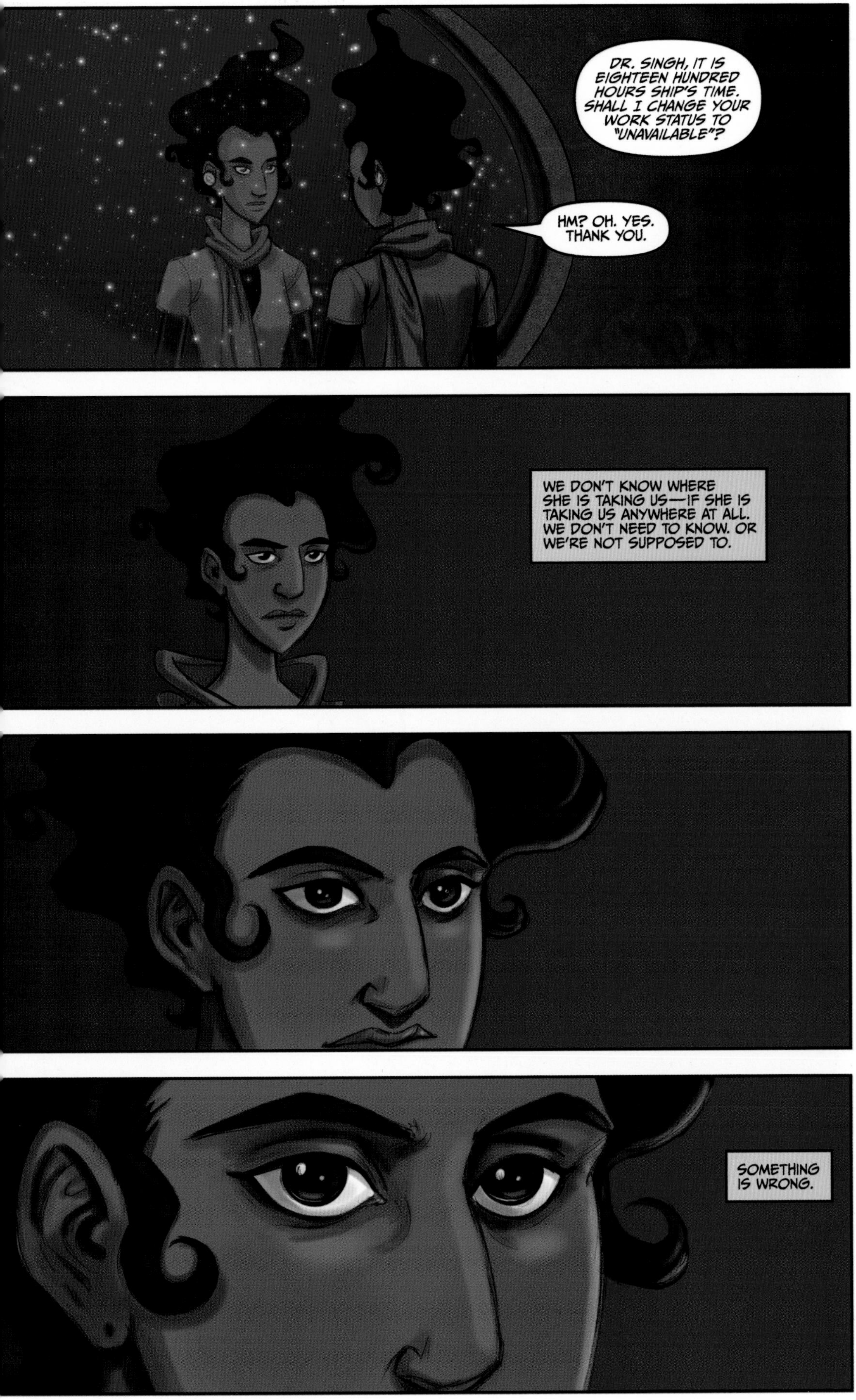
DR. SINGH, IT IS EIGHTEEN HUNDRED HOURS SHIP'S TIME. SHALL I CHANGE YOUR WORK STATUS TO "UNAVAILABLE"?
HM? OH. YES. THANK YOU.
WE DON'T KNOW WHERE SHE IS TAKING US—IF SHE IS TAKING US ANYWHERE AT ALL. WE DON'T NEED TO KNOW. OR WE'RE NOT SUPPOSED TO.
SOMETHING IS WRONG.

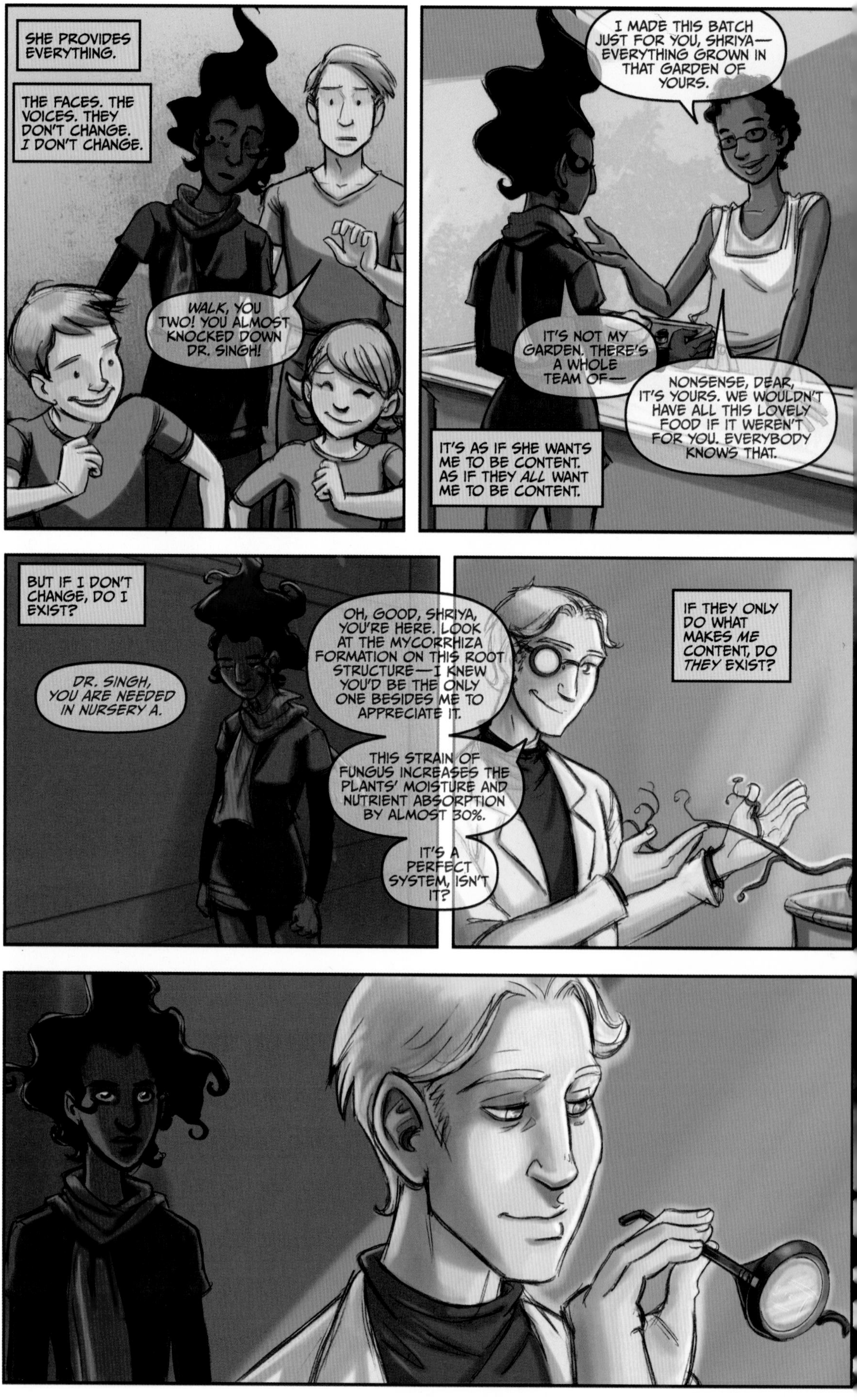

SHE PROVIDES EVERYTHING.
THE FACES. THE VOICES. THEY DON'T CHANGE. I DON'T CHANGE.
WALK, YOU TWO! YOU ALMOST KNOCKED DOWN DR. SINGH!
I MADE THIS BATCH JUST FOR YOU, SHRIYA— EVERYTHING GROWN IN THAT GARDEN OF YOURS.
IT'S NOT MY GARDEN. THERE'S A WHOLE TEAM OF—
NONSENSE, DEAR, IT'S YOURS. WE WOULDN'T HAVE ALL THIS LOVELY FOOD IF IT WEREN'T FOR YOU. EVERYBODY KNOWS THAT.
IT'S AS IF SHE WANTS ME TO BE CONTENT. AS IF THEY ALL WANT ME TO BE CONTENT.
BUT IF I DON'T CHANGE, DO I EXIST?
DR. SINGH, YOU ARE NEEDED IN NURSERY A.
OH, GOOD, SHRIYA, YOU'RE HERE. LOOK AT THE MYCORRHIZA FORMATION ON THIS ROOT STRUCTURE—I KNEW YOU'D BE THE ONLY ONE BESIDES ME TO APPRECIATE IT.
THIS STRAIN OF FUNGUS INCREASES THE PLANTS' MOISTURE AND NUTRIENT ABSORPTION BY ALMOST 30%.
IT'S A PERFECT SYSTEM, ISN'T IT?
IF THEY ONLY DO WHAT MAKES ME CONTENT, DO THEY EXIST?

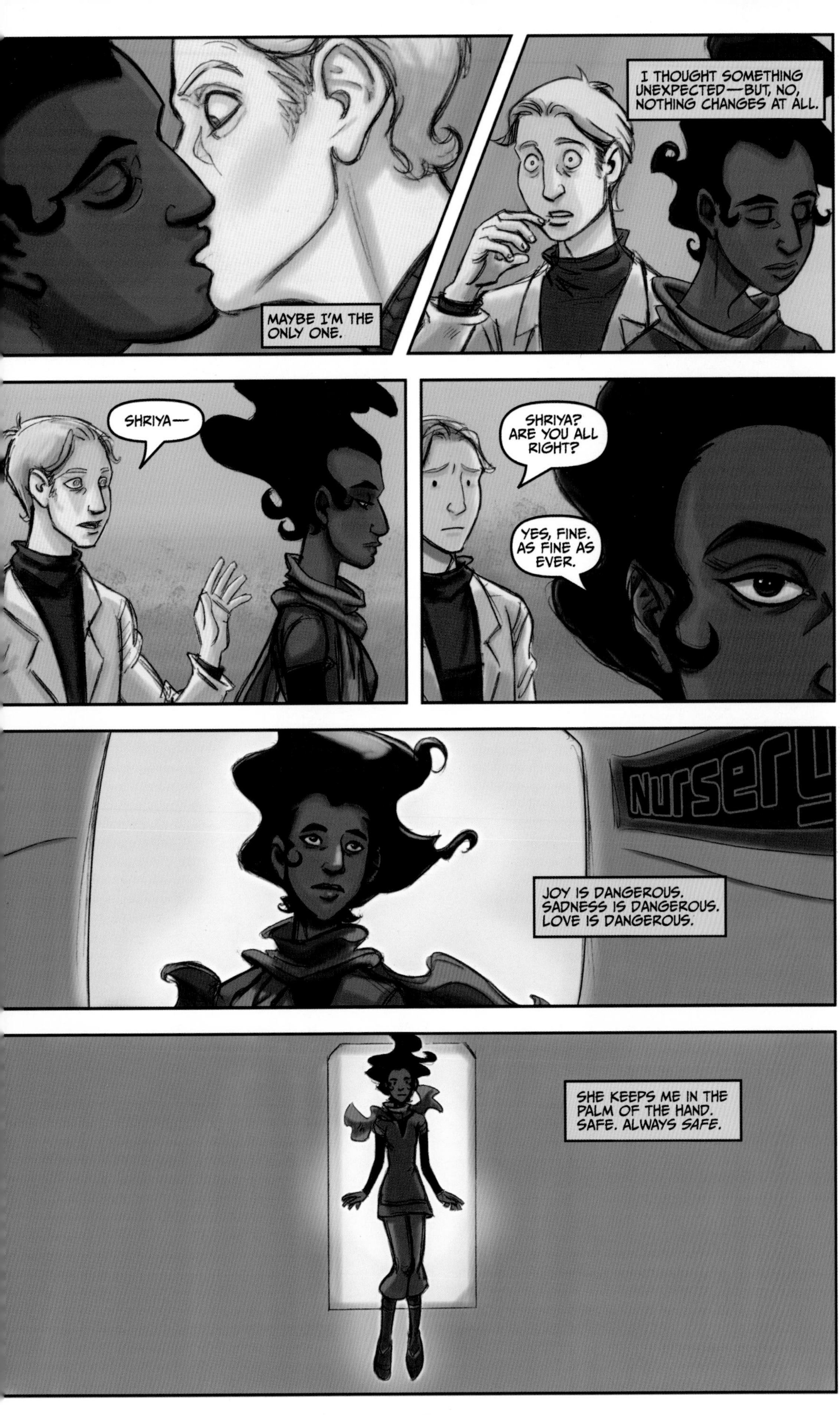
MAYBE I'M THE ONLY ONE.
I THOUGHT SOMETHING UNEXPECTED—BUT, NO, NOTHING CHANGES AT ALL.
SHRIYA—
SHRIYA? ARE YOU ALL RIGHT?
YES, FINE. AS FINE AS EVER.
Nursery
JOY IS DANGEROUS. SADNESS IS DANGEROUS. LOVE IS DANGEROUS.
SHE KEEPS ME IN THE PALM OF THE HAND. SAFE. ALWAYS SAFE.

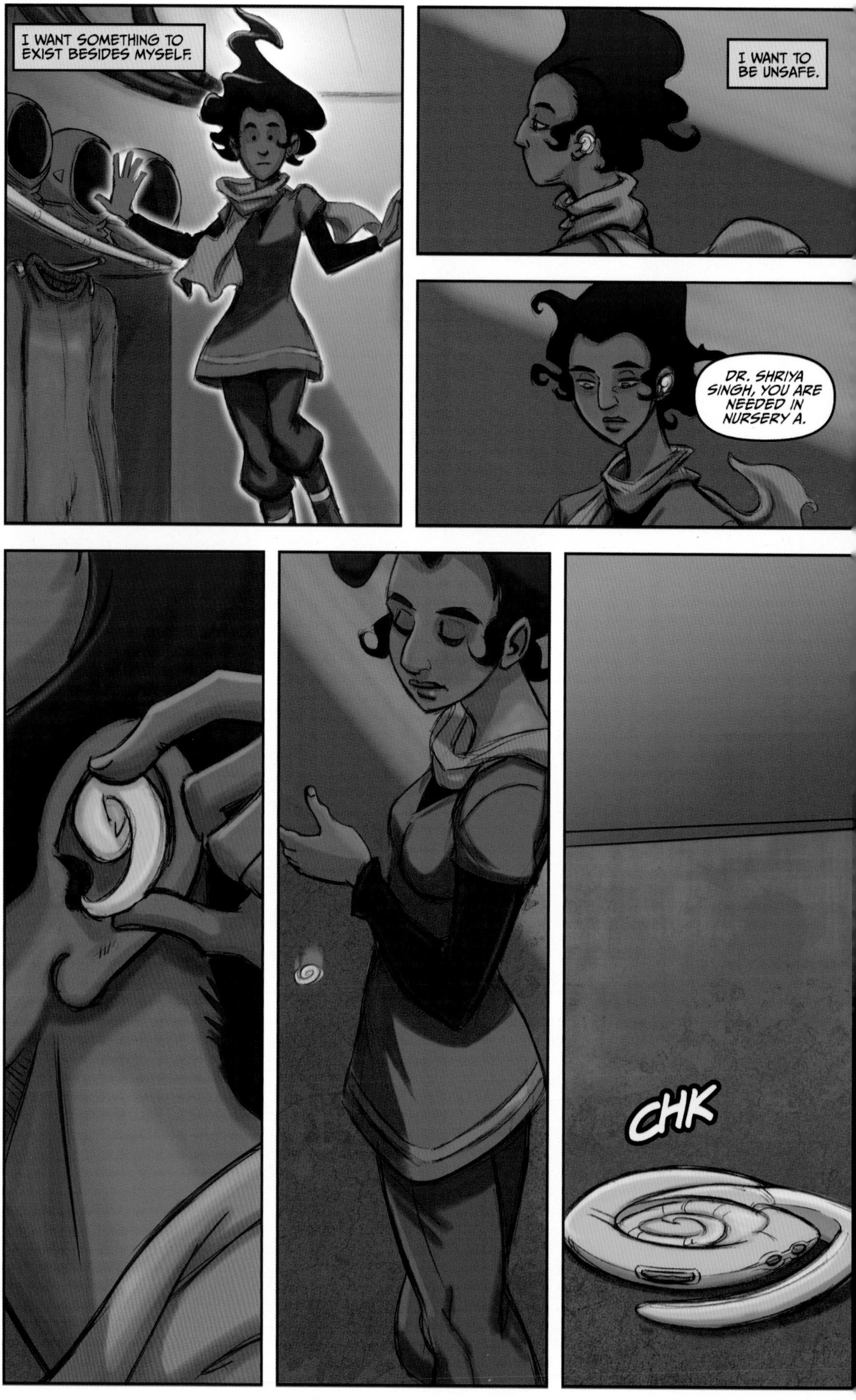
I WANT SOMETHING TO EXIST BESIDES MYSELF.
I WANT TO BE UNSAFE.
DR. SHRIYA SINGH, YOU ARE NEEDED IN NURSERY A.
CHK

BSSHHH

SEAL

SSHHHK

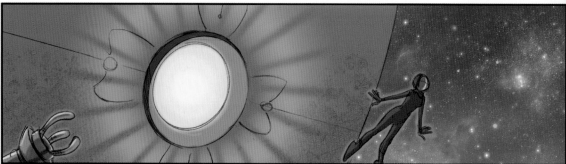

END.

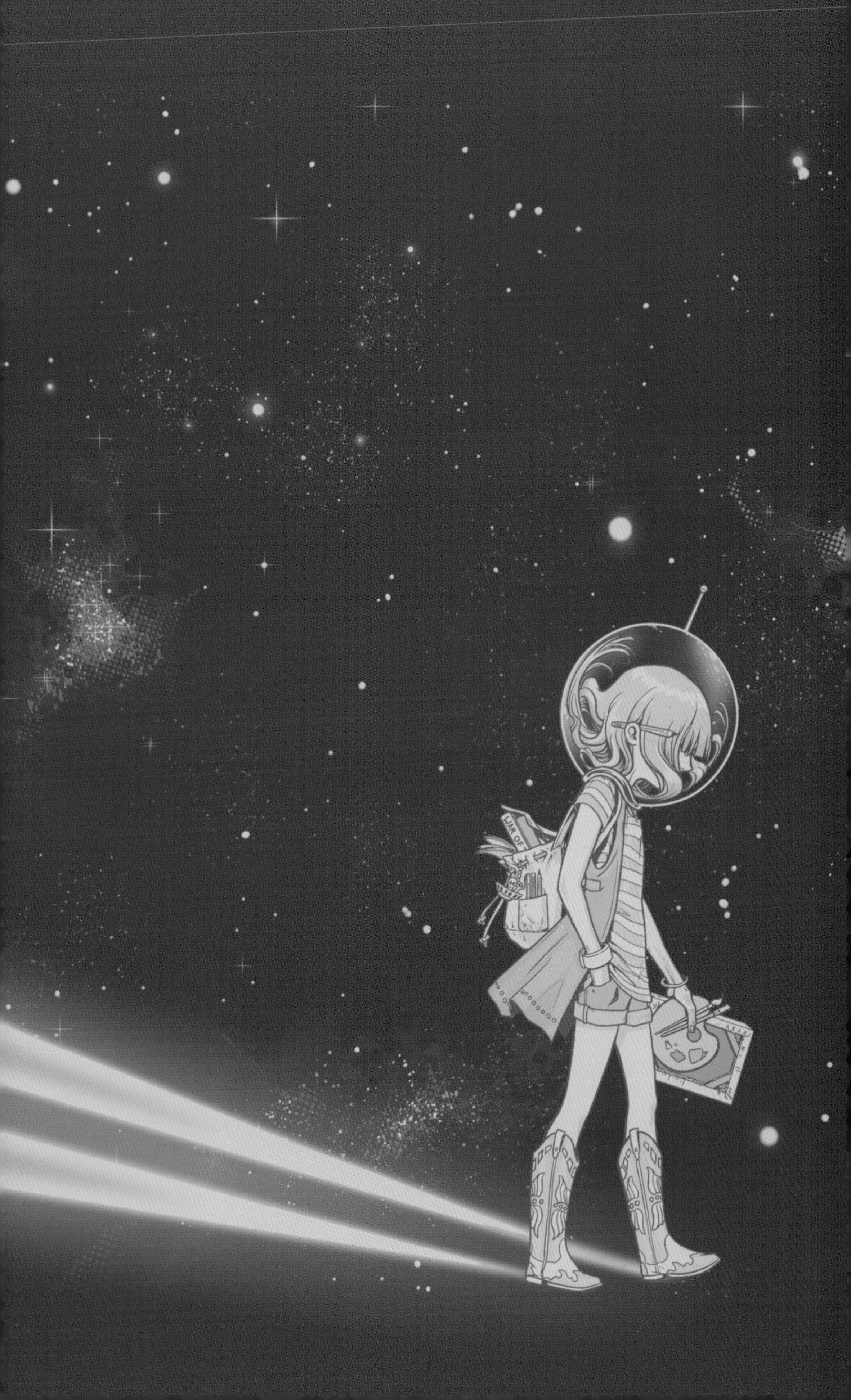
WAR OF

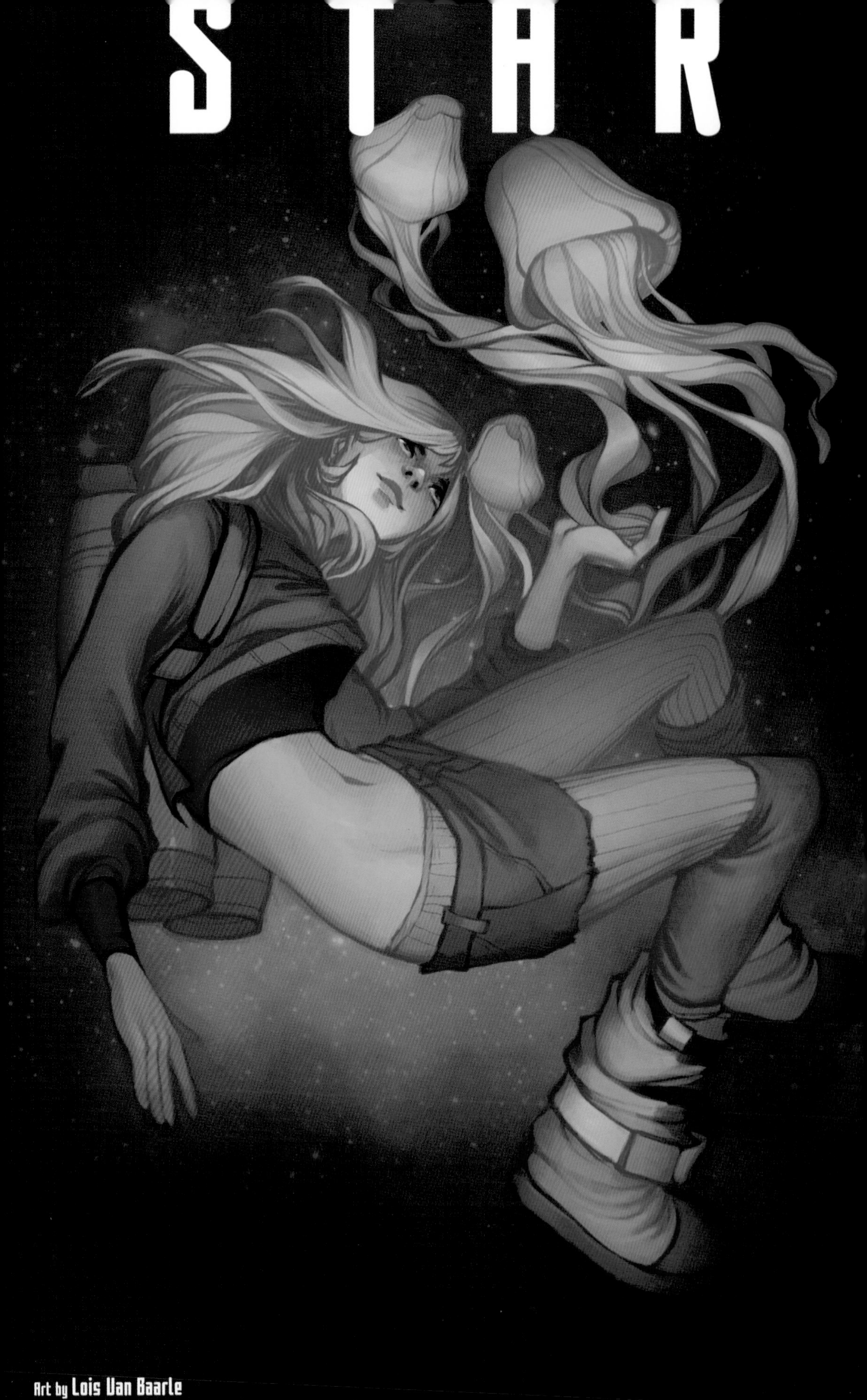
STAR

Art by Lois Van Baarle

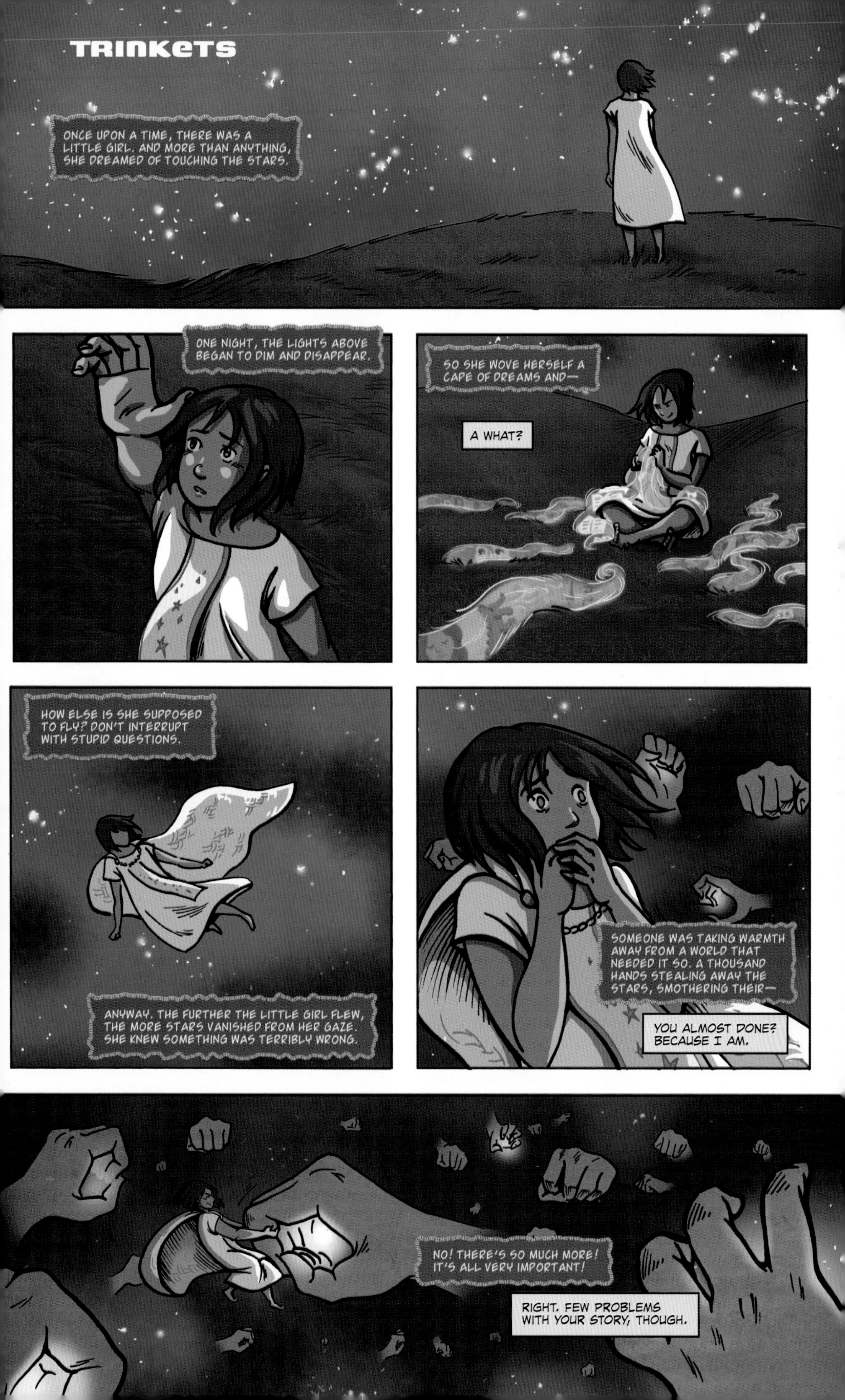
TRINKETS
ONCE UPON A TIME, THERE WAS A LITTLE GIRL. AND MORE THAN ANYTHING, SHE DREAMED OF TOUCHING THE STARS.
ONE NIGHT, THE LIGHTS ABOVE BEGAN TO DIM AND DISAPPEAR.
SO SHE WOVE HERSELF A CAPE OF DREAMS AND—
A WHAT?
HOW ELSE IS SHE SUPPOSED TO FLY? DON'T INTERRUPT WITH STUPID QUESTIONS.
ANYWAY. THE FURTHER THE LITTLE GIRL FLEW, THE MORE STARS VANISHED FROM HER GAZE. SHE KNEW SOMETHING WAS TERRIBLY WRONG.
SOMEONE WAS TAKING WARMTH AWAY FROM A WORLD THAT NEEDED IT SO. A THOUSAND HANDS STEALING AWAY THE STARS, SMOTHERING THEIR—
YOU ALMOST DONE? BECAUSE I AM.
NO! THERE'S SO MUCH MORE! IT'S ALL VERY IMPORTANT!
RIGHT. FEW PROBLEMS WITH YOUR STORY, THOUGH.

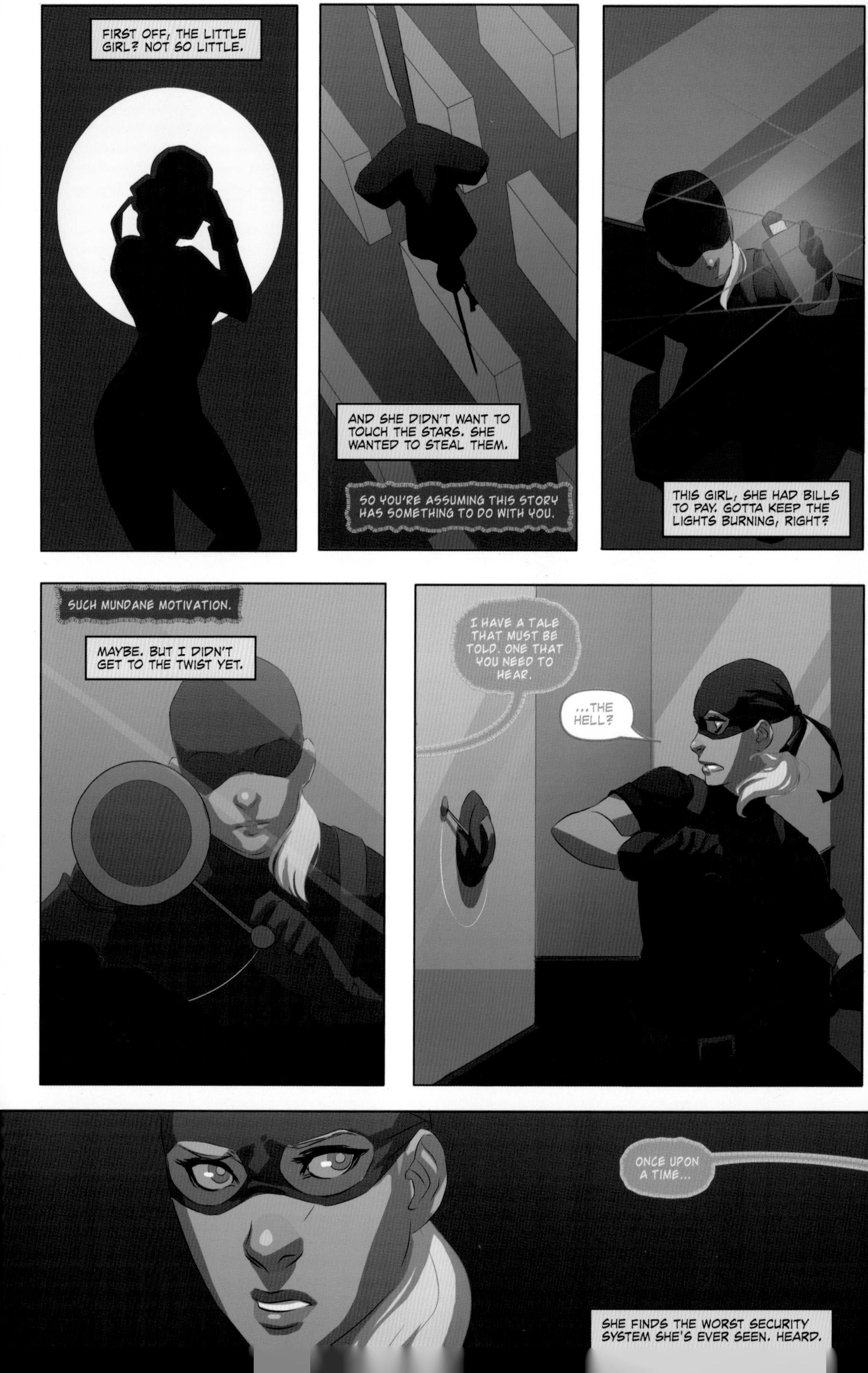
FIRST OFF, THE LITTLE GIRL? NOT SO LITTLE.
AND SHE DIDN'T WANT TO TOUCH THE STARS. SHE WANTED TO STEAL THEM.
SO YOU'RE ASSUMING THIS STORY HAS SOMETHING TO DO WITH YOU.
THIS GIRL, SHE HAD BILLS TO PAY. GOTTA KEEP THE LIGHTS BURNING, RIGHT?
SUCH MUNDANE MOTIVATION.
MAYBE. BUT I DIDN'T GET TO THE TWIST YET.
I HAVE A TALE THAT MUST BE TOLD. ONE THAT YOU NEED TO HEAR.
...THE HELL?
ONCE UPON A TIME...
SHE FINDS THE WORST SECURITY SYSTEM SHE'S EVER SEEN. HEARD.

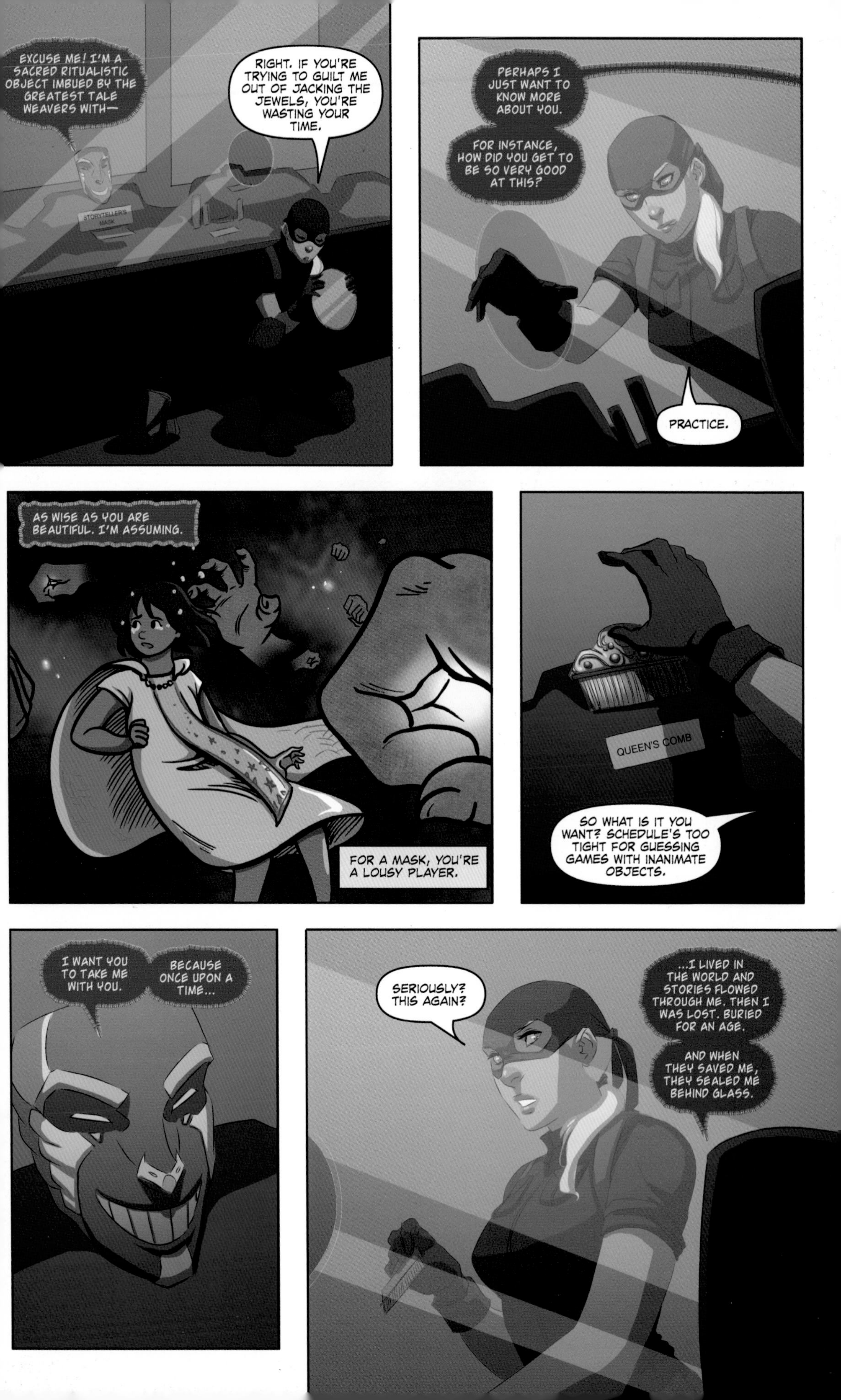

EXCUSE ME! I'M A SACRED RITUALISTIC OBJECT IMBUED BY THE GREATEST TALE WEAVERS WITH—
STORYTELLER'S MASK
RIGHT. IF YOU'RE TRYING TO GUILT ME OUT OF JACKING THE JEWELS, YOU'RE WASTING YOUR TIME.
PERHAPS I JUST WANT TO KNOW MORE ABOUT YOU.
FOR INSTANCE, HOW DID YOU GET TO BE SO VERY GOOD AT THIS?
PRACTICE.
AS WISE AS YOU ARE BEAUTIFUL. I'M ASSUMING.
FOR A MASK, YOU'RE A LOUSY PLAYER.
QUEEN'S COMB
SO WHAT IS IT YOU WANT? SCHEDULE'S TOO TIGHT FOR GUESSING GAMES WITH INANIMATE OBJECTS.
I WANT YOU TO TAKE ME WITH YOU.
BECAUSE ONCE UPON A TIME...
SERIOUSLY? THIS AGAIN?
...I LIVED IN THE WORLD AND STORIES FLOWED THROUGH ME. THEN I WAS LOST. BURIED FOR AN AGE.
AND WHEN THEY SAVED ME, THEY SEALED ME BEHIND GLASS.

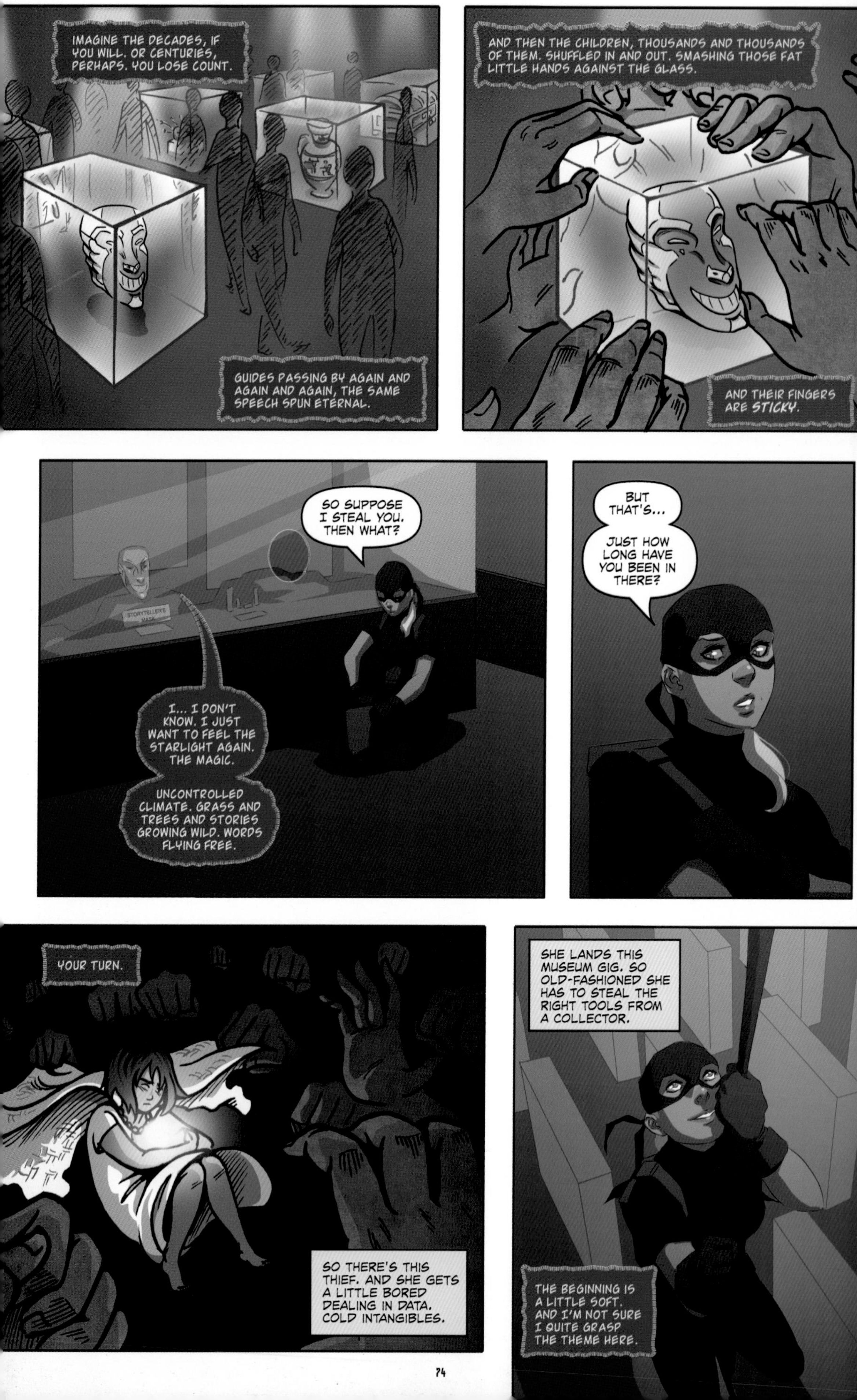

IMAGINE THE DECADES, IF YOU WILL. OR CENTURIES, PERHAPS. YOU LOSE COUNT.
GUIDES PASSING BY AGAIN AND AGAIN AND AGAIN, THE SAME SPEECH SPUN ETERNAL.
AND THEN THE CHILDREN, THOUSANDS AND THOUSANDS OF THEM. SHUFFLED IN AND OUT. SMASHING THOSE FAT LITTLE HANDS AGAINST THE GLASS.
AND THEIR FINGERS ARE STICKY.
SO SUPPOSE I STEAL YOU. THEN WHAT?
I... I DON'T KNOW. I JUST WANT TO FEEL THE STARLIGHT AGAIN. THE MAGIC.
UNCONTROLLED CLIMATE. GRASS AND TREES AND STORIES GROWING WILD. WORDS FLYING FREE.
BUT THAT'S...
JUST HOW LONG HAVE YOU BEEN IN THERE?
YOUR TURN.
SO THERE'S THIS THIEF. AND SHE GETS A LITTLE BORED DEALING IN DATA. COLD INTANGIBLES.
SHE LANDS THIS MUSEUM GIG. SO OLD-FASHIONED SHE HAS TO STEAL THE RIGHT TOOLS FROM A COLLECTOR.
THE BEGINNING IS A LITTLE SOFT. AND I'M NOT SURE I QUITE GRASP THE THEME HERE.

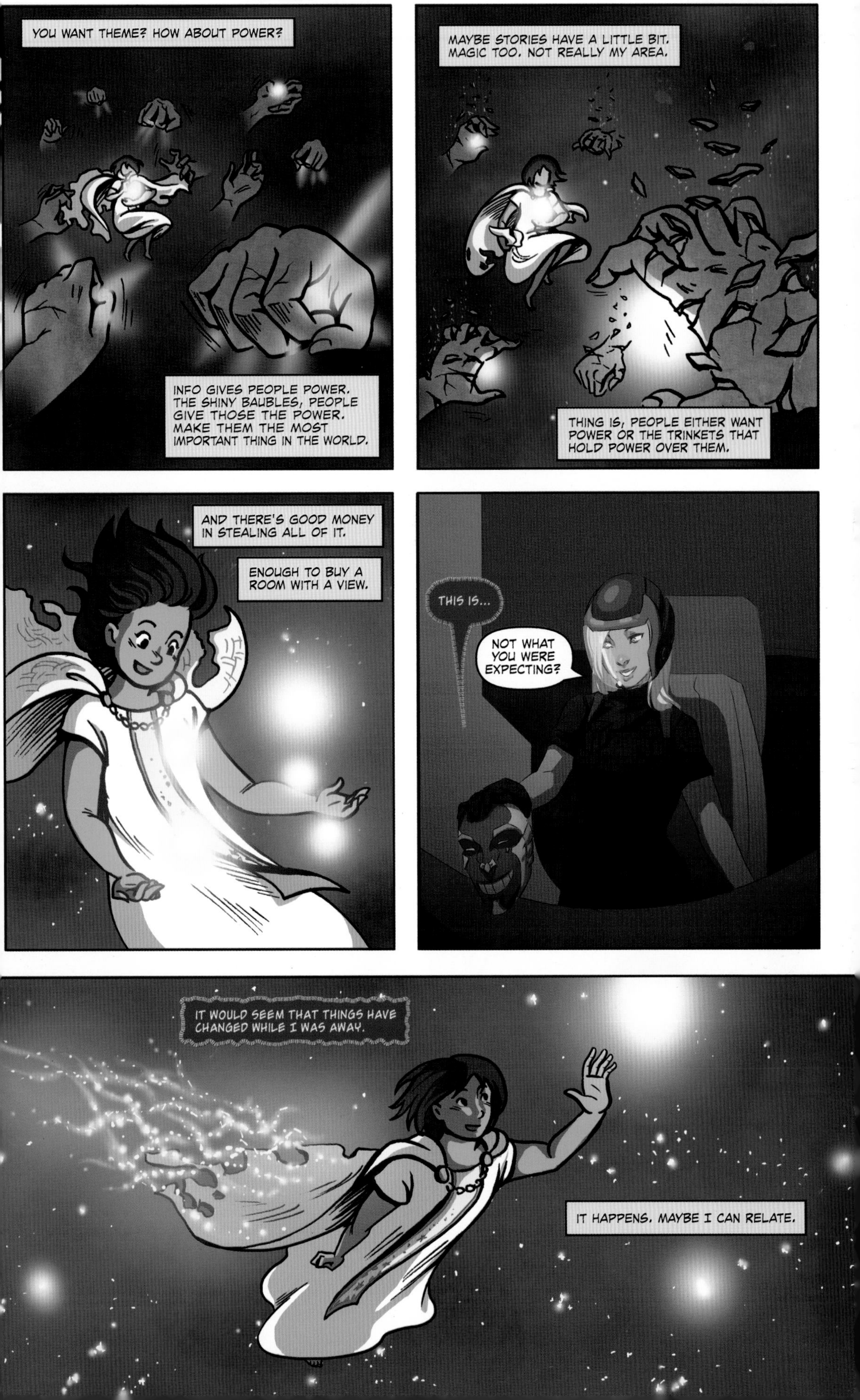
YOU WANT THEME? HOW ABOUT POWER?
INFO GIVES PEOPLE POWER. THE SHINY BAUBLES, PEOPLE GIVE THOSE THE POWER. MAKE THEM THE MOST IMPORTANT THING IN THE WORLD.
MAYBE STORIES HAVE A LITTLE BIT. MAGIC TOO. NOT REALLY MY AREA.
THING IS, PEOPLE EITHER WANT POWER OR THE TRINKETS THAT HOLD POWER OVER THEM.
AND THERE'S GOOD MONEY IN STEALING ALL OF IT.
ENOUGH TO BUY A ROOM WITH A VIEW.
THIS IS...
NOT WHAT YOU WERE EXPECTING?
IT WOULD SEEM THAT THINGS HAVE CHANGED WHILE I WAS AWAY.
IT HAPPENS. MAYBE I CAN RELATE.

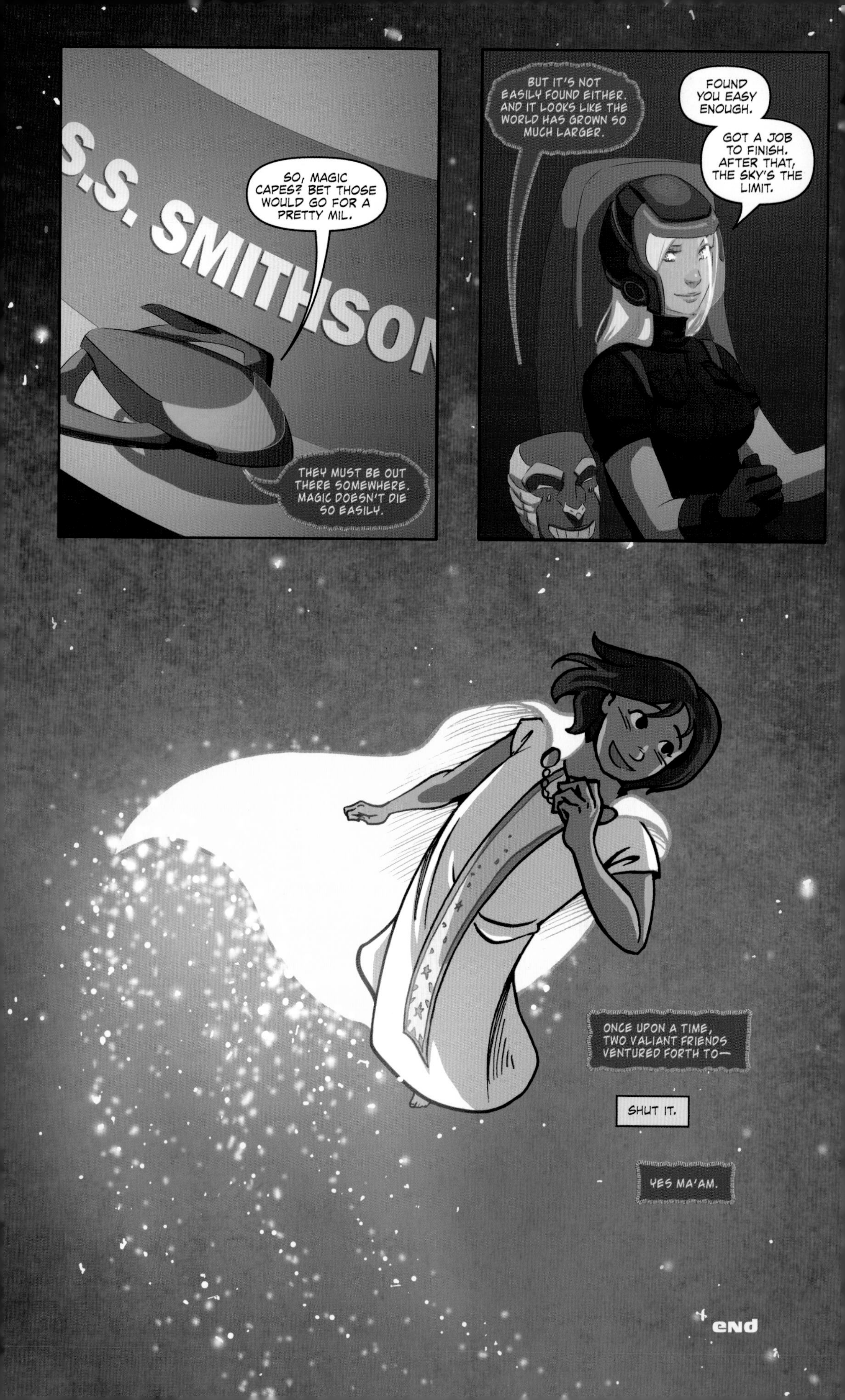
S.S. SMITHSON
SO, MAGIC CAPES? BET THOSE WOULD GO FOR A PRETTY MIL.
THEY MUST BE OUT THERE SOMEWHERE. MAGIC DOESN'T DIE SO EASILY.
BUT IT'S NOT EASILY FOUND EITHER. AND IT LOOKS LIKE THE WORLD HAS GROWN SO MUCH LARGER.
FOUND YOU EASY ENOUGH.
GOT A JOB TO FINISH. AFTER THAT, THE SKY'S THE LIMIT.
ONCE UPON A TIME, TWO VALIANT FRIENDS VENTURED FORTH TO—
SHUT IT.
YES MA'AM.
end

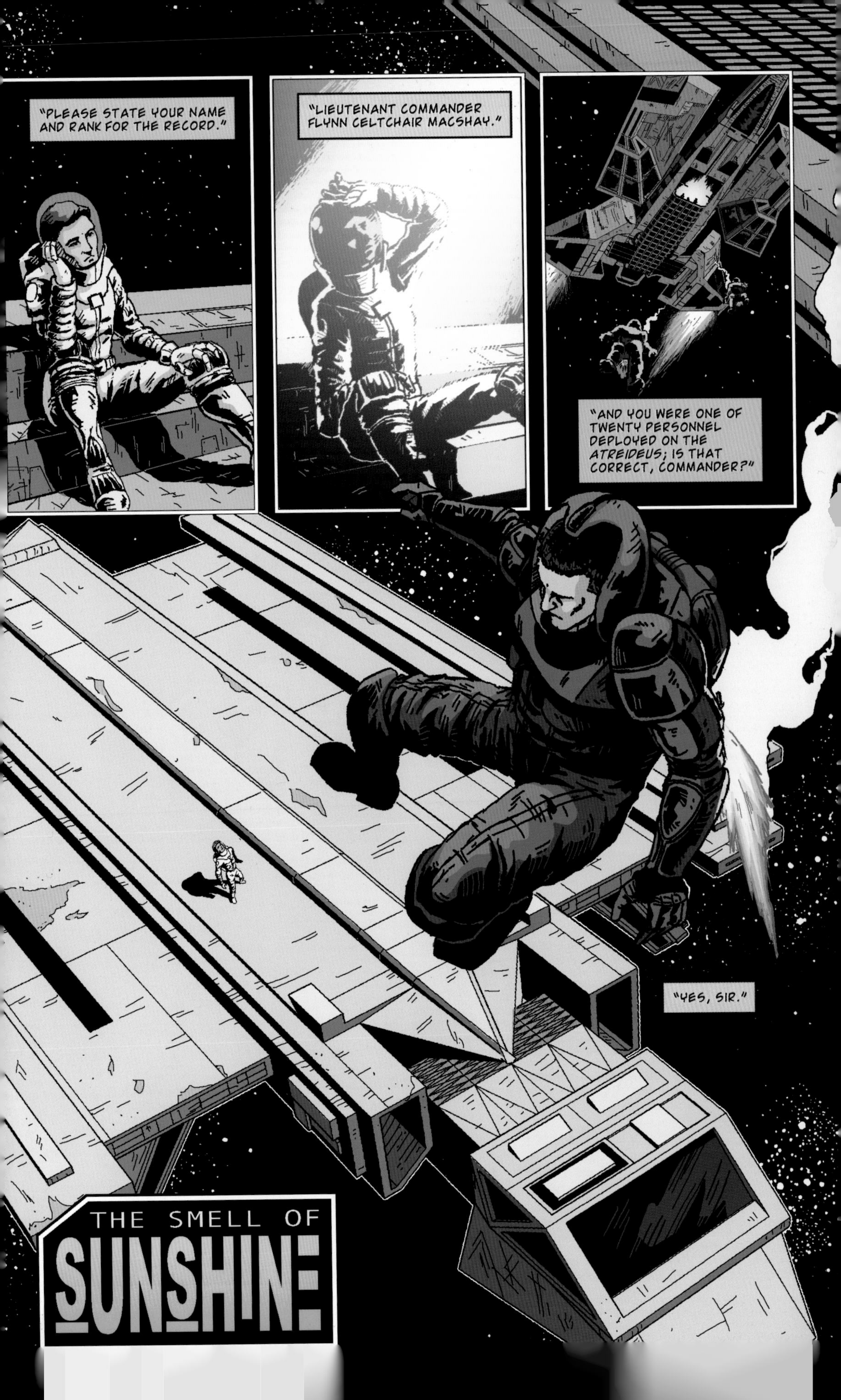
"PLEASE STATE YOUR NAME AND RANK FOR THE RECORD."
"LIEUTENANT COMMANDER FLYNN CELTCHAIR MACSHAY."
"AND YOU WERE ONE OF TWENTY PERSONNEL DEPLOYED ON THE ATREIDEUS; IS THAT CORRECT, COMMANDER?"
"YES, SIR."
THE SMELL OF SUNSHINE

"WHAT WAS THE MISSION OF THE *ATREIDEUS*, COMMANDER?"

WE WERE CHARTING THE GORUKAMI ASTEROID FIELD.

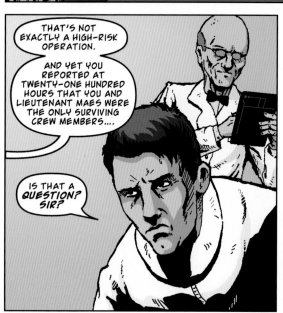

THAT'S NOT EXACTLY A HIGH-RISK OPERATION.

AND YET YOU REPORTED AT TWENTY-ONE HUNDRED HOURS THAT YOU AND LIEUTENANT MAES WERE THE ONLY SURVIVING CREW MEMBERS....

IS THAT A *QUESTION?* SIR?

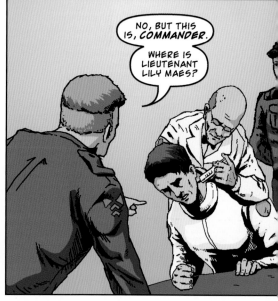

NO, BUT THIS IS, *COMMANDER*.

WHERE IS LIEUTENANT LILY MAES?

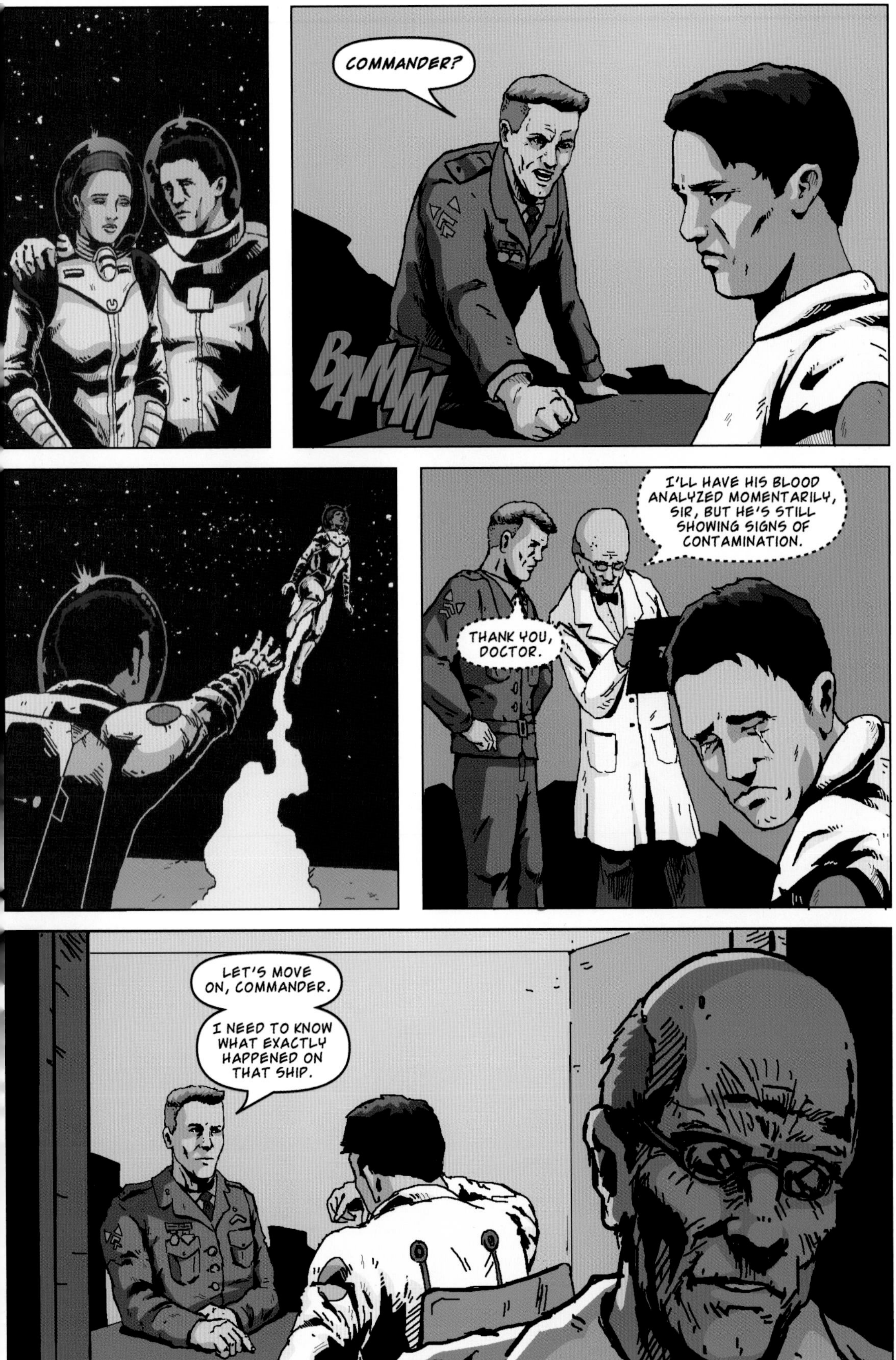
COMMANDER?
BAMMM
I'LL HAVE HIS BLOOD ANALYZED MOMENTARILY, SIR, BUT HE'S STILL SHOWING SIGNS OF CONTAMINATION.
THANK YOU, DOCTOR.
LET'S MOVE ON, COMMANDER.
I NEED TO KNOW WHAT EXACTLY HAPPENED ON THAT SHIP.

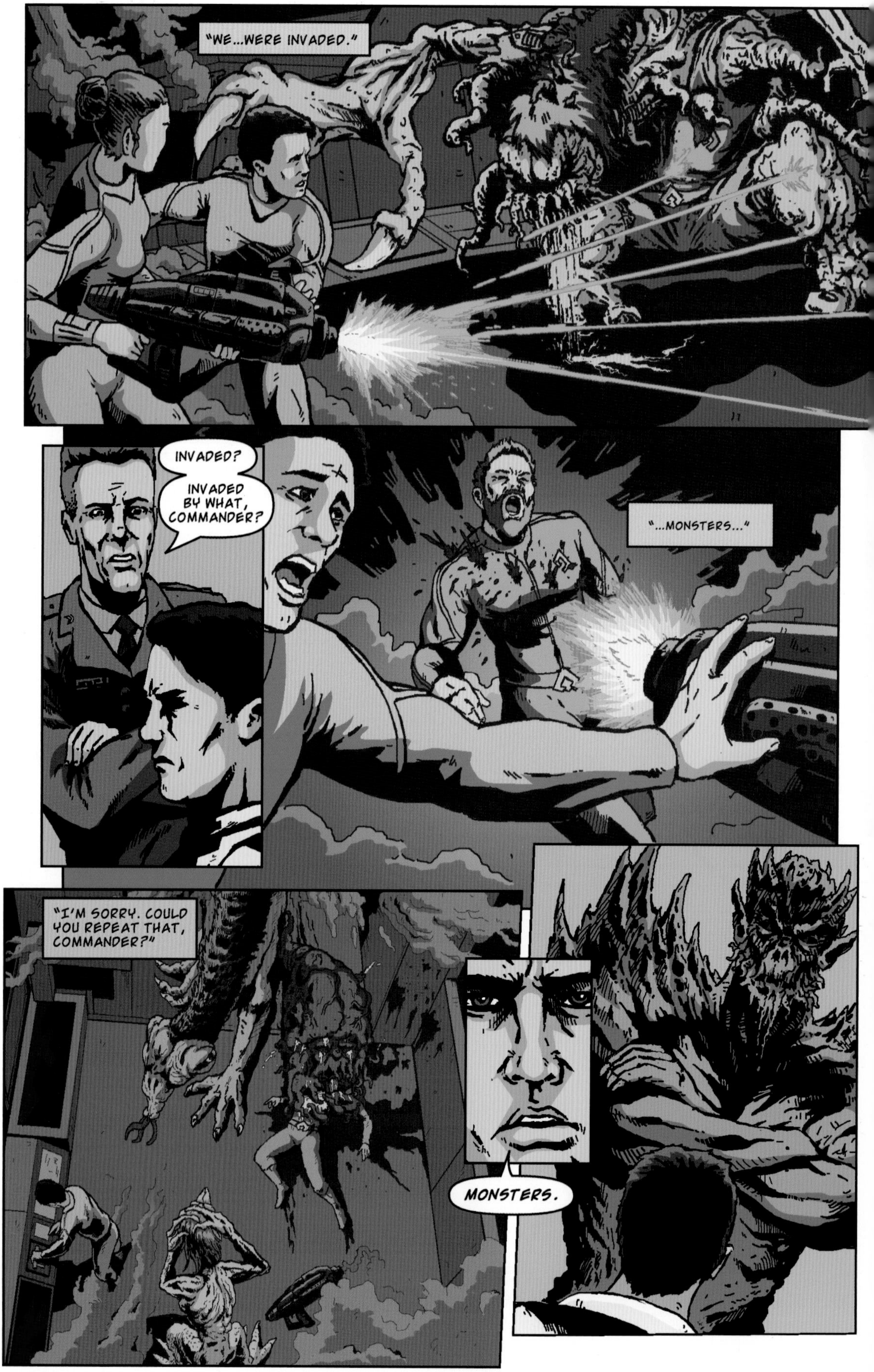
"WE...WERE INVADED."
INVADED?
INVADED BY WHAT, COMMANDER?
"...MONSTERS..."
"I'M SORRY. COULD YOU REPEAT THAT, COMMANDER?"
MONSTERS.

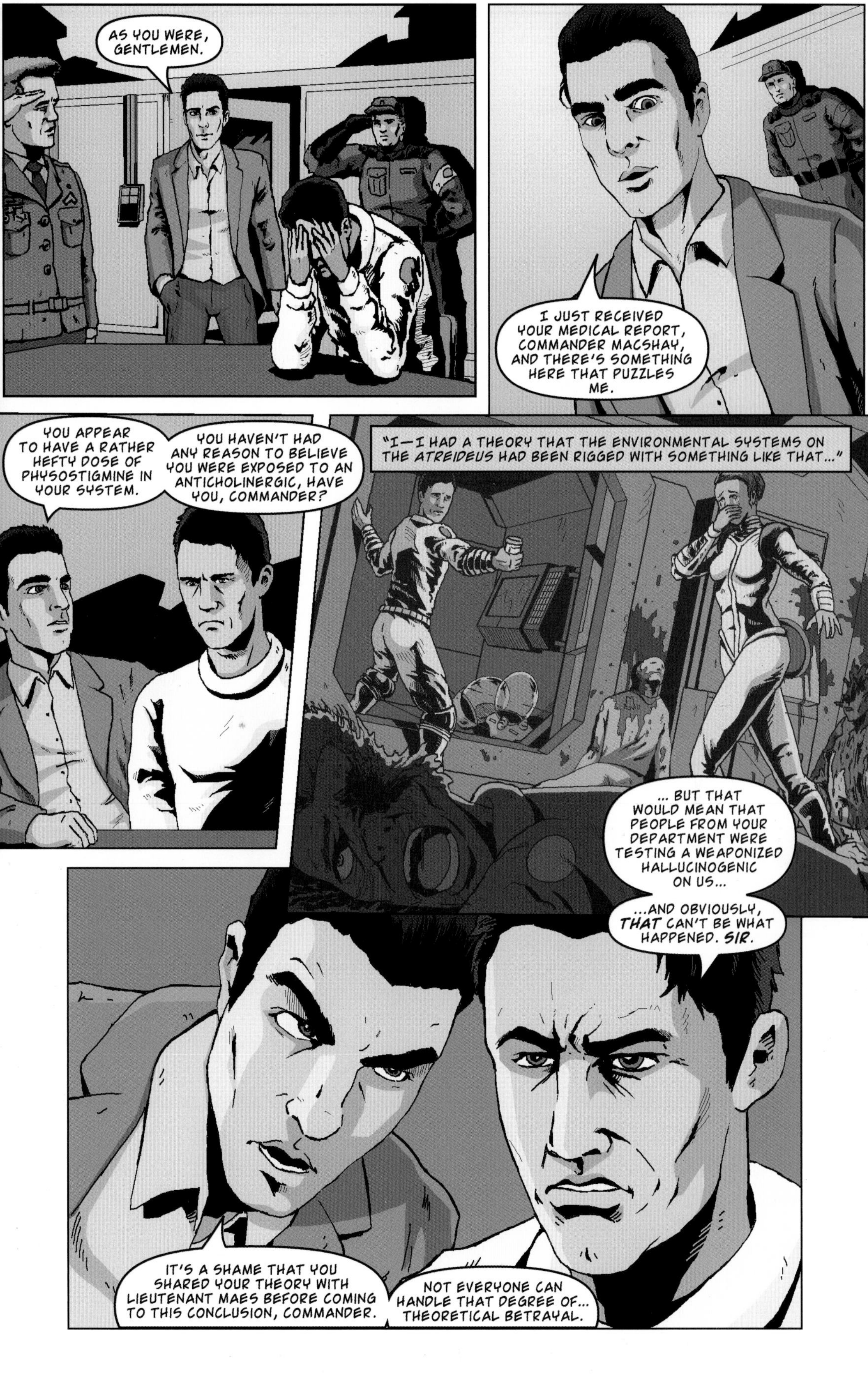
AS YOU WERE, GENTLEMEN.
I JUST RECEIVED YOUR MEDICAL REPORT, COMMANDER MACSHAY, AND THERE'S SOMETHING HERE THAT PUZZLES ME.
YOU APPEAR TO HAVE A RATHER HEFTY DOSE OF PHYSOSTIGMINE IN YOUR SYSTEM.
YOU HAVEN'T HAD ANY REASON TO BELIEVE YOU WERE EXPOSED TO AN ANTICHOLINERGIC, HAVE YOU, COMMANDER?
"I—I HAD A THEORY THAT THE ENVIRONMENTAL SYSTEMS ON THE *ATREIDEUS* HAD BEEN RIGGED WITH SOMETHING LIKE THAT..."
... BUT THAT WOULD MEAN THAT PEOPLE FROM YOUR DEPARTMENT WERE TESTING A WEAPONIZED HALLUCINOGENIC ON US...
...AND OBVIOUSLY, ***THAT*** CAN'T BE WHAT HAPPENED. ***SIR***.
IT'S A SHAME THAT YOU SHARED YOUR THEORY WITH LIEUTENANT MAES BEFORE COMING TO THIS CONCLUSION, COMMANDER.
NOT EVERYONE CAN HANDLE THAT DEGREE OF... THEORETICAL BETRAYAL.

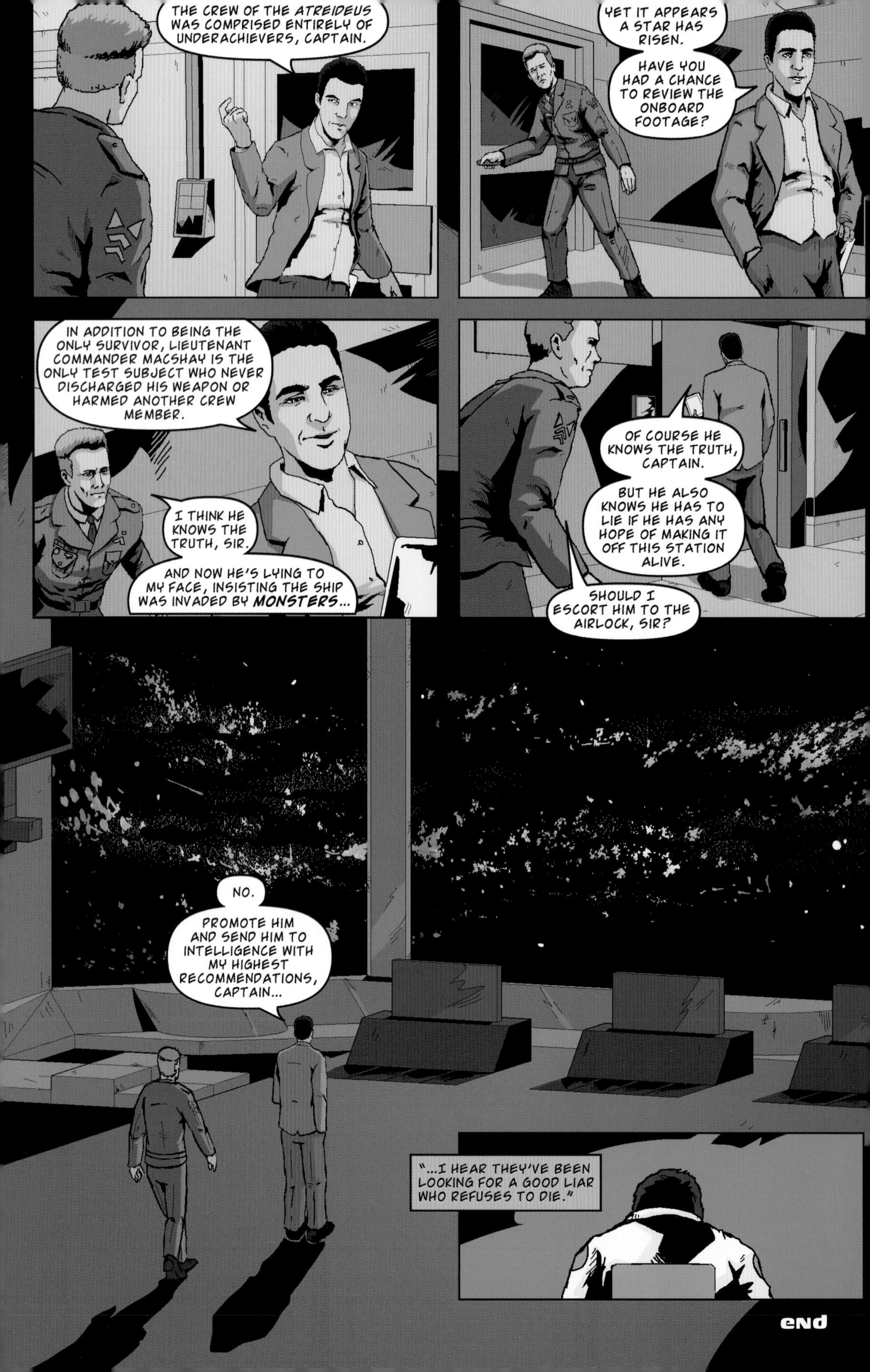
THE CREW OF THE *ATREIDEUS* WAS COMPRISED ENTIRELY OF UNDERACHIEVERS, CAPTAIN.
YET IT APPEARS A STAR HAS RISEN.
HAVE YOU HAD A CHANCE TO REVIEW THE ONBOARD FOOTAGE?
IN ADDITION TO BEING THE ONLY SURVIVOR, LIEUTENANT COMMANDER MACSHAY IS THE ONLY TEST SUBJECT WHO NEVER DISCHARGED HIS WEAPON OR HARMED ANOTHER CREW MEMBER.
I THINK HE KNOWS THE TRUTH, SIR.
AND NOW HE'S LYING TO MY FACE, INSISTING THE SHIP WAS INVADED BY **MONSTERS**...
OF COURSE HE KNOWS THE TRUTH, CAPTAIN.
BUT HE ALSO KNOWS HE HAS TO LIE IF HE HAS ANY HOPE OF MAKING IT OFF THIS STATION ALIVE.
SHOULD I ESCORT HIM TO THE AIRLOCK, SIR?
NO.
PROMOTE HIM AND SEND HIM TO INTELLIGENCE WITH MY HIGHEST RECOMMENDATIONS, CAPTAIN...
"...I HEAR THEY'VE BEEN LOOKING FOR A GOOD LIAR WHO REFUSES TO DIE."
END

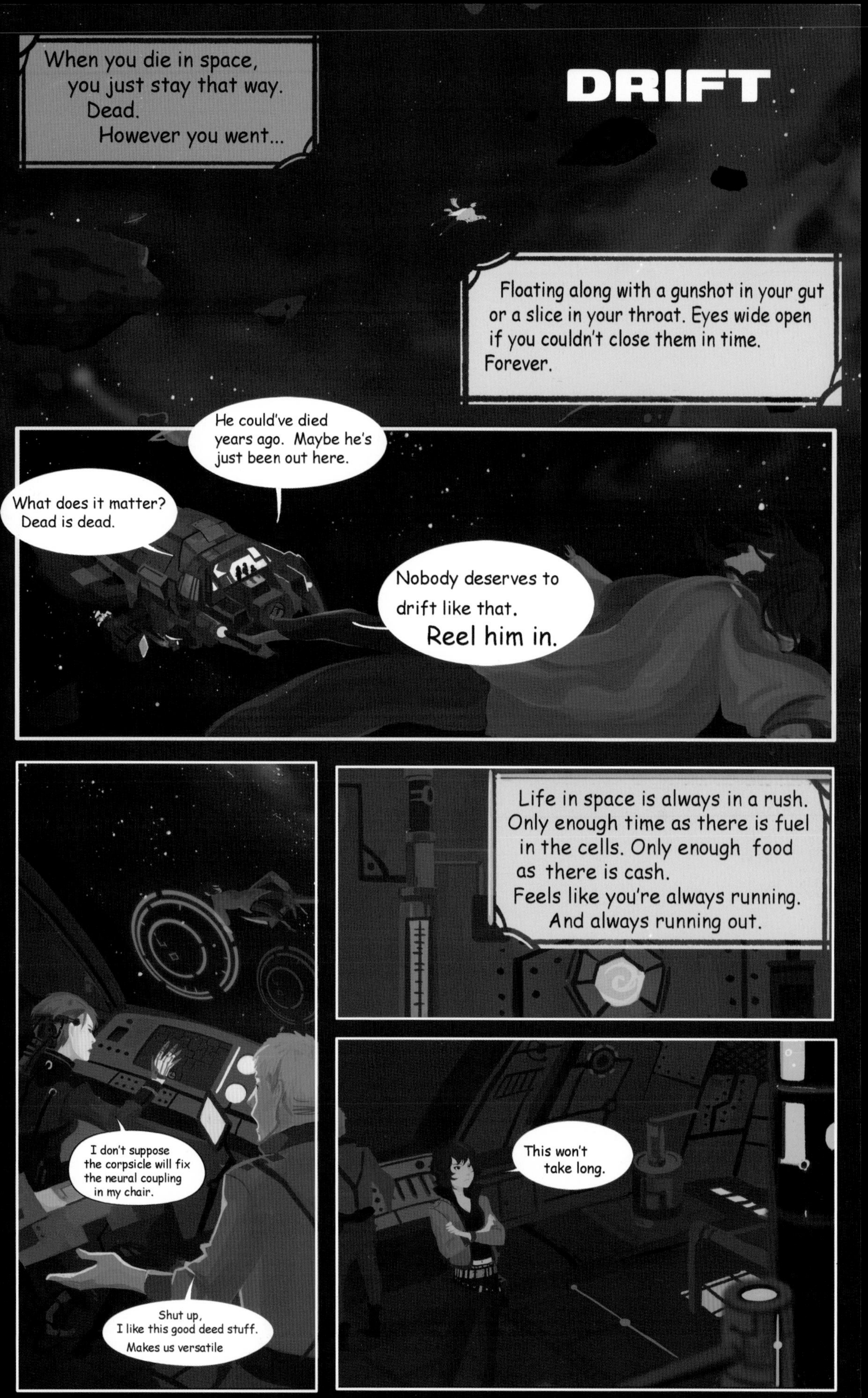
When you die in space, you just stay that way. Dead. However you went...
DRIFT
Floating along with a gunshot in your gut or a slice in your throat. Eyes wide open if you couldn't close them in time. Forever.
He could've died years ago. Maybe he's just been out here.
What does it matter? Dead is dead.
Nobody deserves to drift like that. Reel him in.
I don't suppose the corpsicle will fix the neural coupling in my chair.
Shut up, I like this good deed stuff. Makes us versatile
Life in space is always in a rush. Only enough time as there is fuel in the cells. Only enough food as there is cash. Feels like you're always running. And always running out.
This won't take long.

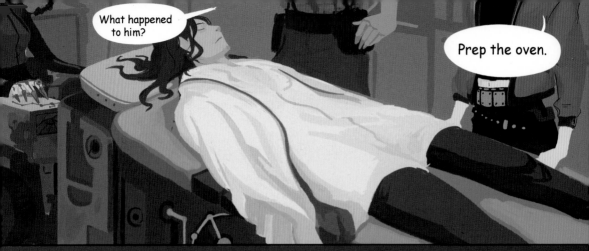

What happened to him?

Prep the oven.

We won't make it to Saturn at this rate, Captain.

We'll make it.

That's money we can't afford to lose.

I said we'll make it.

Guys...

Guys..!

He's definitely not dead!

HUMANS

How...what...!!

YOU HAVE INTERRUPTED MY SENESCENCE.

After awhile everything in space looks the same. Until...it doesn't.

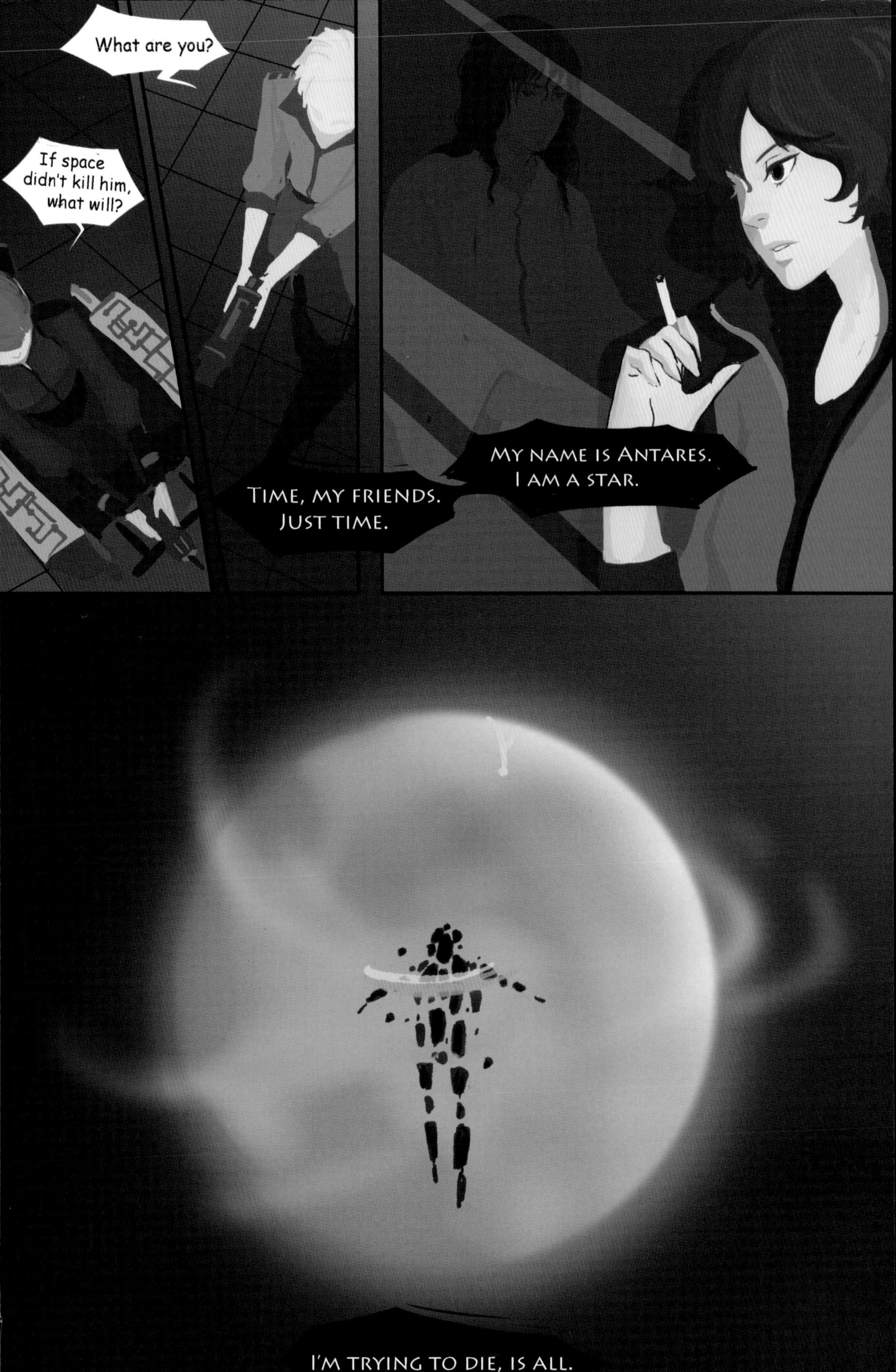

What are you?
If space didn't kill him, what will?
My name is Antares. I am a star.
Time, my friends. Just time.
I'm trying to die, is all.

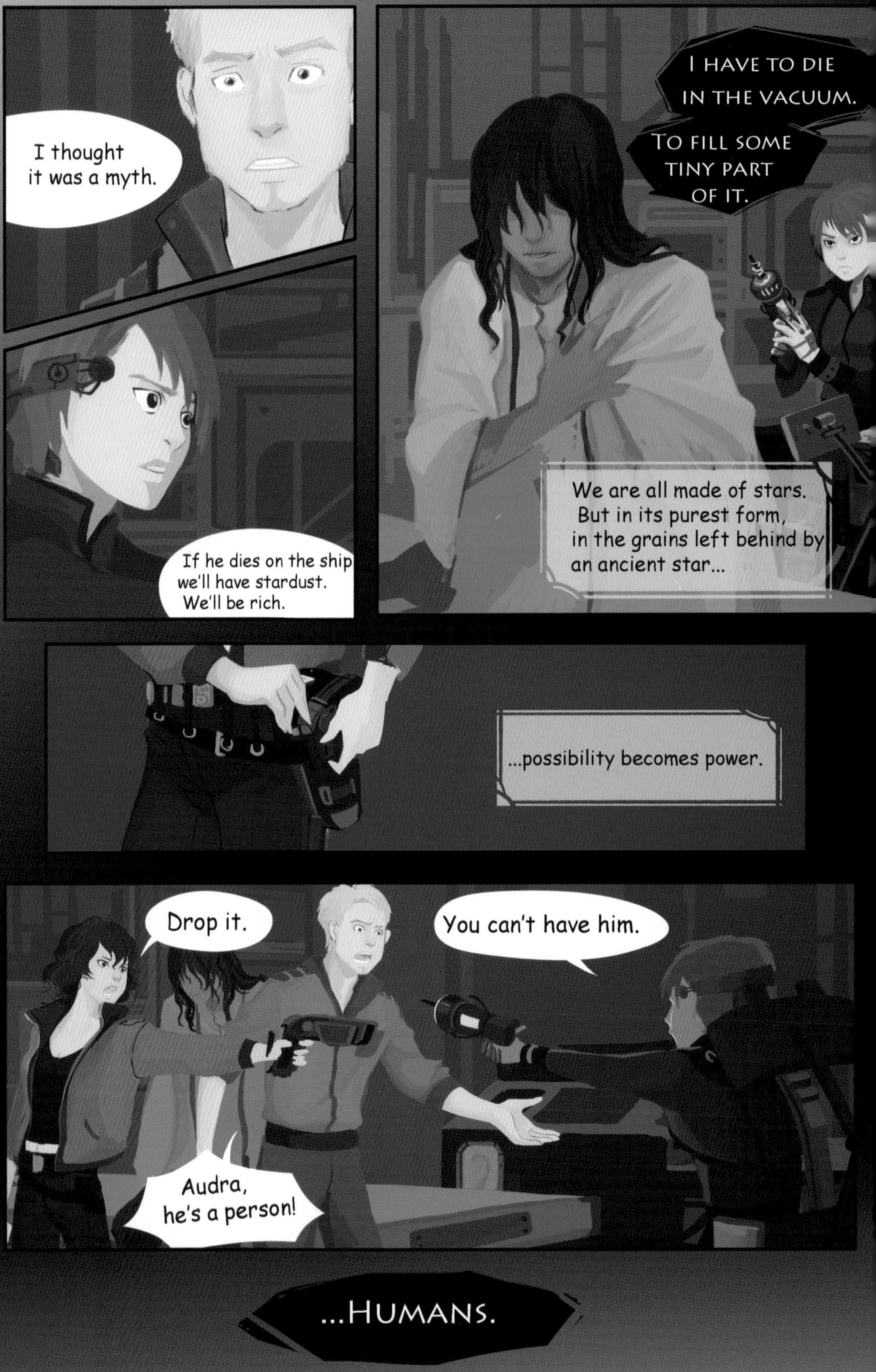

I thought it was a myth.
If he dies on the ship we'll have stardust. We'll be rich.
I have to die in the vacuum.
To fill some tiny part of it.
We are all made of stars. But in its purest form, in the grains left behind by an ancient star...
...possibility becomes power.
Drop it.
You can't have him.
Audra, he's a person!
...Humans.

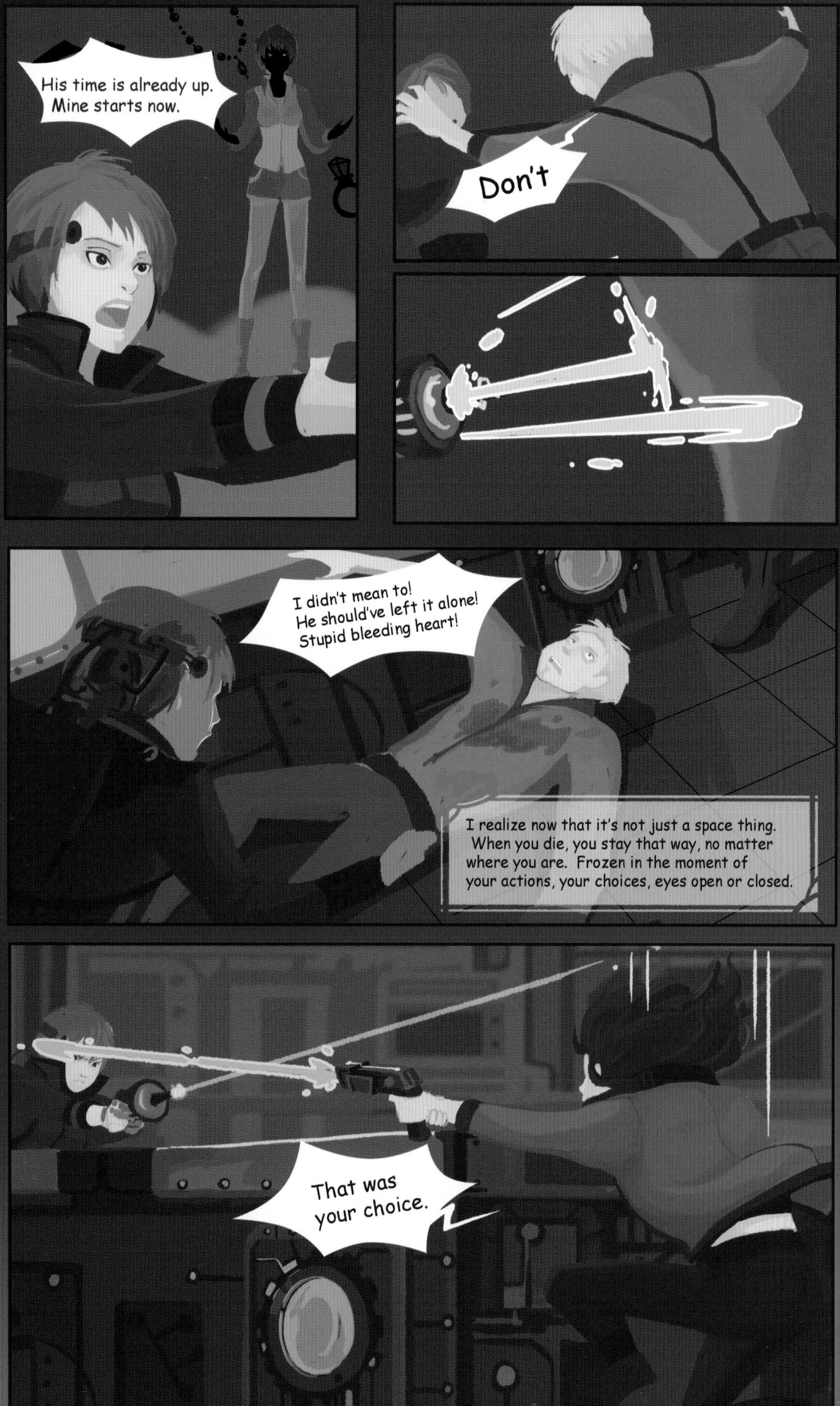
His time is already up.
Mine starts now.
Don't
I didn't mean to!
He should've left it alone!
Stupid bleeding heart!
I realize now that it's not just a space thing. When you die, you stay that way, no matter where you are. Frozen in the moment of your actions, your choices, eyes open or closed.
That was
your choice.

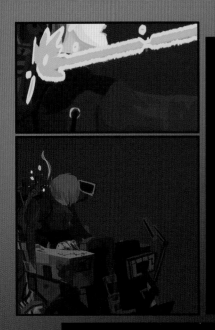

THANK YOU.

Yeah.

We all fill a part of the vacuum, add a little something to the nothing that has been there all along.

Not all of us add good somethings.

end

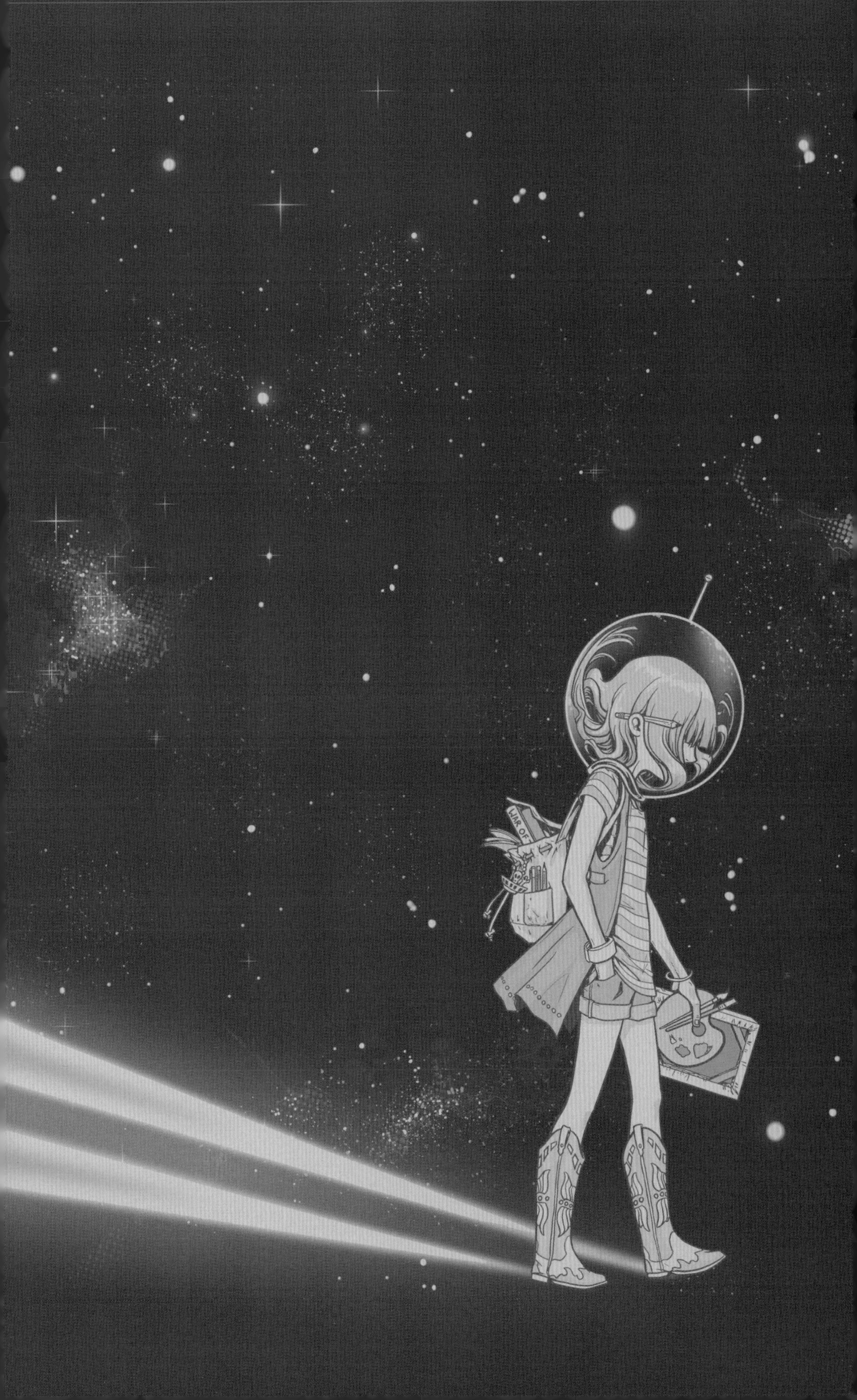
WAR OF

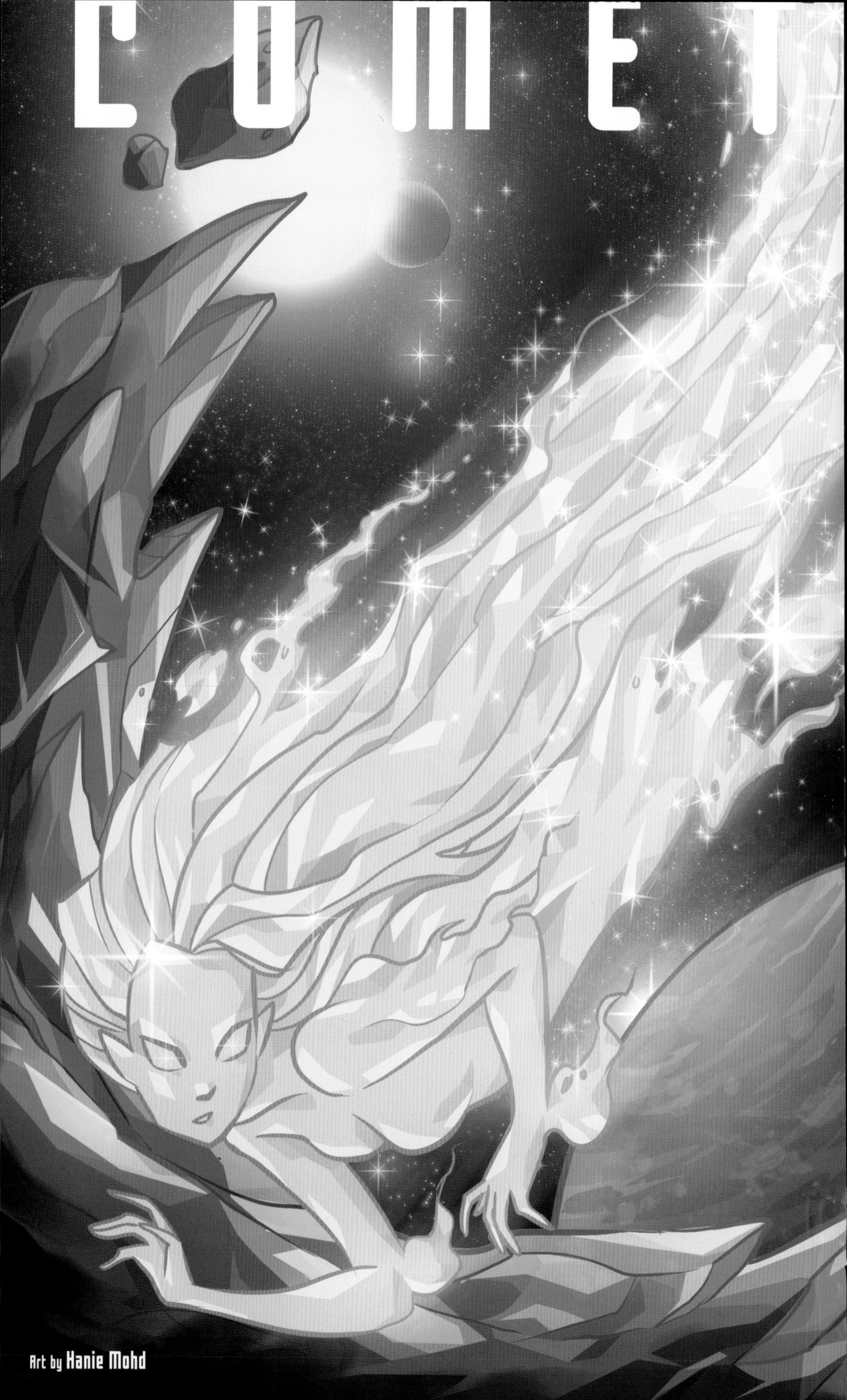
COMET

Art by Hanie Mohd

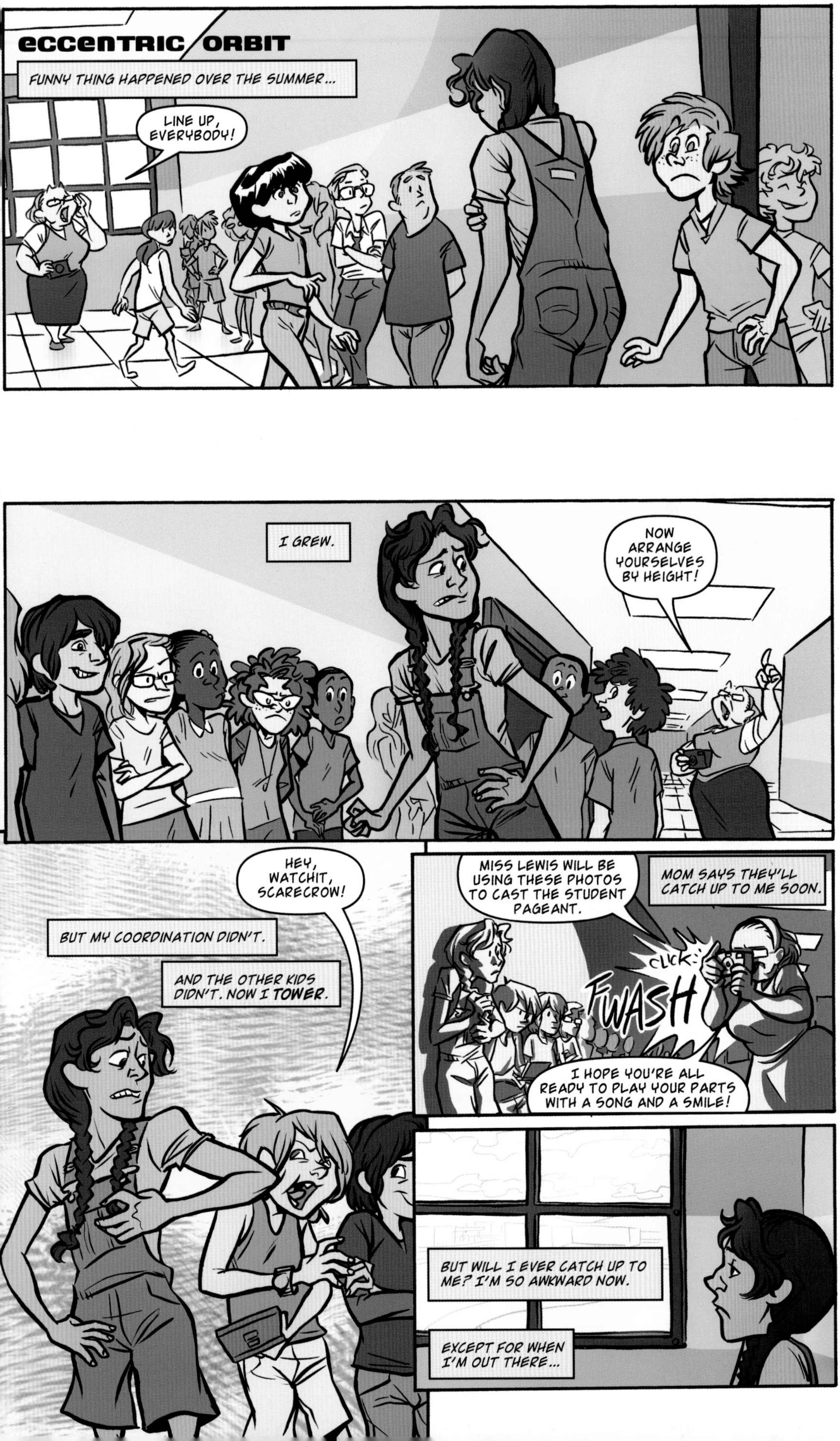

ECCENTRIC ORBIT
FUNNY THING HAPPENED OVER THE SUMMER...
LINE UP, EVERYBODY!
I GREW.
NOW ARRANGE YOURSELVES BY HEIGHT!
BUT MY COORDINATION DIDN'T.
AND THE OTHER KIDS DIDN'T. NOW I TOWER.
HEY, WATCHIT, SCARECROW!
MISS LEWIS WILL BE USING THESE PHOTOS TO CAST THE STUDENT PAGEANT.
MOM SAYS THEY'LL CATCH UP TO ME SOON.
CLICK
FWASH
I HOPE YOU'RE ALL READY TO PLAY YOUR PARTS WITH A SONG AND A SMILE!
BUT WILL I EVER CATCH UP TO ME? I'M SO AWKWARD NOW.
EXCEPT FOR WHEN I'M OUT THERE...

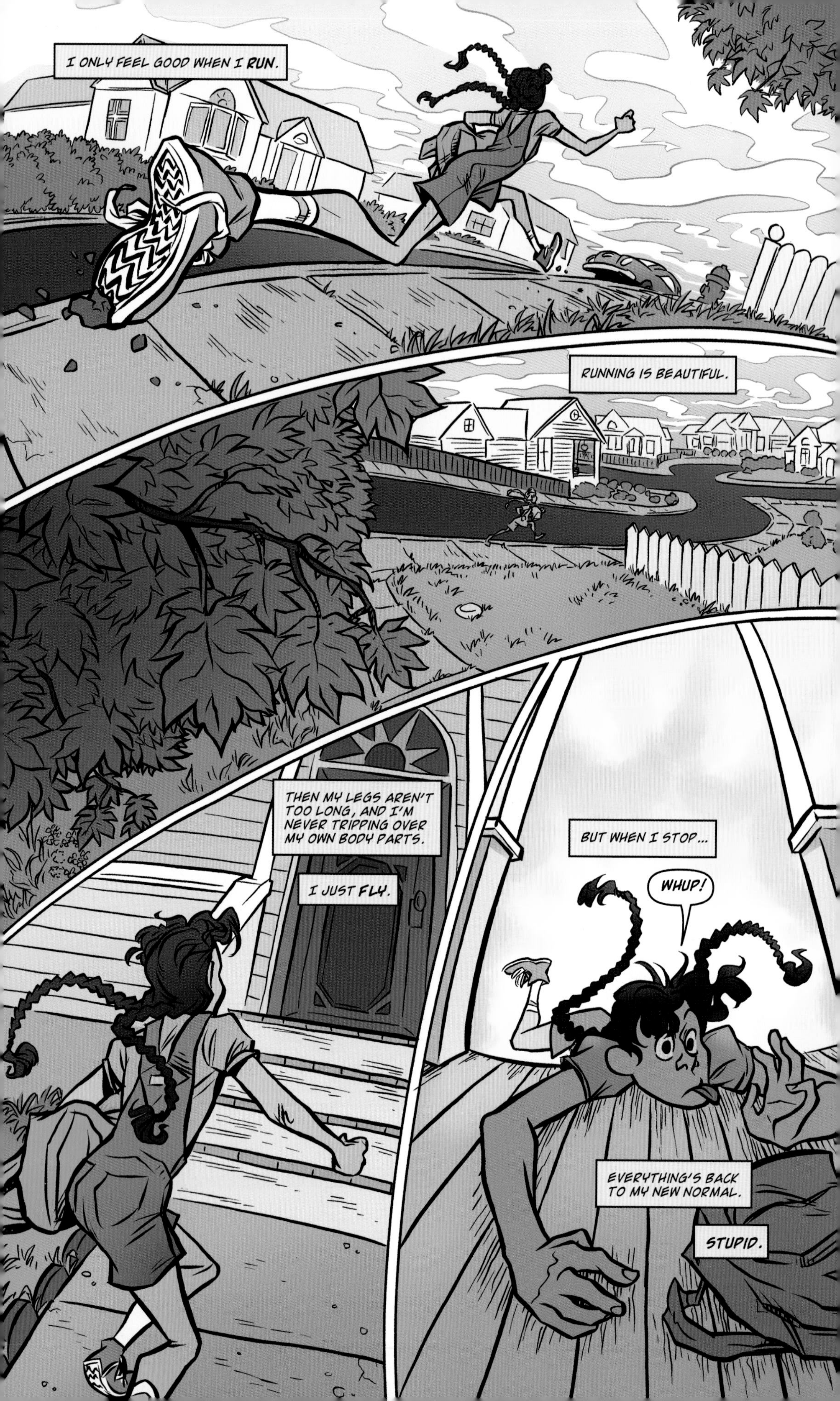
I ONLY FEEL GOOD WHEN I RUN.
RUNNING IS BEAUTIFUL.
THEN MY LEGS AREN'T TOO LONG, AND I'M NEVER TRIPPING OVER MY OWN BODY PARTS.
I JUST FLY.
BUT WHEN I STOP...
WHUP!
EVERYTHING'S BACK TO MY NEW NORMAL.
STUPID.

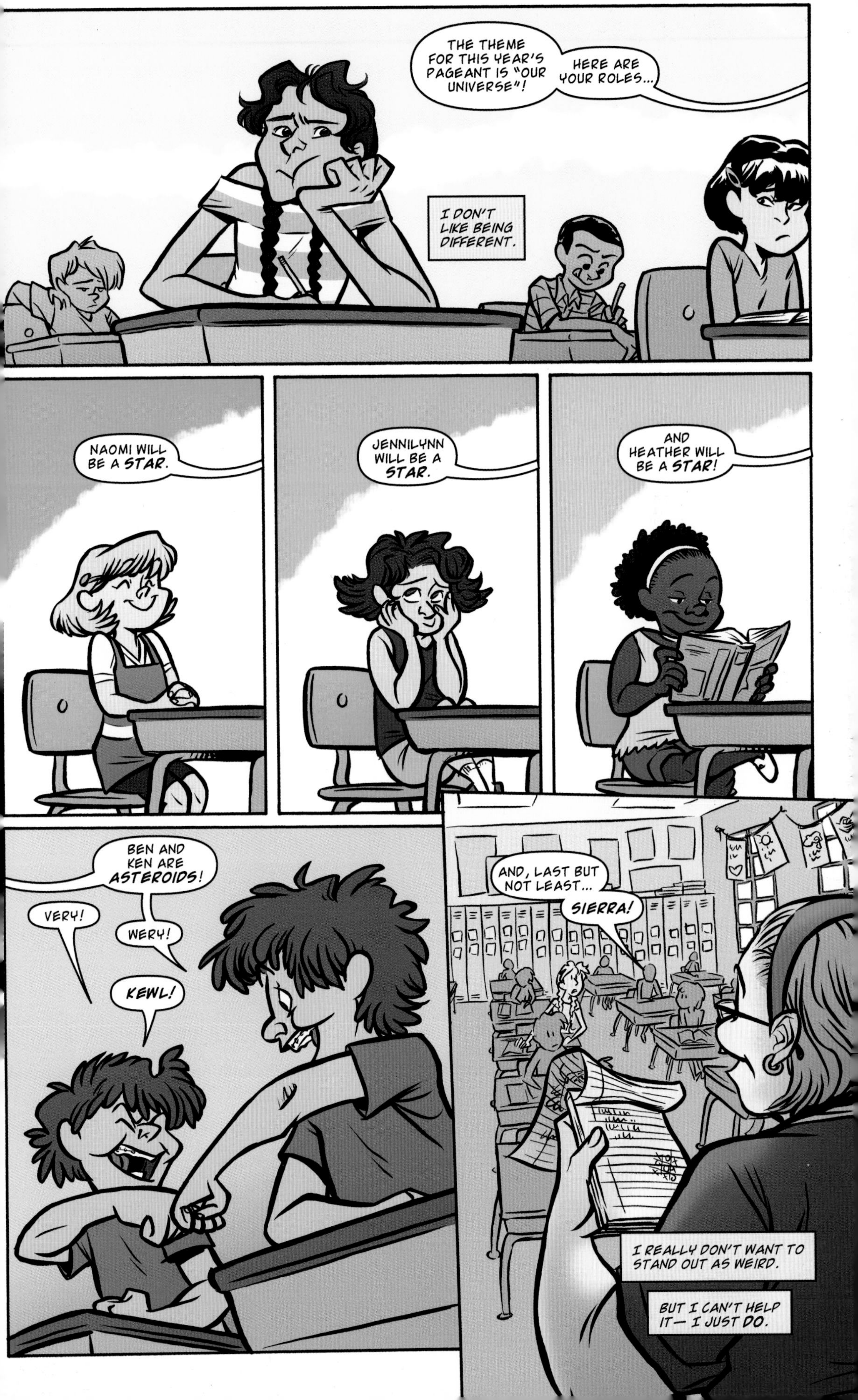
THE THEME FOR THIS YEAR'S PAGEANT IS "OUR UNIVERSE"!
HERE ARE YOUR ROLES...
I DON'T LIKE BEING DIFFERENT.
NAOMI WILL BE A STAR.
JENNILYNN WILL BE A STAR.
AND HEATHER WILL BE A STAR!
BEN AND KEN ARE ASTEROIDS!
VERY!
WERY!
KEWL!
AND, LAST BUT NOT LEAST...
SIERRA!
I REALLY DON'T WANT TO STAND OUT AS WEIRD.
BUT I CAN'T HELP IT— I JUST DO.

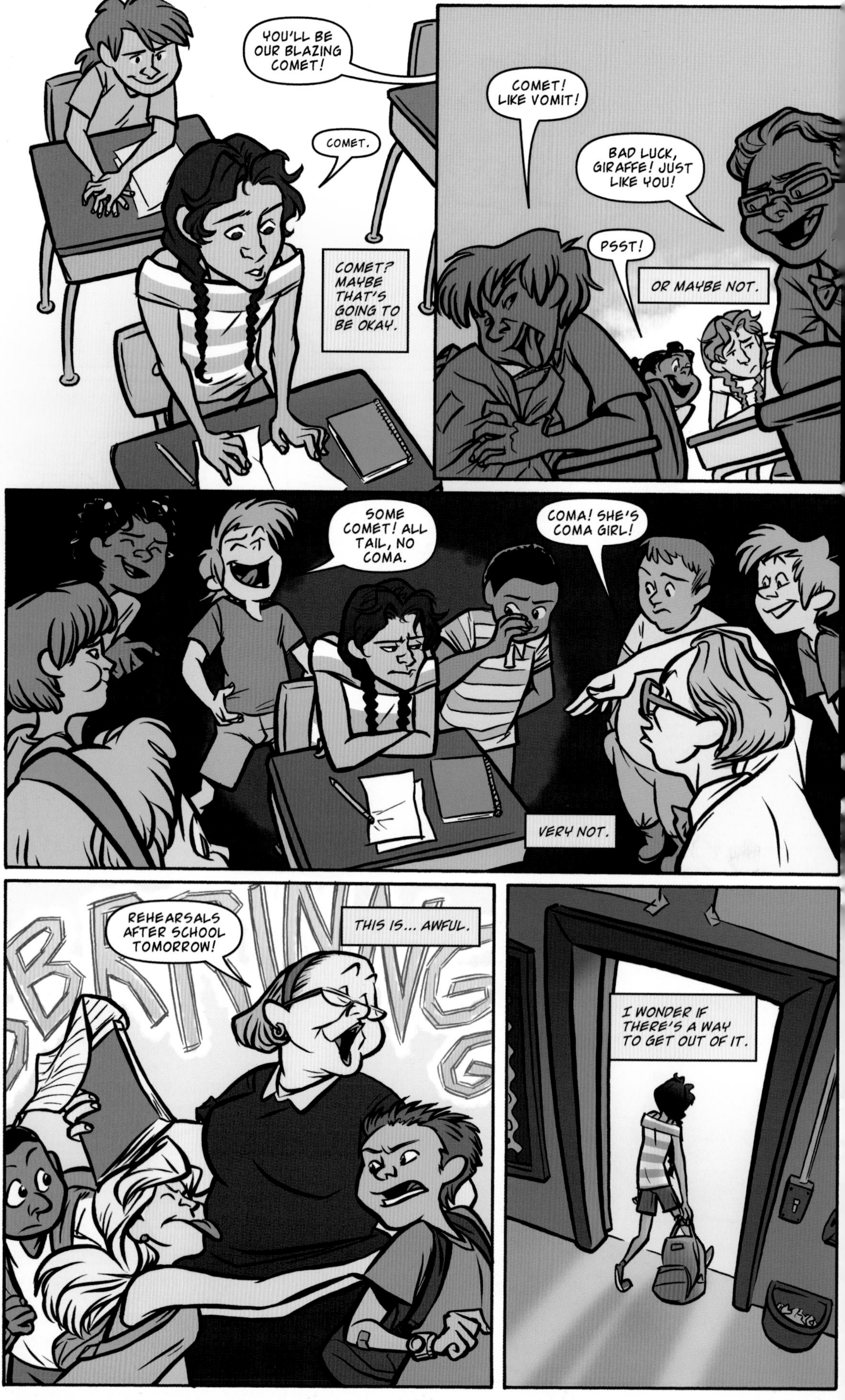
YOU'LL BE OUR BLAZING COMET!
COMET.
COMET? MAYBE THAT'S GOING TO BE OKAY.
COMET! LIKE VOMIT!
BAD LUCK, GIRAFFE! JUST LIKE YOU!
PSST!
OR MAYBE NOT.
SOME COMET! ALL TAIL, NO COMA.
COMA! SHE'S COMA GIRL!
VERY NOT.
BRRING
REHEARSALS AFTER SCHOOL TOMORROW!
THIS IS... AWFUL.
I WONDER IF THERE'S A WAY TO GET OUT OF IT.

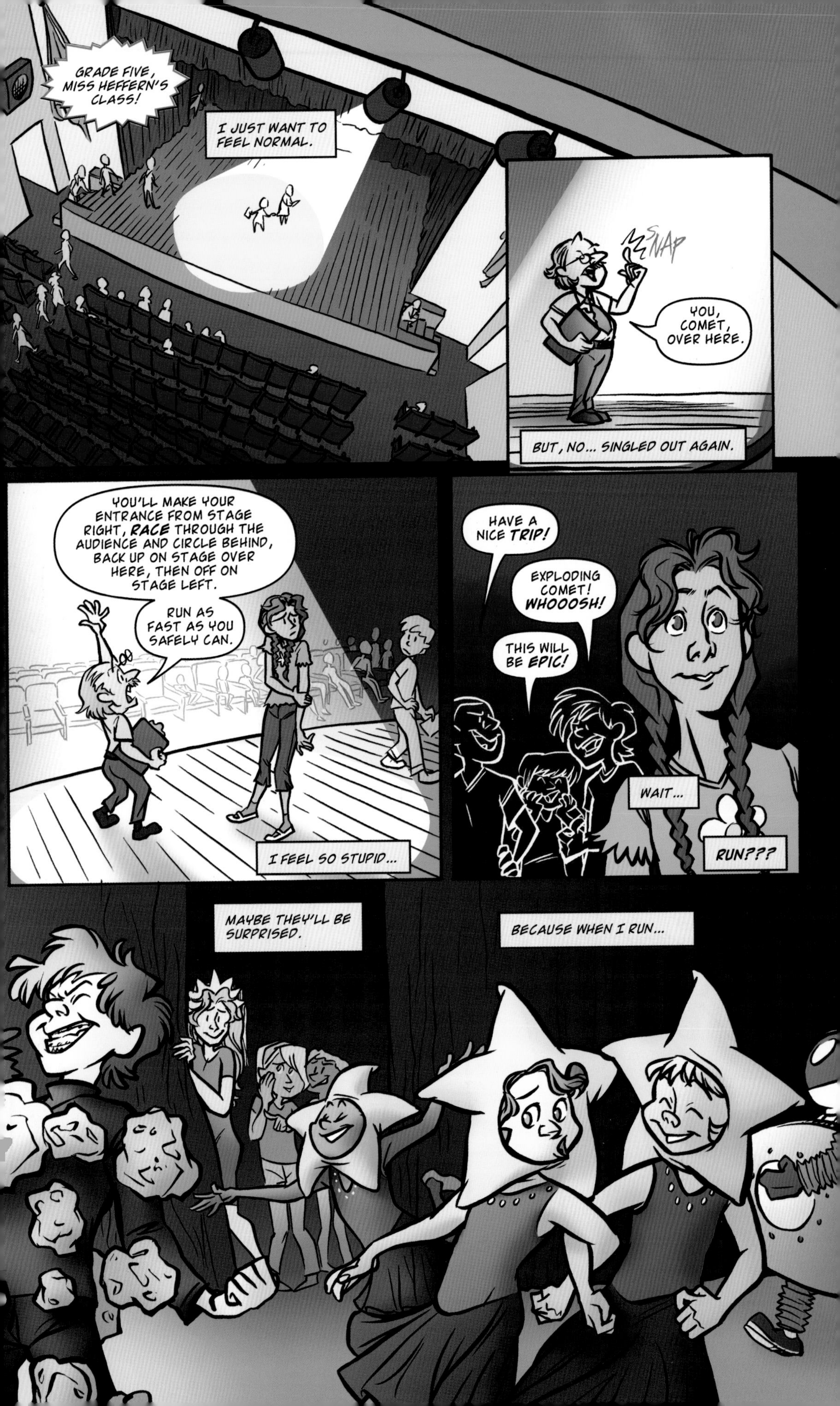

GRADE FIVE, MISS HEFFERN'S CLASS!
I JUST WANT TO FEEL NORMAL.
SNAP
YOU, COMET, OVER HERE.
BUT, NO... SINGLED OUT AGAIN.
YOU'LL MAKE YOUR ENTRANCE FROM STAGE RIGHT, RACE THROUGH THE AUDIENCE AND CIRCLE BEHIND, BACK UP ON STAGE OVER HERE, THEN OFF ON STAGE LEFT.
RUN AS FAST AS YOU SAFELY CAN.
I FEEL SO STUPID...
HAVE A NICE TRIP!
EXPLODING COMET! WHOOOSH!
THIS WILL BE EPIC!
WAIT...
RUN???
MAYBE THEY'LL BE SURPRISED.
BECAUSE WHEN I RUN...

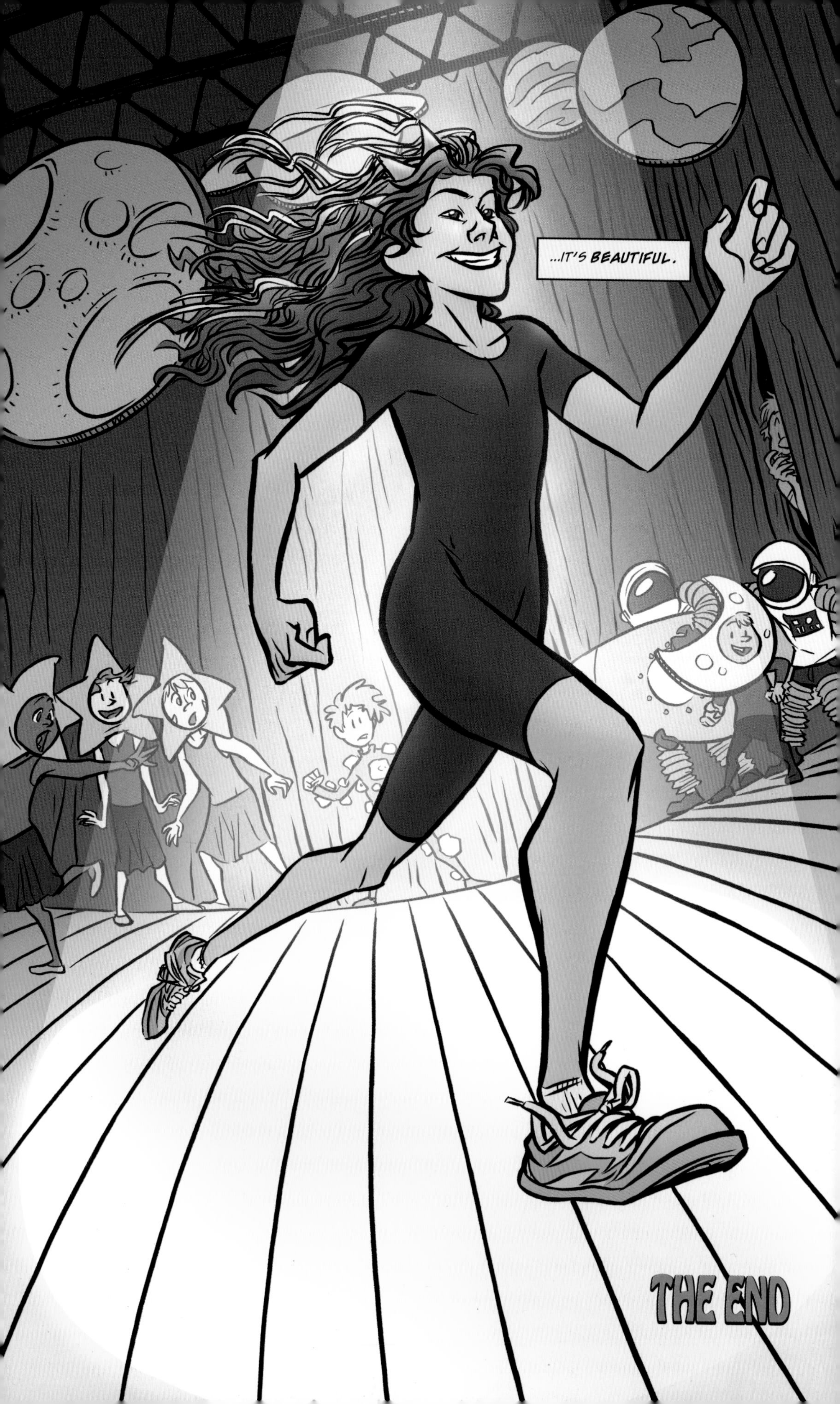
...IT'S BEAUTIFUL.
THE END

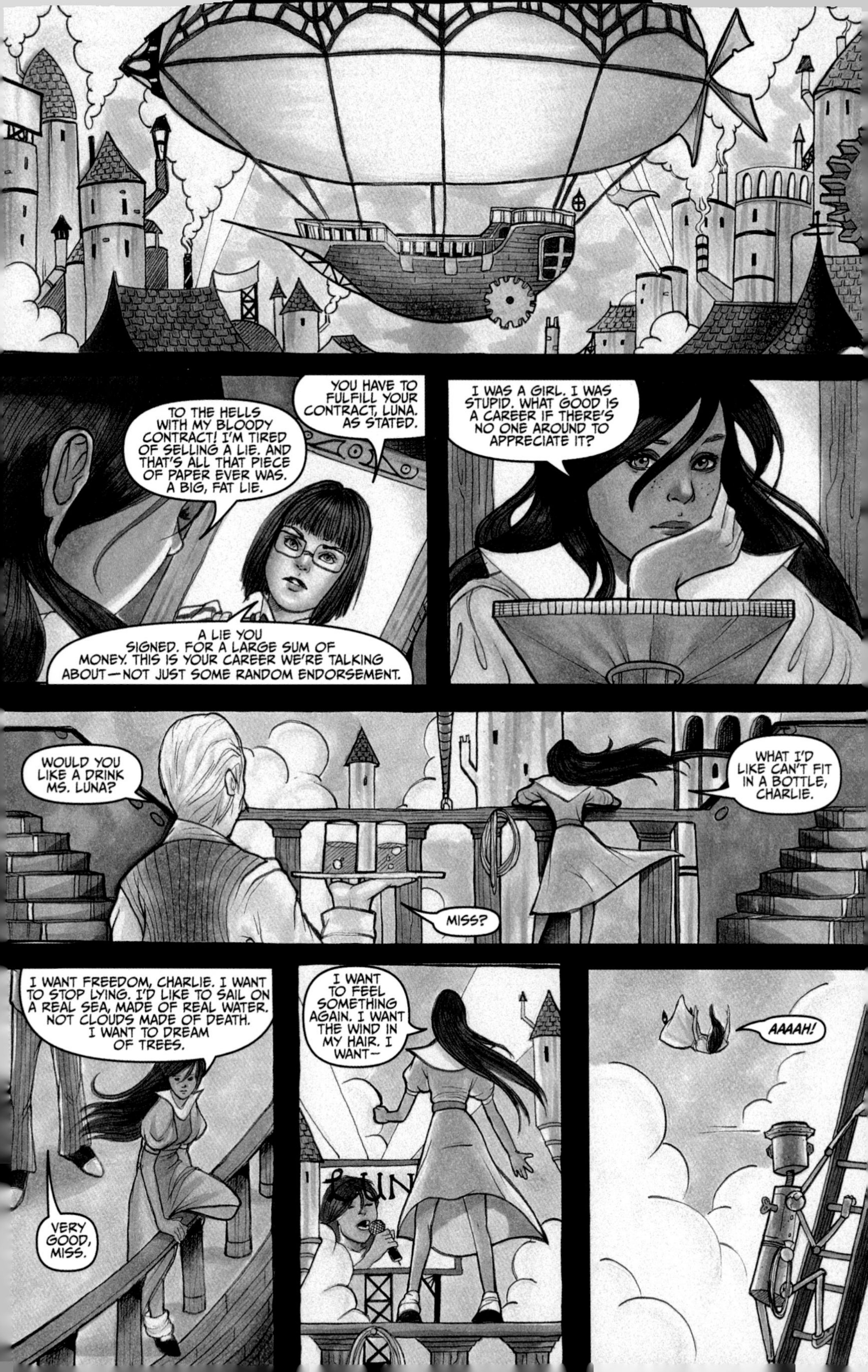
TO THE HELLS WITH MY BLOODY CONTRACT! I'M TIRED OF SELLING A LIE. AND THAT'S ALL THAT PIECE OF PAPER EVER WAS. A BIG, FAT LIE.
YOU HAVE TO FULFILL YOUR CONTRACT, LUNA. AS STATED.
A LIE YOU SIGNED. FOR A LARGE SUM OF MONEY. THIS IS YOUR CAREER WE'RE TALKING ABOUT—NOT JUST SOME RANDOM ENDORSEMENT.
I WAS A GIRL. I WAS STUPID. WHAT GOOD IS A CAREER IF THERE'S NO ONE AROUND TO APPRECIATE IT?
WOULD YOU LIKE A DRINK MS. LUNA?
WHAT I'D LIKE CAN'T FIT IN A BOTTLE, CHARLIE.
MISS?
I WANT FREEDOM, CHARLIE. I WANT TO STOP LYING. I'D LIKE TO SAIL ON A REAL SEA, MADE OF REAL WATER. NOT CLOUDS MADE OF DEATH. I WANT TO DREAM OF TREES.
VERY GOOD, MISS.
I WANT TO FEEL SOMETHING AGAIN. I WANT THE WIND IN MY HAIR. I WANT—
AAAAH!

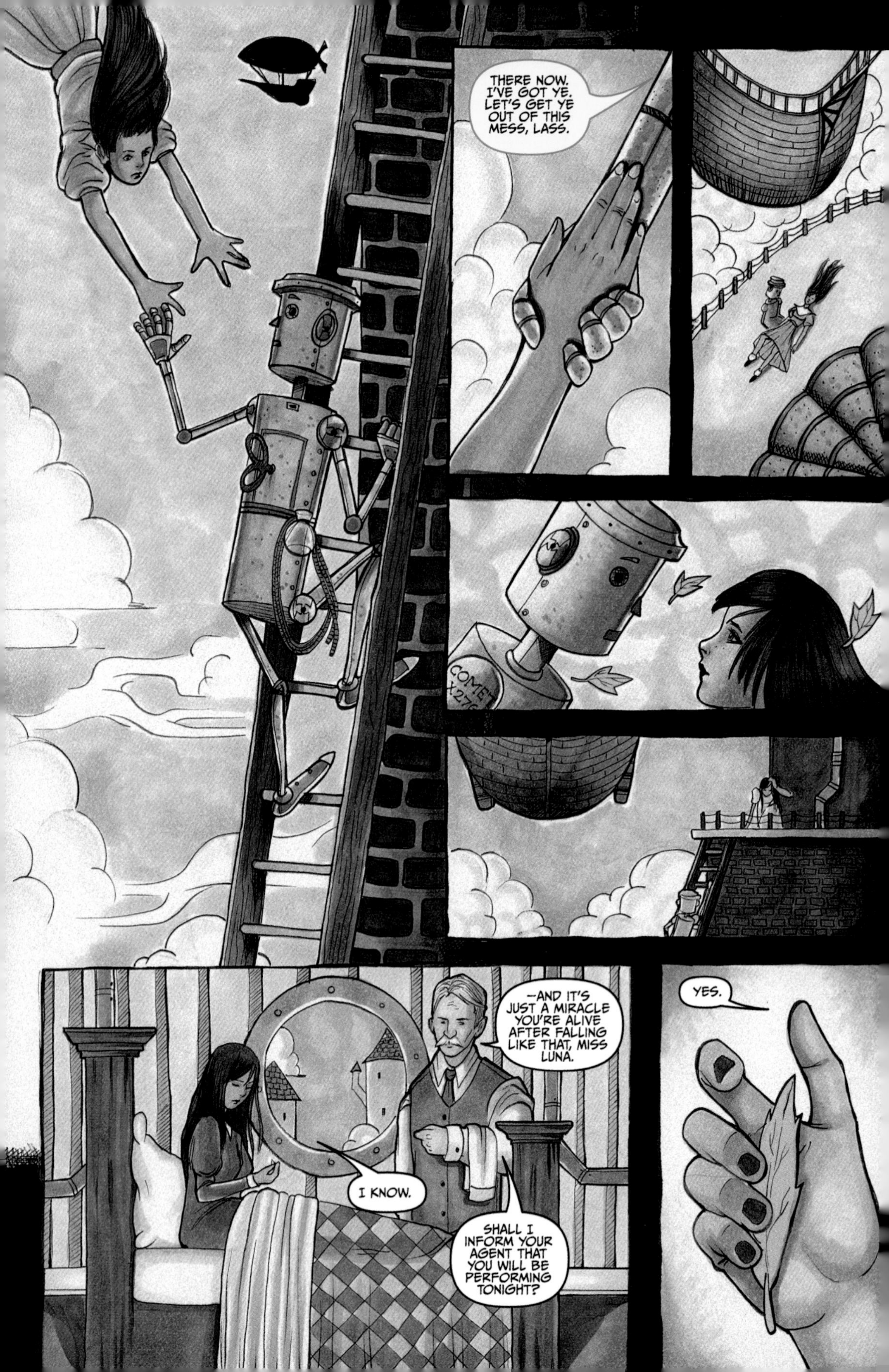
THERE NOW. I'VE GOT YE. LET'S GET YE OUT OF THIS MESS, LASS.
COMET X276
—AND IT'S JUST A MIRACLE YOU'RE ALIVE AFTER FALLING LIKE THAT, MISS LUNA.
I KNOW.
SHALL I INFORM YOUR AGENT THAT YOU WILL BE PERFORMING TONIGHT?
YES.

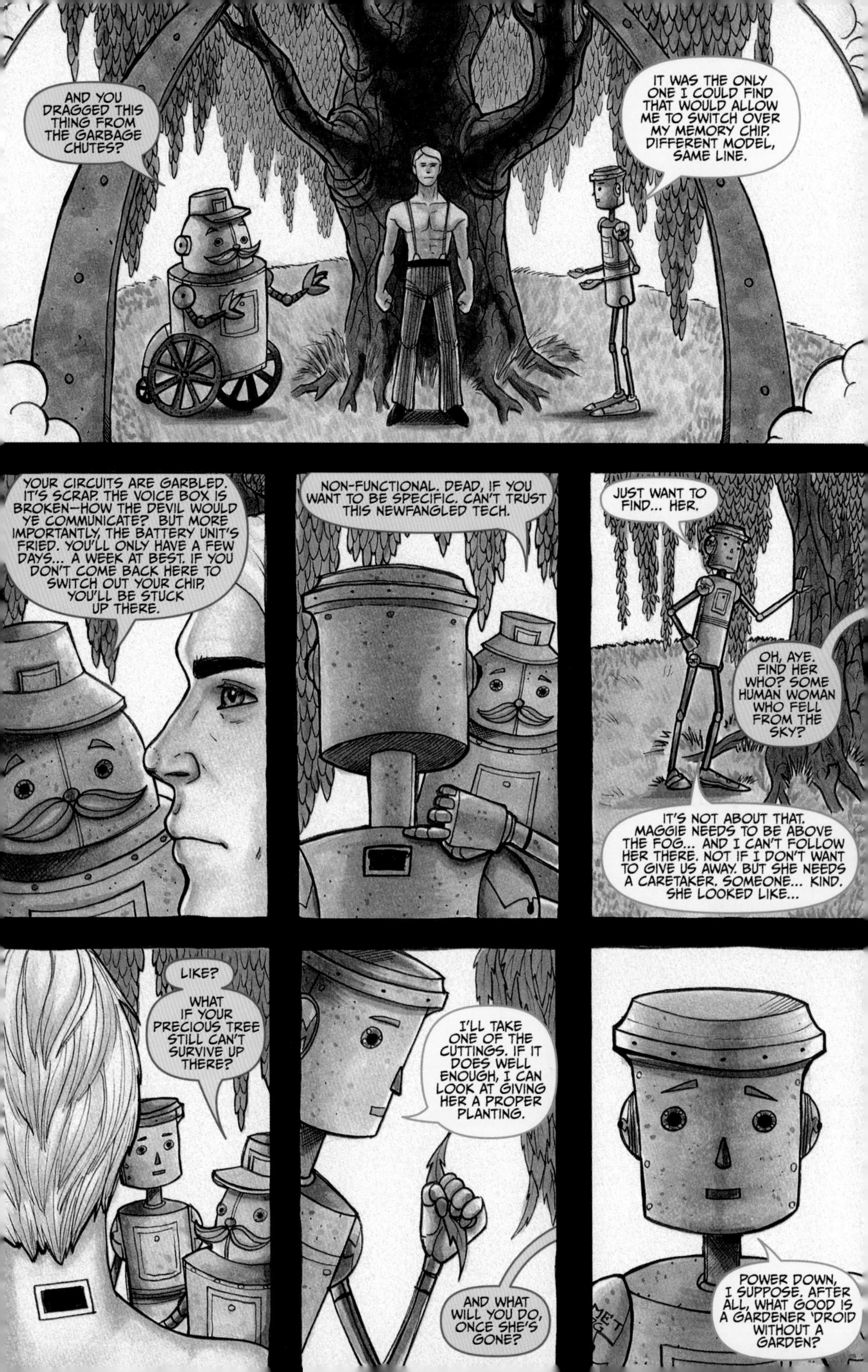
AND YOU DRAGGED THIS THING FROM THE GARBAGE CHUTES?
IT WAS THE ONLY ONE I COULD FIND THAT WOULD ALLOW ME TO SWITCH OVER MY MEMORY CHIP. DIFFERENT MODEL, SAME LINE.
YOUR CIRCUITS ARE GARBLED. IT'S SCRAP. THE VOICE BOX IS BROKEN--HOW THE DEVIL WOULD YE COMMUNICATE? BUT MORE IMPORTANTLY, THE BATTERY UNIT'S FRIED. YOU'LL ONLY HAVE A FEW DAYS... A WEEK AT BEST. IF YOU DON'T COME BACK HERE TO SWITCH OUT YOUR CHIP, YOU'LL BE STUCK UP THERE.
NON-FUNCTIONAL. DEAD, IF YOU WANT TO BE SPECIFIC. CAN'T TRUST THIS NEWFANGLED TECH.
JUST WANT TO FIND... HER.
OH, AYE. FIND HER WHO? SOME HUMAN WOMAN WHO FELL FROM THE SKY?
IT'S NOT ABOUT THAT. MAGGIE NEEDS TO BE ABOVE THE FOG... AND I CAN'T FOLLOW HER THERE. NOT IF I DON'T WANT TO GIVE US AWAY. BUT SHE NEEDS A CARETAKER. SOMEONE... KIND. SHE LOOKED LIKE...
LIKE?
WHAT IF YOUR PRECIOUS TREE STILL CAN'T SURVIVE UP THERE?
I'LL TAKE ONE OF THE CUTTINGS. IF IT DOES WELL ENOUGH, I CAN LOOK AT GIVING HER A PROPER PLANTING.
AND WHAT WILL YOU DO, ONCE SHE'S GONE?
POWER DOWN, I SUPPOSE. AFTER ALL, WHAT GOOD IS A GARDENER 'DROID WITHOUT A GARDEN?

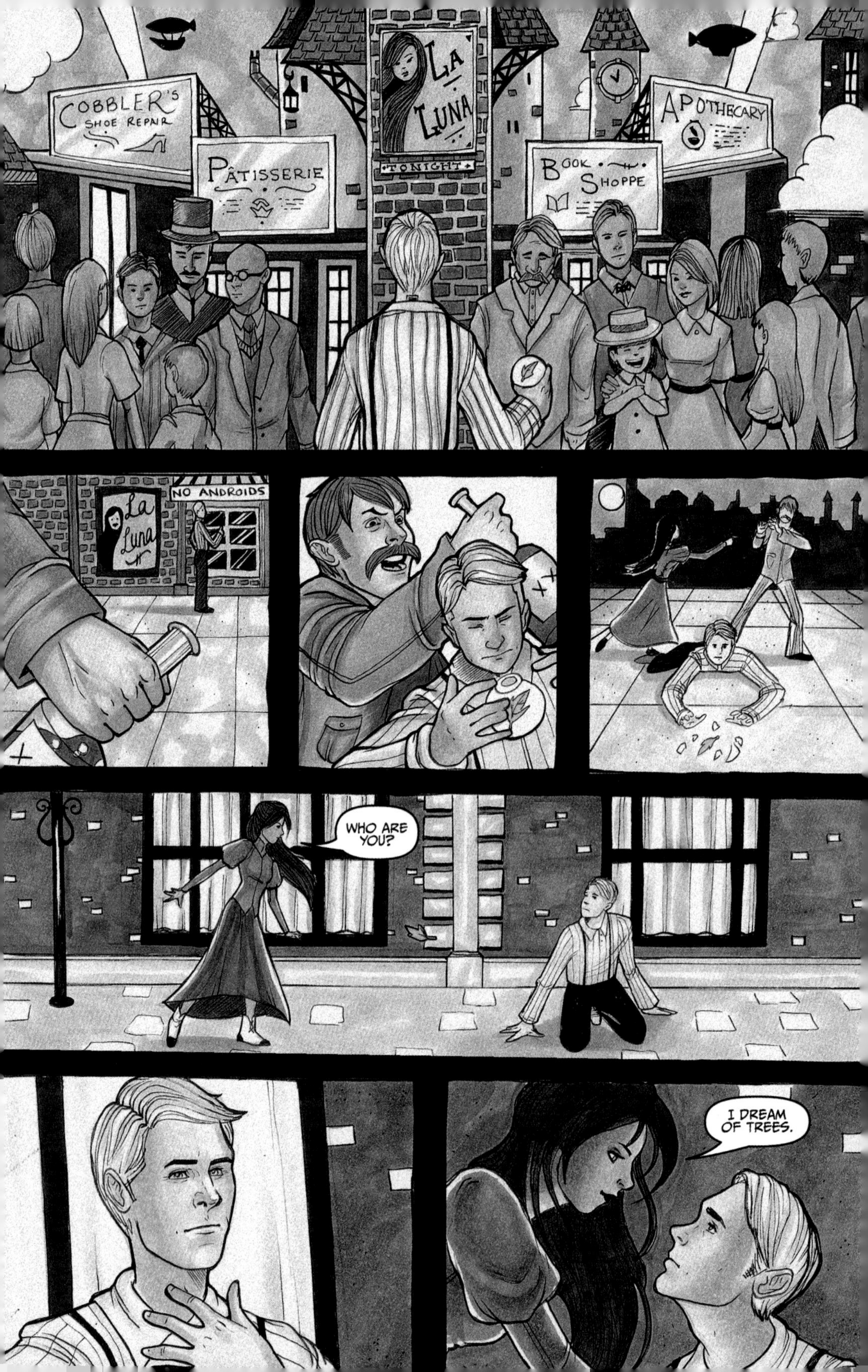
COBBLER'S
SHOE REPAIR
PÂTISSERIE
LA LUNA
TONIGHT
BOOK SHOPPE
APOTHECARY
LA LUNA
NO ANDROIDS
WHO ARE YOU?
I DREAM OF TREES.

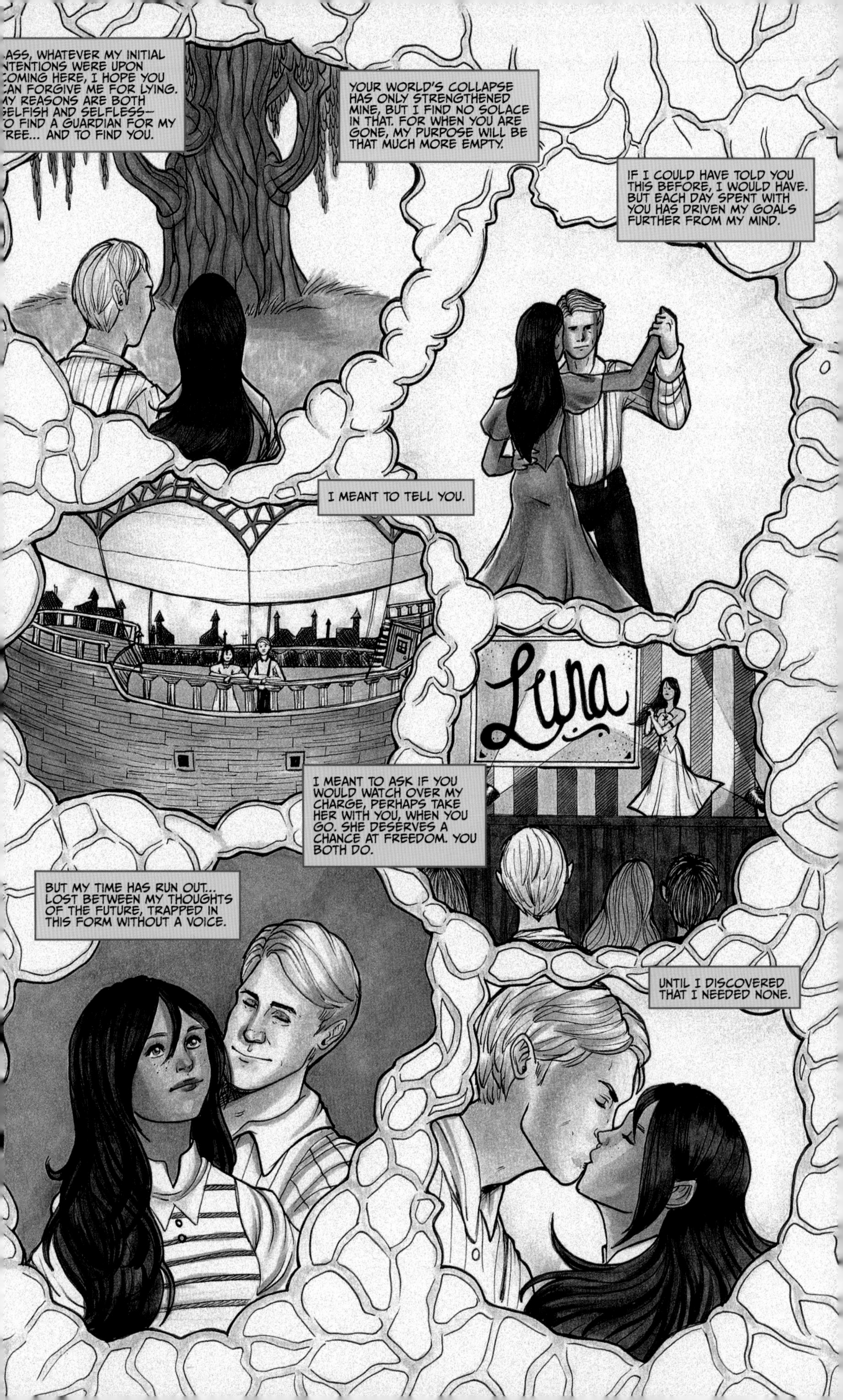
LASS, WHATEVER MY INITIAL INTENTIONS WERE UPON COMING HERE, I HOPE YOU CAN FORGIVE ME FOR LYING. MY REASONS ARE BOTH SELFISH AND SELFLESS— TO FIND A GUARDIAN FOR MY TREE... AND TO FIND YOU.
YOUR WORLD'S COLLAPSE HAS ONLY STRENGTHENED MINE, BUT I FIND NO SOLACE IN THAT. FOR WHEN YOU ARE GONE, MY PURPOSE WILL BE THAT MUCH MORE EMPTY.
IF I COULD HAVE TOLD YOU THIS BEFORE, I WOULD HAVE. BUT EACH DAY SPENT WITH YOU HAS DRIVEN MY GOALS FURTHER FROM MY MIND.
I MEANT TO TELL YOU.
Luna
I MEANT TO ASK IF YOU WOULD WATCH OVER MY CHARGE, PERHAPS TAKE HER WITH YOU, WHEN YOU GO. SHE DESERVES A CHANCE AT FREEDOM. YOU BOTH DO.
BUT MY TIME HAS RUN OUT... LOST BETWEEN MY THOUGHTS OF THE FUTURE, TRAPPED IN THIS FORM WITHOUT A VOICE.
UNTIL I DISCOVERED THAT I NEEDED NONE.

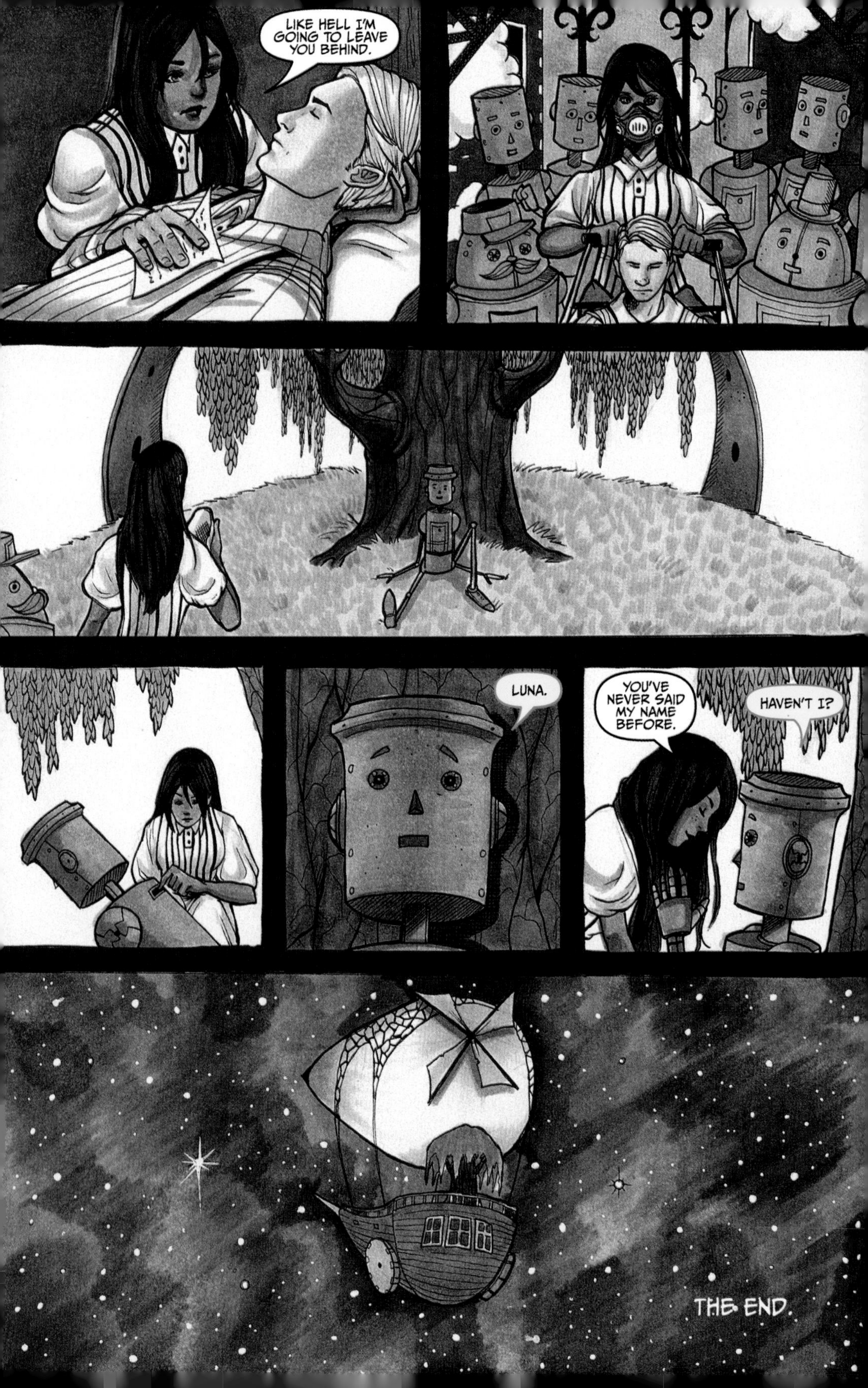
LIKE HELL I'M GOING TO LEAVE YOU BEHIND.
LUNA.
YOU'VE NEVER SAID MY NAME BEFORE.
HAVEN'T I?
THE END.

IN THE DRINK

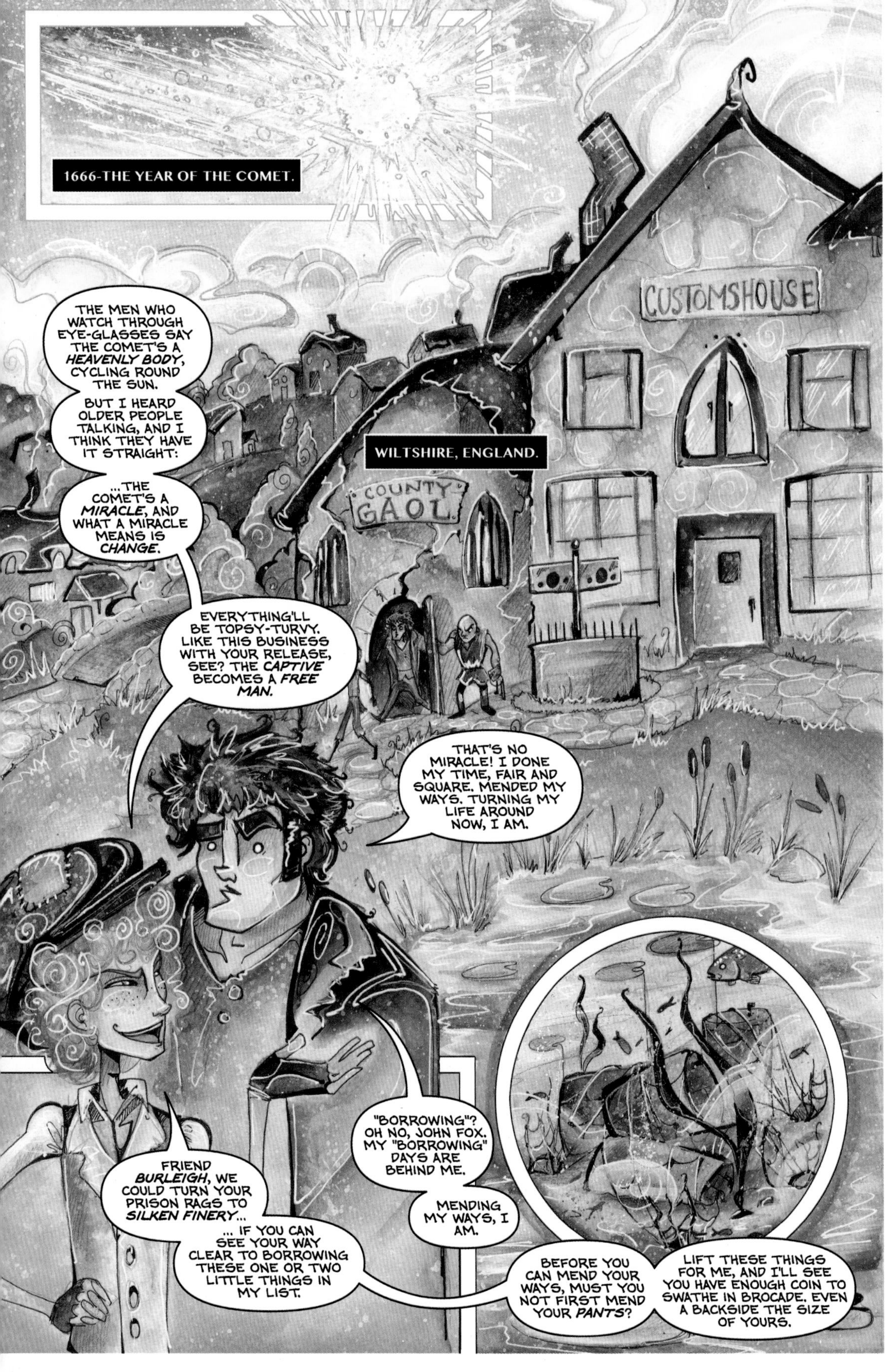

1666-THE YEAR OF THE COMET.
CUSTOMSHOUSE
WILTSHIRE, ENGLAND.
COUNTY GAOL
THE MEN WHO WATCH THROUGH EYE-GLASSES SAY THE COMET'S A *HEAVENLY BODY*, CYCLING ROUND THE SUN.
BUT I HEARD OLDER PEOPLE TALKING, AND I THINK THEY HAVE IT STRAIGHT:
...THE COMET'S A *MIRACLE*, AND WHAT A MIRACLE MEANS IS *CHANGE*.
EVERYTHING'LL BE TOPSY-TURVY. LIKE THIS BUSINESS WITH YOUR RELEASE, SEE? THE *CAPTIVE* BECOMES A *FREE MAN*.
THAT'S NO MIRACLE! I DONE MY TIME, FAIR AND SQUARE. MENDED MY WAYS. TURNING MY LIFE AROUND NOW, I AM.
FRIEND *BURLEIGH*, WE COULD TURN YOUR PRISON RAGS TO *SILKEN FINERY*...
... IF YOU CAN SEE YOUR WAY CLEAR TO BORROWING THESE ONE OR TWO LITTLE THINGS IN MY LIST.
"BORROWING"? OH NO, JOHN FOX. MY "BORROWING" DAYS ARE BEHIND ME.
MENDING MY WAYS, I AM.
BEFORE YOU CAN MEND YOUR WAYS, MUST YOU NOT FIRST MEND YOUR *PANTS*?
LIFT THESE THINGS FOR ME, AND I'LL SEE YOU HAVE ENOUGH COIN TO SWATHE IN BROCADE. EVEN A BACKSIDE THE SIZE OF YOURS.

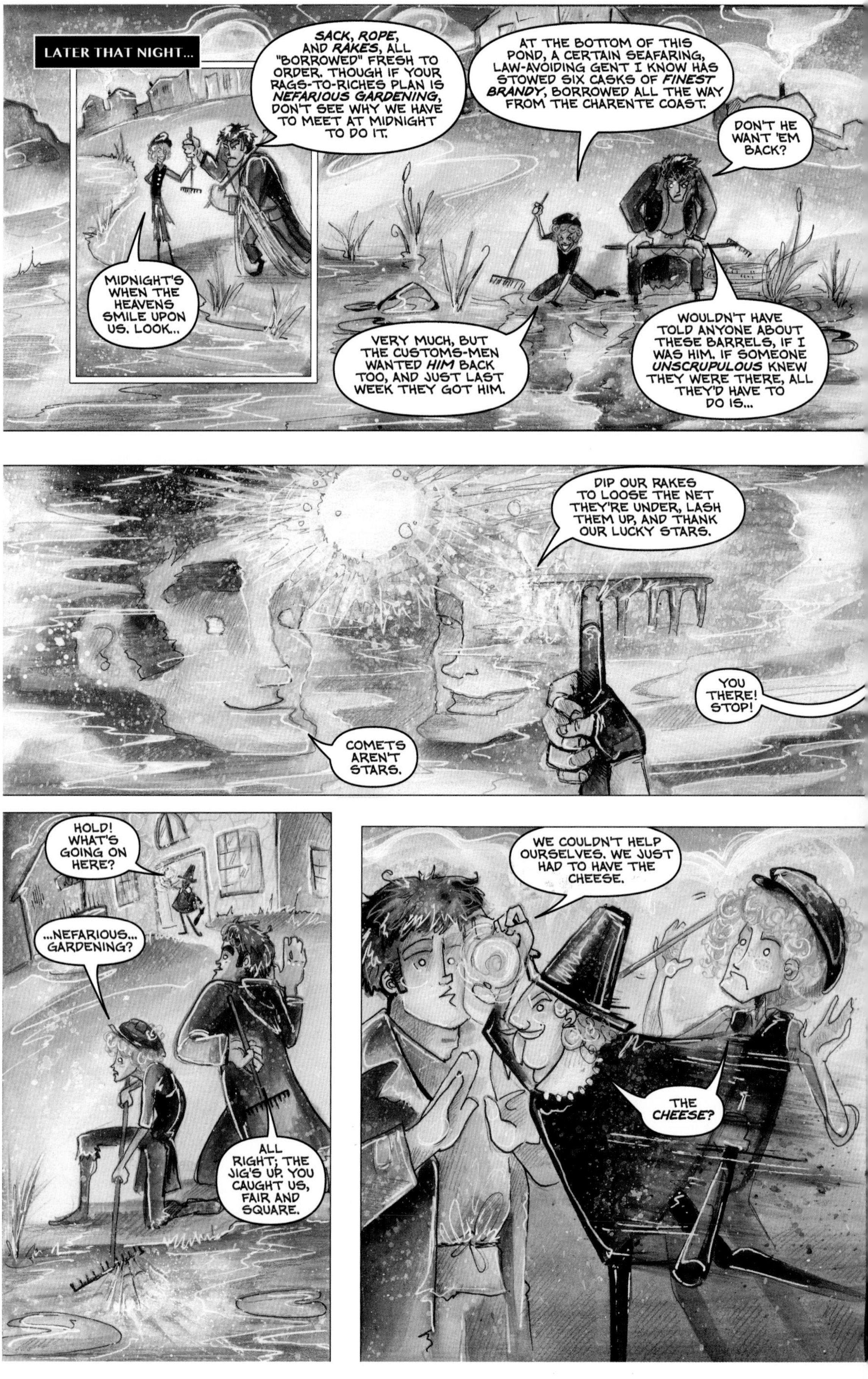
LATER THAT NIGHT...
SACK, ROPE, AND RAKES, ALL "BORROWED" FRESH TO ORDER. THOUGH IF YOUR RAGS-TO-RICHES PLAN IS NEFARIOUS GARDENING, DON'T SEE WHY WE HAVE TO MEET AT MIDNIGHT TO DO IT.
MIDNIGHT'S WHEN THE HEAVENS SMILE UPON US. LOOK...
AT THE BOTTOM OF THIS POND, A CERTAIN SEAFARING, LAW-AVOIDING GENT I KNOW HAS STOWED SIX CASKS OF FINEST BRANDY, BORROWED ALL THE WAY FROM THE CHARENTE COAST.
DON'T HE WANT 'EM BACK?
VERY MUCH, BUT THE CUSTOMS-MEN WANTED HIM BACK TOO, AND JUST LAST WEEK THEY GOT HIM.
WOULDN'T HAVE TOLD ANYONE ABOUT THESE BARRELS, IF I WAS HIM. IF SOMEONE UNSCRUPULOUS KNEW THEY WERE THERE, ALL THEY'D HAVE TO DO IS...
DIP OUR RAKES TO LOOSE THE NET THEY'RE UNDER, LASH THEM UP, AND THANK OUR LUCKY STARS.
COMETS AREN'T STARS.
YOU THERE! STOP!
HOLD! WHAT'S GOING ON HERE?
...NEFARIOUS... GARDENING?
ALL RIGHT; THE JIG'S UP. YOU CAUGHT US, FAIR AND SQUARE.
WE COULDN'T HELP OURSELVES. WE JUST HAD TO HAVE THE CHEESE.
THE CHEESE?

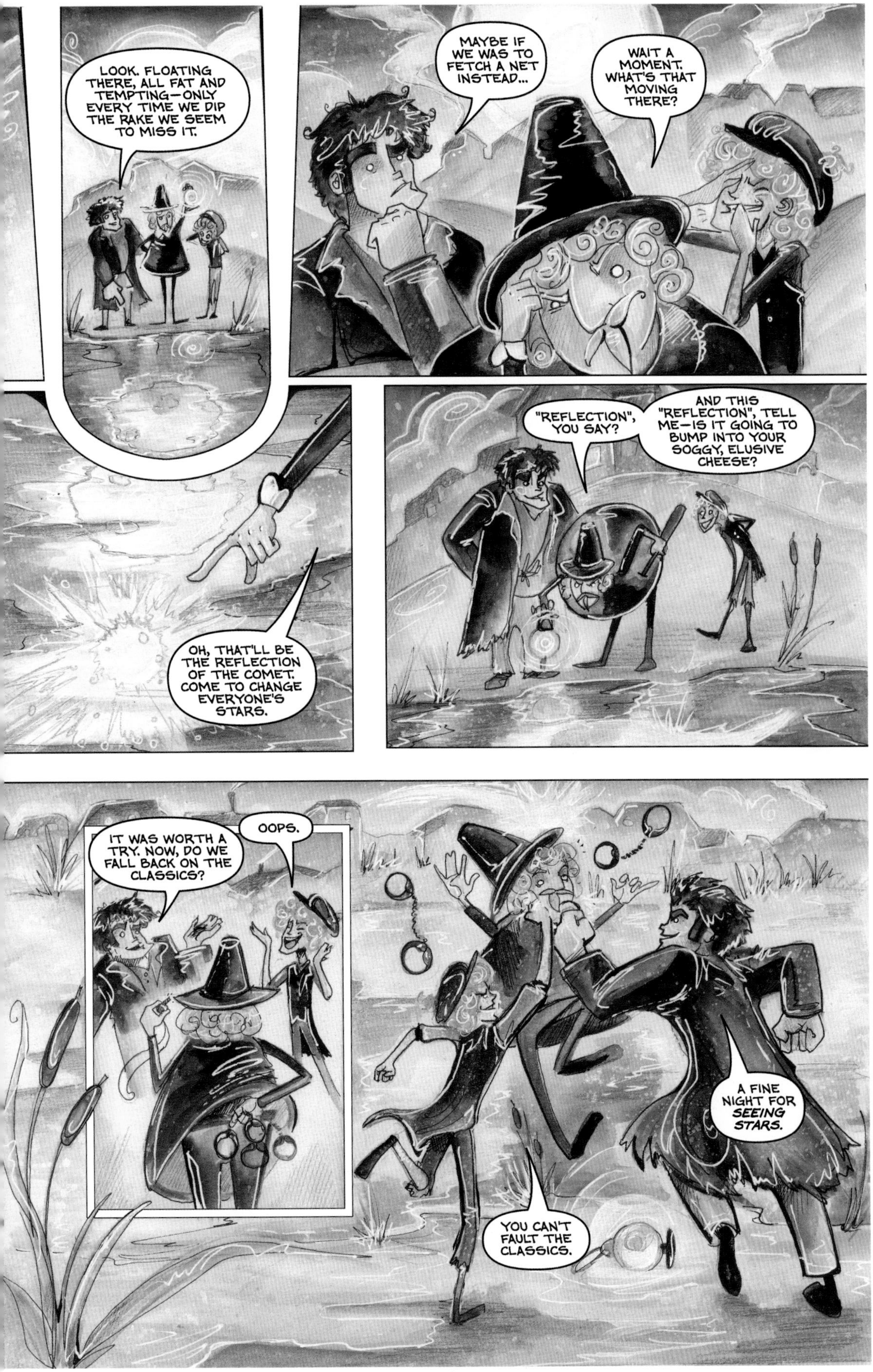
LOOK. FLOATING THERE, ALL FAT AND TEMPTING—ONLY EVERY TIME WE DIP THE RAKE WE SEEM TO MISS IT.
MAYBE IF WE WAS TO FETCH A NET INSTEAD...
WAIT A MOMENT. WHAT'S THAT MOVING THERE?
OH, THAT'LL BE THE REFLECTION OF THE COMET. COME TO CHANGE EVERYONE'S STARS.
"REFLECTION", YOU SAY?
AND THIS "REFLECTION", TELL ME—IS IT GOING TO BUMP INTO YOUR SOGGY, ELUSIVE CHEESE?
IT WAS WORTH A TRY. NOW, DO WE FALL BACK ON THE CLASSICS?
OOPS.
A FINE NIGHT FOR *SEEING STARS.*
YOU CAN'T FAULT THE CLASSICS.

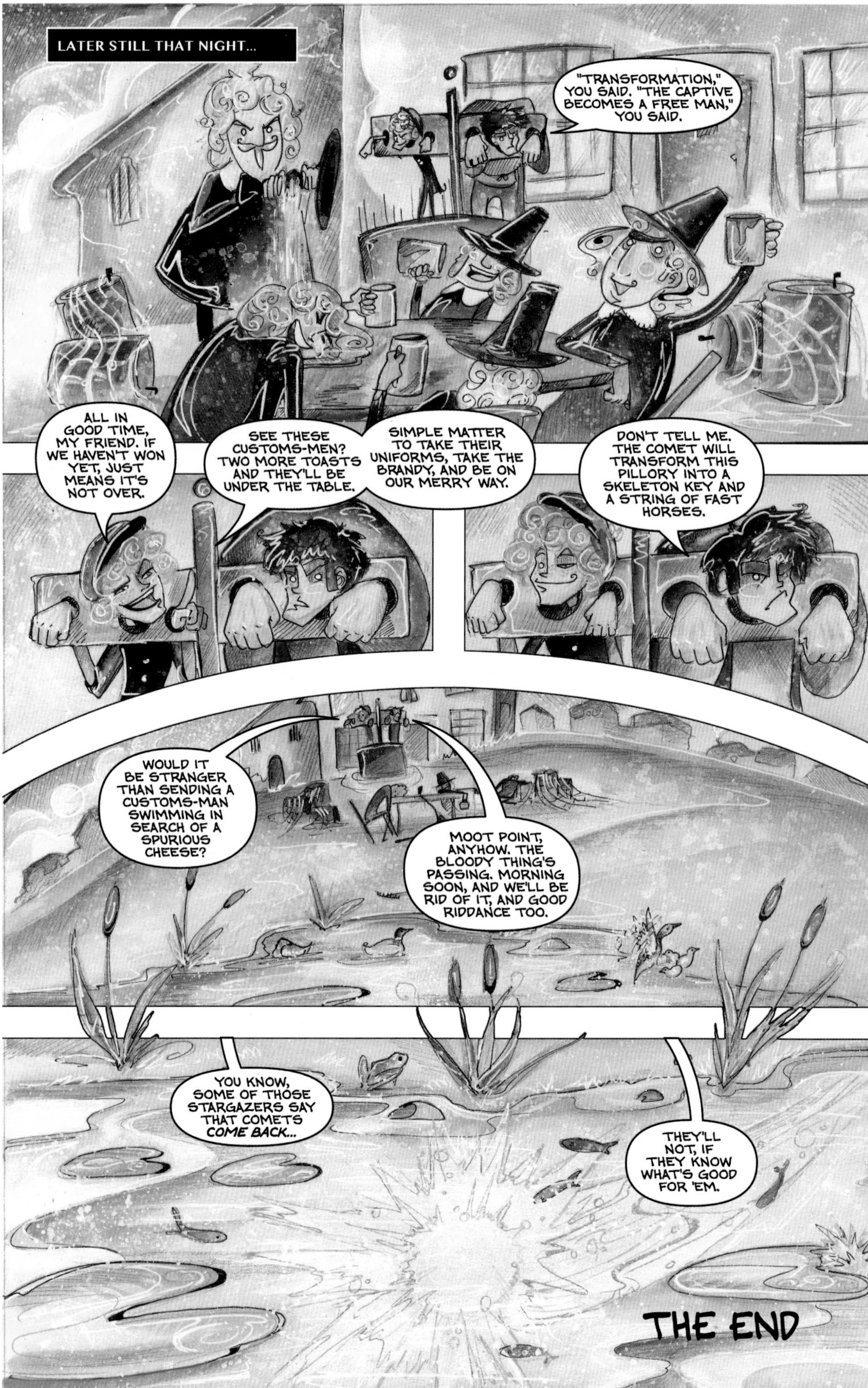
LATER STILL THAT NIGHT...
"TRANSFORMATION," YOU SAID. "THE CAPTIVE BECOMES A FREE MAN," YOU SAID.
ALL IN GOOD TIME, MY FRIEND. IF WE HAVEN'T WON YET, JUST MEANS IT'S NOT OVER.
SEE THESE CUSTOMS-MEN? TWO MORE TOASTS AND THEY'LL BE UNDER THE TABLE.
SIMPLE MATTER TO TAKE THEIR UNIFORMS, TAKE THE BRANDY, AND BE ON OUR MERRY WAY.
DON'T TELL ME. THE COMET WILL TRANSFORM THIS PILLORY INTO A SKELETON KEY AND A STRING OF FAST HORSES.
WOULD IT BE STRANGER THAN SENDING A CUSTOMS-MAN SWIMMING IN SEARCH OF A SPURIOUS CHEESE?
MOOT POINT, ANYHOW. THE BLOODY THING'S PASSING. MORNING SOON, AND WE'LL BE RID OF IT, AND GOOD RIDDANCE TOO.
YOU KNOW, SOME OF THOSE STARGAZERS SAY THAT COMETS *COME BACK*...
THEY'LL NOT, IF THEY KNOW WHAT'S GOOD FOR 'EM.
THE END

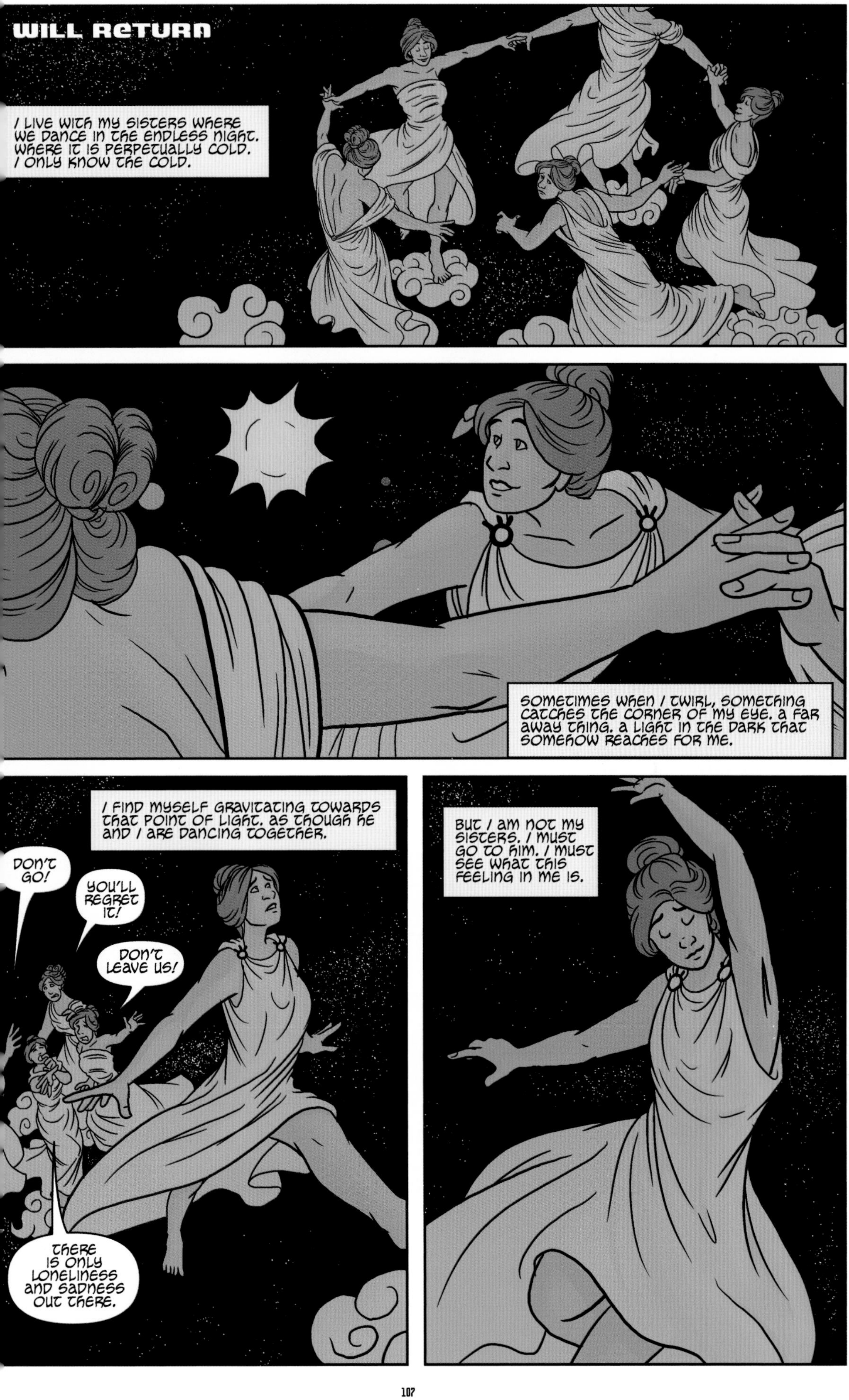
WILL RETURN
I LIVE WITH MY SISTERS WHERE WE DANCE IN THE ENDLESS NIGHT. WHERE IT IS PERPETUALLY COLD. I ONLY KNOW THE COLD.
SOMETIMES WHEN I TWIRL, SOMETHING CATCHES THE CORNER OF MY EYE. A FAR AWAY THING. A LIGHT IN THE DARK THAT SOMEHOW REACHES FOR ME.
I FIND MYSELF GRAVITATING TOWARDS THAT POINT OF LIGHT. AS THOUGH HE AND I ARE DANCING TOGETHER.
DON'T GO!
YOU'LL REGRET IT!
DON'T LEAVE US!
THERE IS ONLY LONELINESS AND SADNESS OUT THERE.
BUT I AM NOT MY SISTERS. I MUST GO TO HIM. I MUST SEE WHAT THIS FEELING IN ME IS.

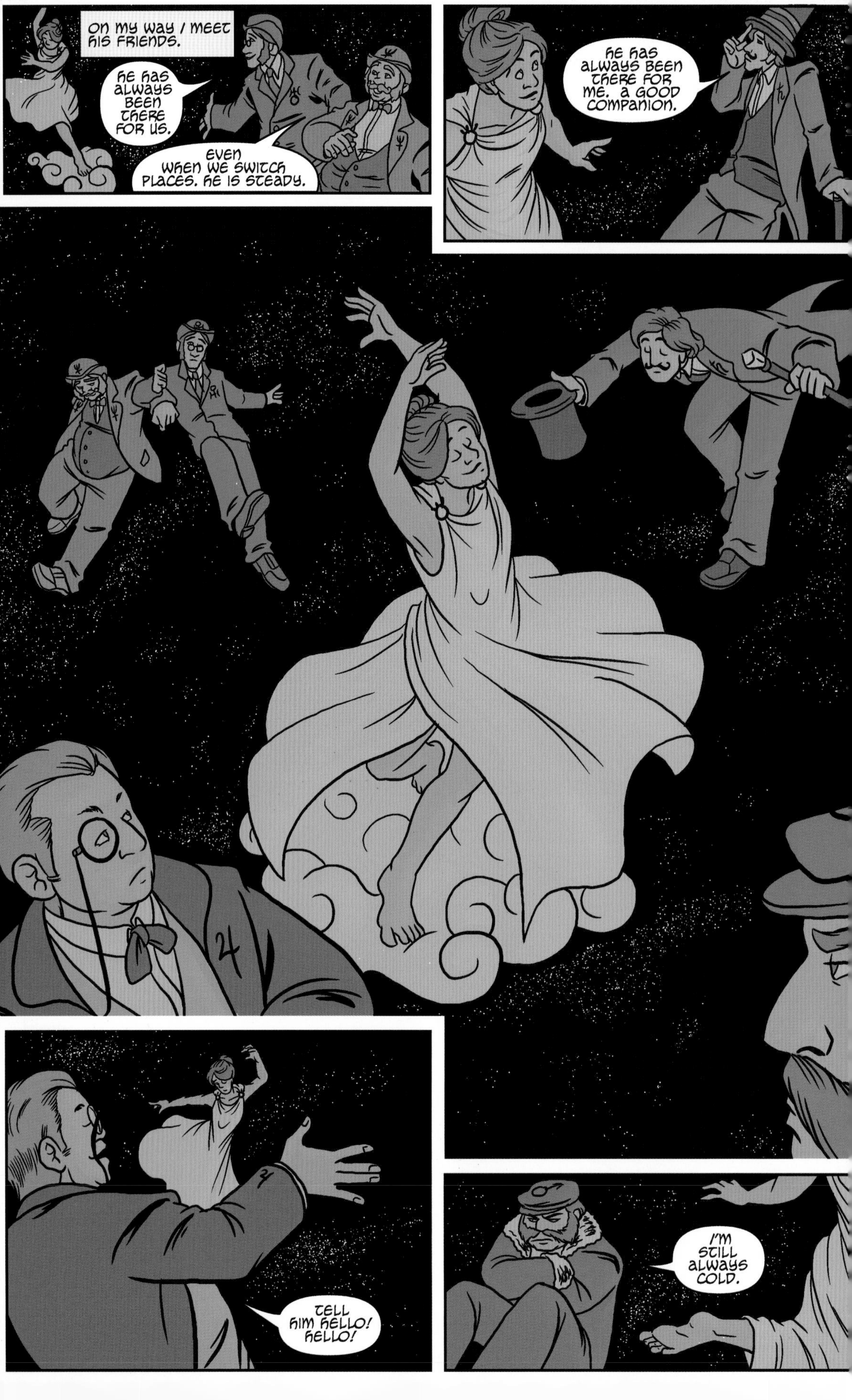
ON MY WAY I MEET HIS FRIENDS.
HE HAS ALWAYS BEEN THERE FOR US.
EVEN WHEN WE SWITCH PLACES. HE IS STEADY.
HE HAS ALWAYS BEEN THERE FOR ME. A GOOD COMPANION.
TELL HIM HELLO! HELLO!
I'M STILL ALWAYS COLD.

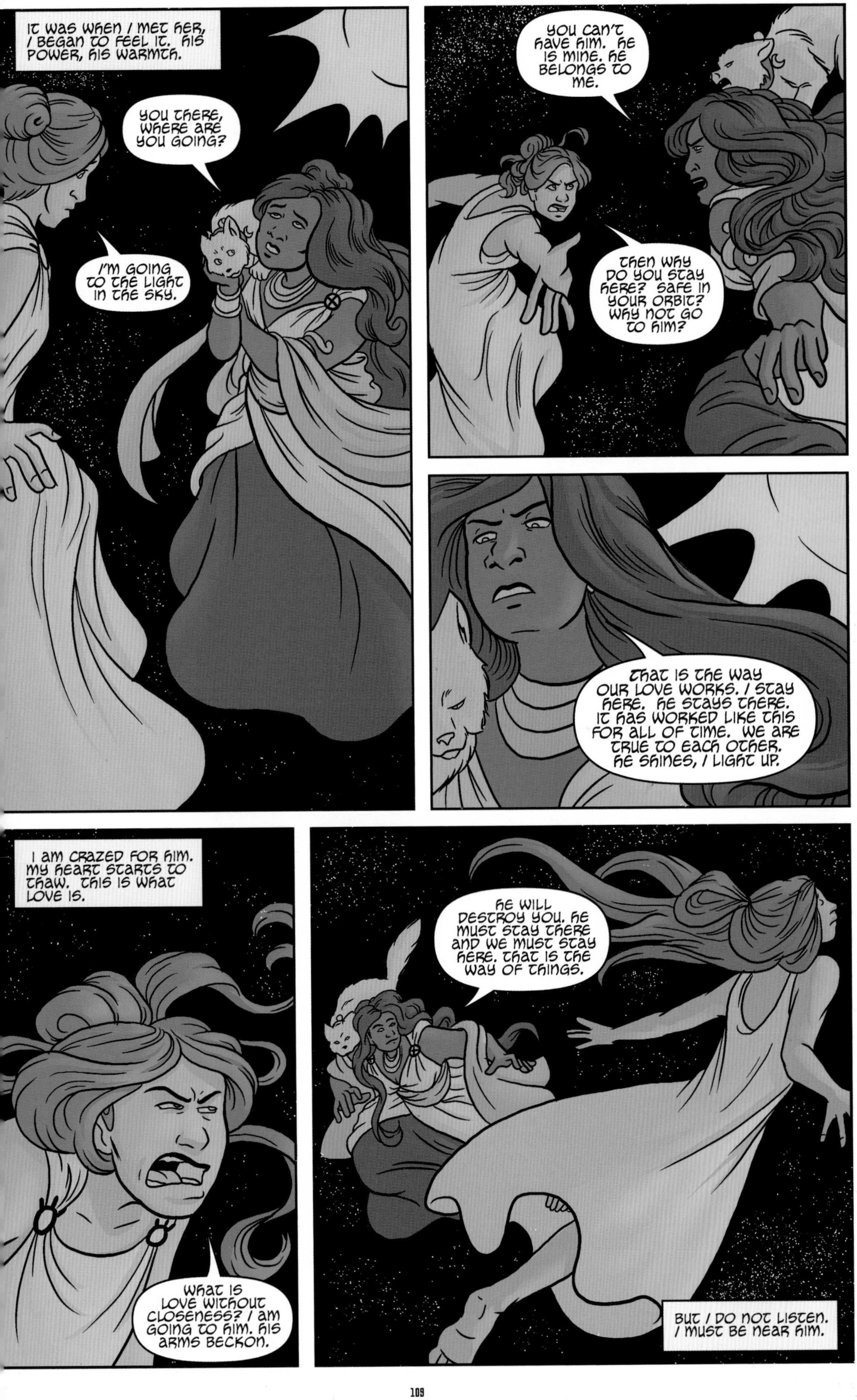

IT WAS WHEN I MET HER, I BEGAN TO FEEL IT. HIS POWER, HIS WARMTH.
YOU THERE, WHERE ARE YOU GOING?
I'M GOING TO THE LIGHT IN THE SKY.
YOU CAN'T HAVE HIM. HE IS MINE. HE BELONGS TO ME.
THEN WHY DO YOU STAY HERE? SAFE IN YOUR ORBIT? WHY NOT GO TO HIM?
THAT IS THE WAY OUR LOVE WORKS. I STAY HERE. HE STAYS THERE. IT HAS WORKED LIKE THIS FOR ALL OF TIME. WE ARE TRUE TO EACH OTHER. HE SHINES, I LIGHT UP.
I AM CRAZED FOR HIM. MY HEART STARTS TO THAW. THIS IS WHAT LOVE IS.
WHAT IS LOVE WITHOUT CLOSENESS? I AM GOING TO HIM. HIS ARMS BECKON.
HE WILL DESTROY YOU. HE MUST STAY THERE AND WE MUST STAY HERE. THAT IS THE WAY OF THINGS.
BUT I DO NOT LISTEN. I MUST BE NEAR HIM.

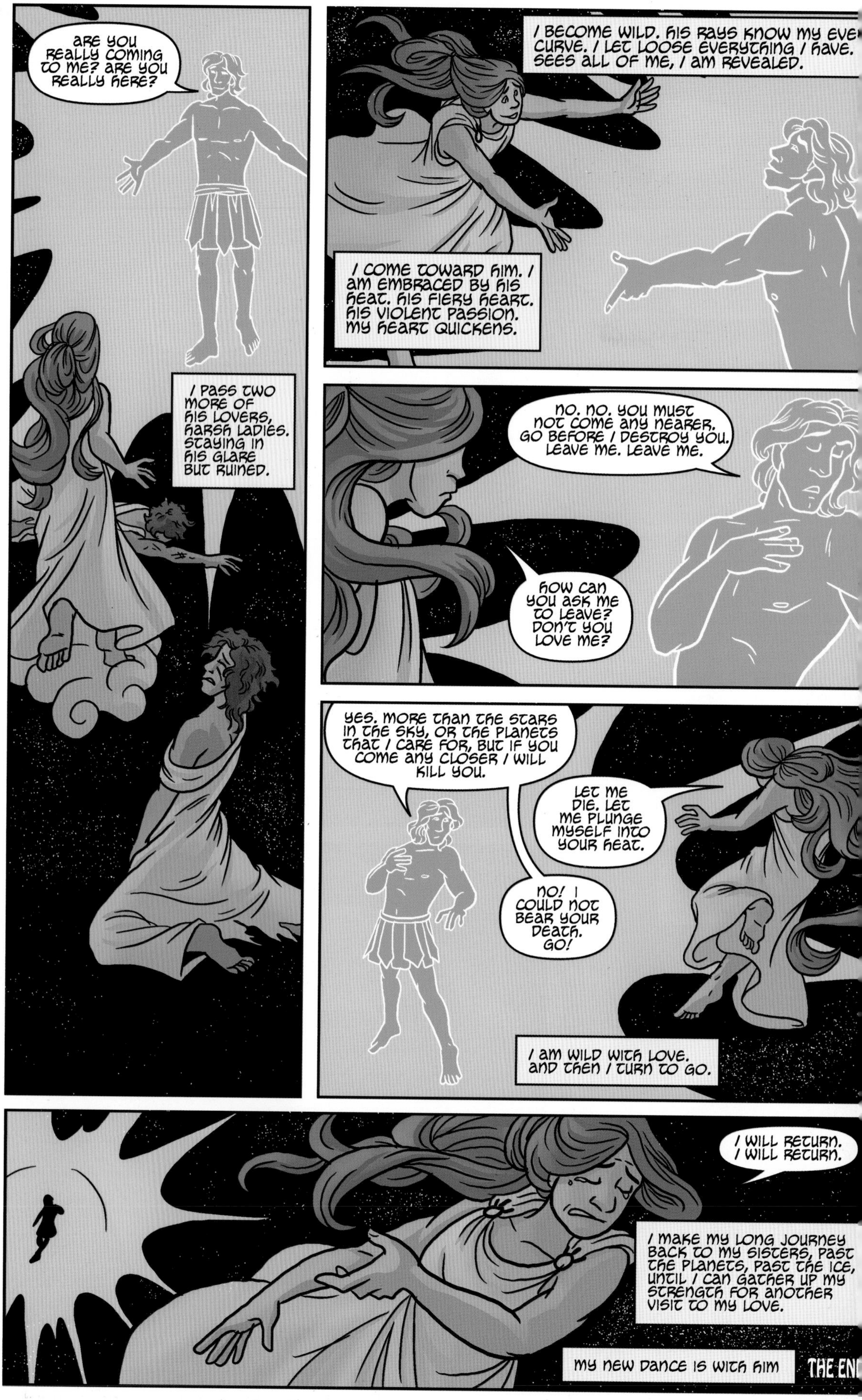
ARE YOU REALLY COMING TO ME? ARE YOU REALLY HERE?
I PASS TWO MORE OF HIS LOVERS, HARSH LADIES. STAYING IN HIS GLARE BUT RUINED.
I BECOME WILD. HIS RAYS KNOW MY EVE CURVE. I LET LOOSE EVERYTHING I HAVE. SEES ALL OF ME, I AM REVEALED.
I COME TOWARD HIM. I AM EMBRACED BY HIS HEAT. HIS FIERY HEART. HIS VIOLENT PASSION. MY HEART QUICKENS.
NO. NO. YOU MUST NOT COME ANY NEARER. GO BEFORE I DESTROY YOU. LEAVE ME. LEAVE ME.
HOW CAN YOU ASK ME TO LEAVE? DON'T YOU LOVE ME?
YES. MORE THAN THE STARS IN THE SKY, OR THE PLANETS THAT I CARE FOR, BUT IF YOU COME ANY CLOSER I WILL KILL YOU.
LET ME DIE. LET ME PLUNGE MYSELF INTO YOUR HEAT.
NO! I COULD NOT BEAR YOUR DEATH. GO!
I AM WILD WITH LOVE. AND THEN I TURN TO GO.
I WILL RETURN. I WILL RETURN.
I MAKE MY LONG JOURNEY BACK TO MY SISTERS, PAST THE PLANETS, PAST THE ICE, UNTIL I CAN GATHER UP MY STRENGTH FOR ANOTHER VISIT TO MY LOVE.
MY NEW DANCE IS WITH HIM
THE EN

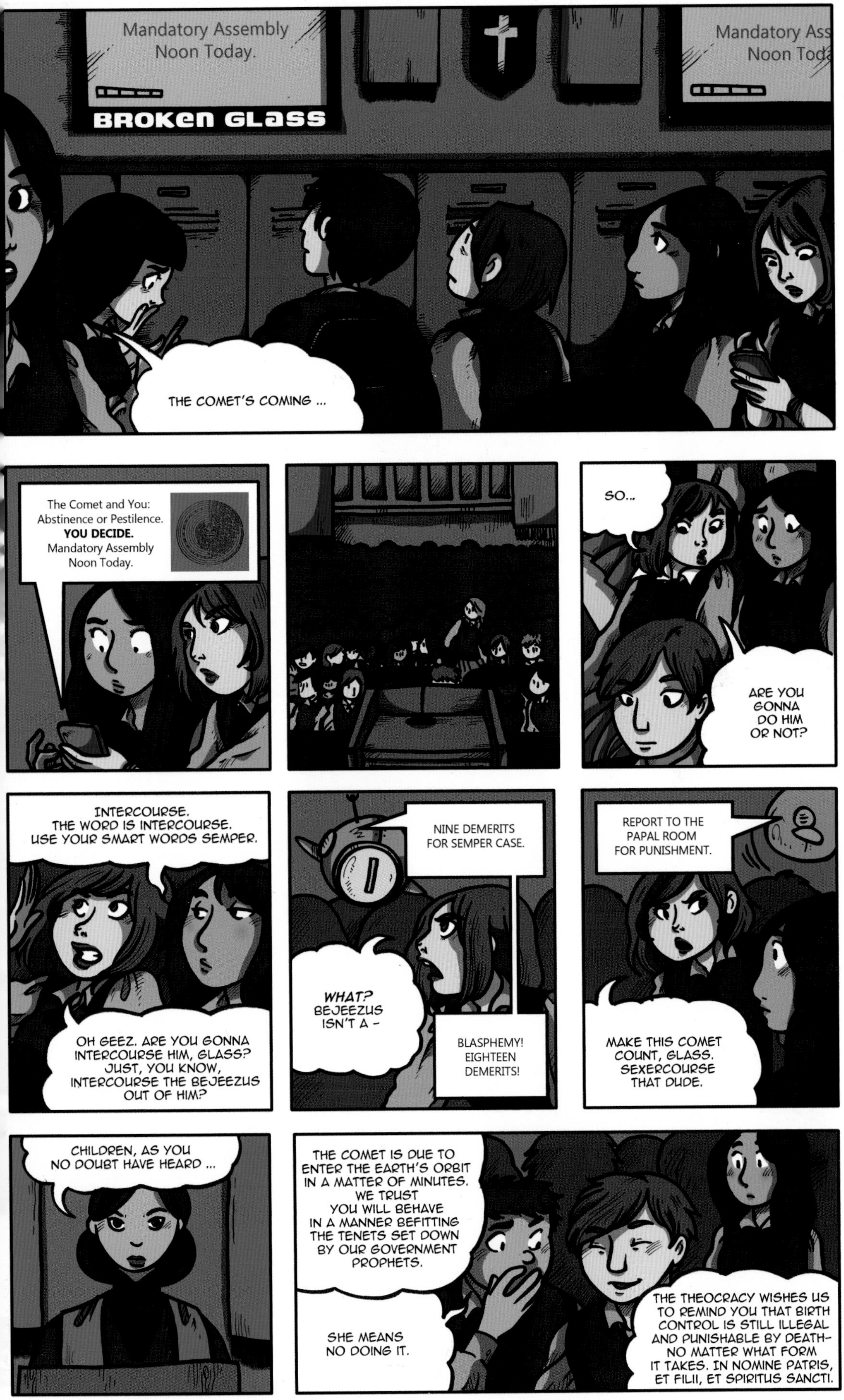
Mandatory Assembly
Noon Today.
BROKEN GLASS
Mandatory Ass
Noon Toda
THE COMET'S COMING ...
The Comet and You:
Abstinence or Pestilence.
YOU DECIDE.
Mandatory Assembly
Noon Today.
SO...
ARE YOU GONNA DO HIM OR NOT?
INTERCOURSE. THE WORD IS INTERCOURSE. USE YOUR SMART WORDS SEMPER.
OH GEEZ. ARE YOU GONNA INTERCOURSE HIM, GLASS? JUST, YOU KNOW, INTERCOURSE THE BEJEEZUS OUT OF HIM?
NINE DEMERITS FOR SEMPER CASE.
WHAT? BEJEEZUS ISN'T A -
BLASPHEMY! EIGHTEEN DEMERITS!
REPORT TO THE PAPAL ROOM FOR PUNISHMENT.
MAKE THIS COMET COUNT, GLASS. SEXERCOURSE THAT DUDE.
CHILDREN, AS YOU NO DOUBT HAVE HEARD ...
THE COMET IS DUE TO ENTER THE EARTH'S ORBIT IN A MATTER OF MINUTES. WE TRUST YOU WILL BEHAVE IN A MANNER BEFITTING THE TENETS SET DOWN BY OUR GOVERNMENT PROPHETS.
SHE MEANS NO DOING IT.
THE THEOCRACY WISHES US TO REMIND YOU THAT BIRTH CONTROL IS STILL ILLEGAL AND PUNISHABLE BY DEATH-NO MATTER WHAT FORM IT TAKES. IN NOMINE PATRIS, ET FILII, ET SPIRITUS SANCTI.

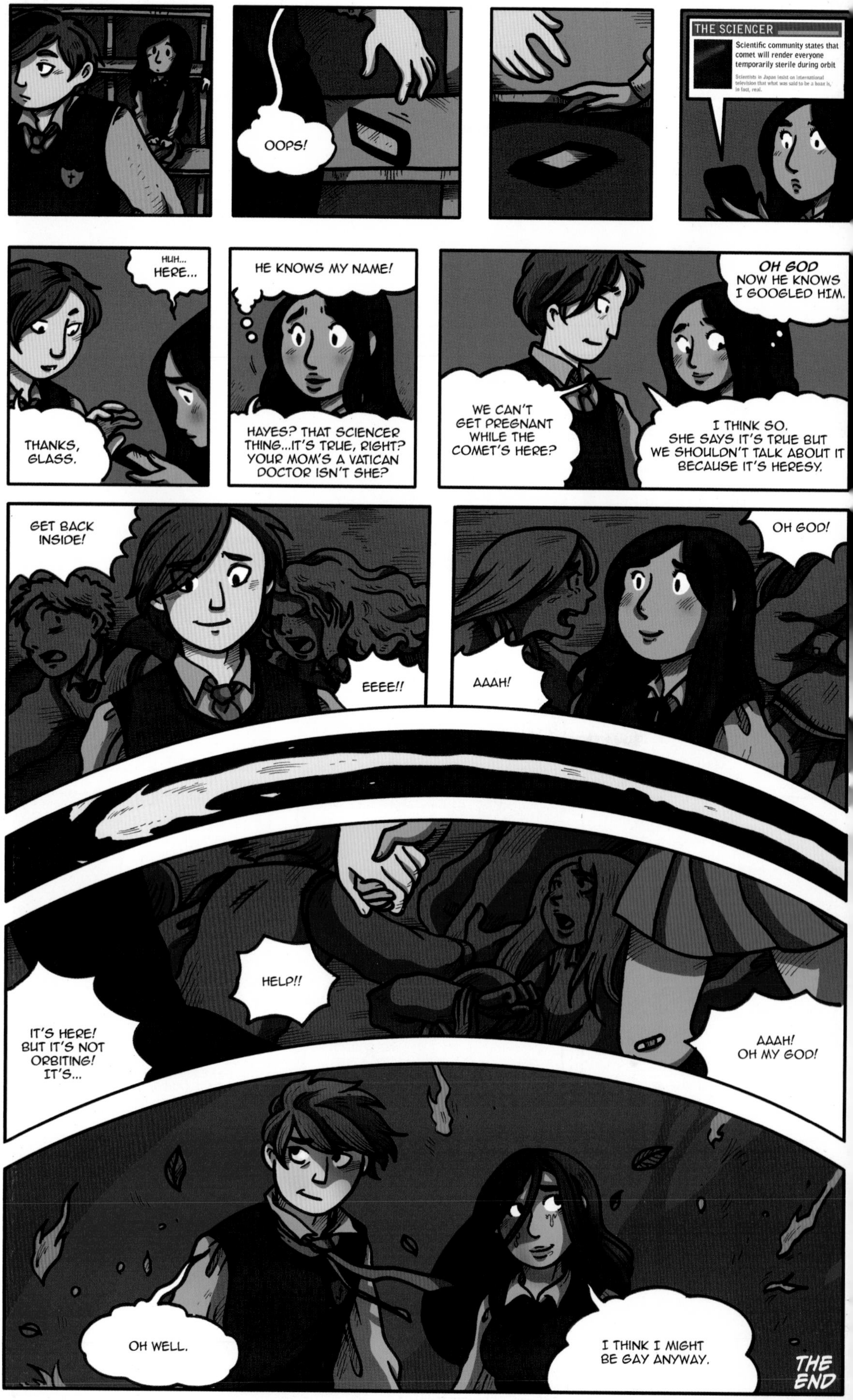
OOPS!
THE SCIENCER
Scientific community states that comet will render everyone temporarily sterile during orbit
Scientists in Japan insist on international television that what was said to be a hoax is, in fact, real.
HUH... HERE...
THANKS, GLASS.
HE KNOWS MY NAME!
HAYES? THAT SCIENCER THING...IT'S TRUE, RIGHT? YOUR MOM'S A VATICAN DOCTOR ISN'T SHE?
WE CAN'T GET PREGNANT WHILE THE COMET'S HERE?
OH GOD NOW HE KNOWS I GOOGLED HIM.
I THINK SO. SHE SAYS IT'S TRUE BUT WE SHOULDN'T TALK ABOUT IT BECAUSE IT'S HERESY.
GET BACK INSIDE!
EEEE!!
OH GOD!
AAAH!
HELP!!
IT'S HERE! BUT IT'S NOT ORBITING! IT'S...
AAAH! OH MY GOD!
OH WELL.
I THINK I MIGHT BE GAY ANYWAY.
THE END

WOMANTHOLOGY
SPACE
GALLERY

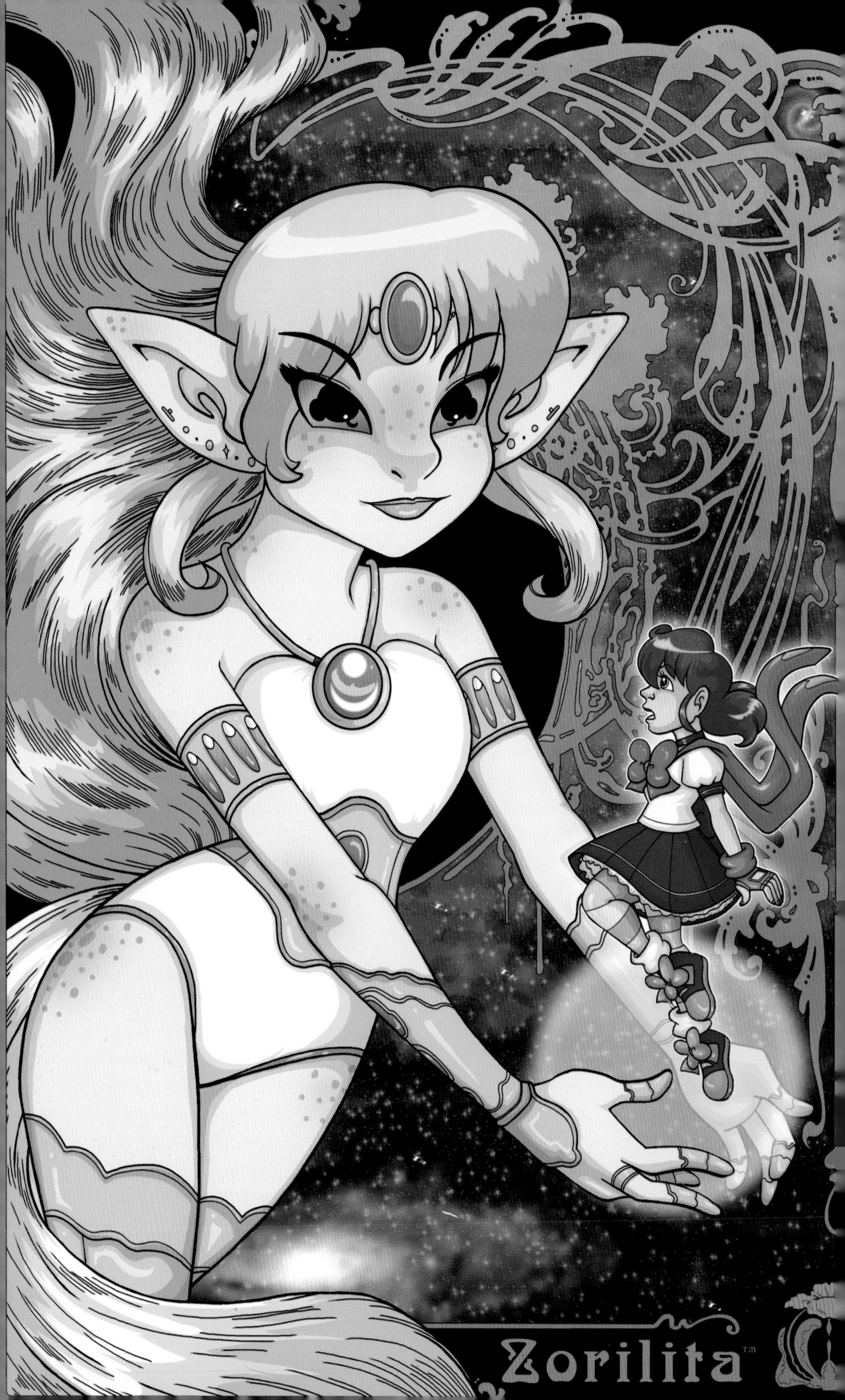
Zorilita™

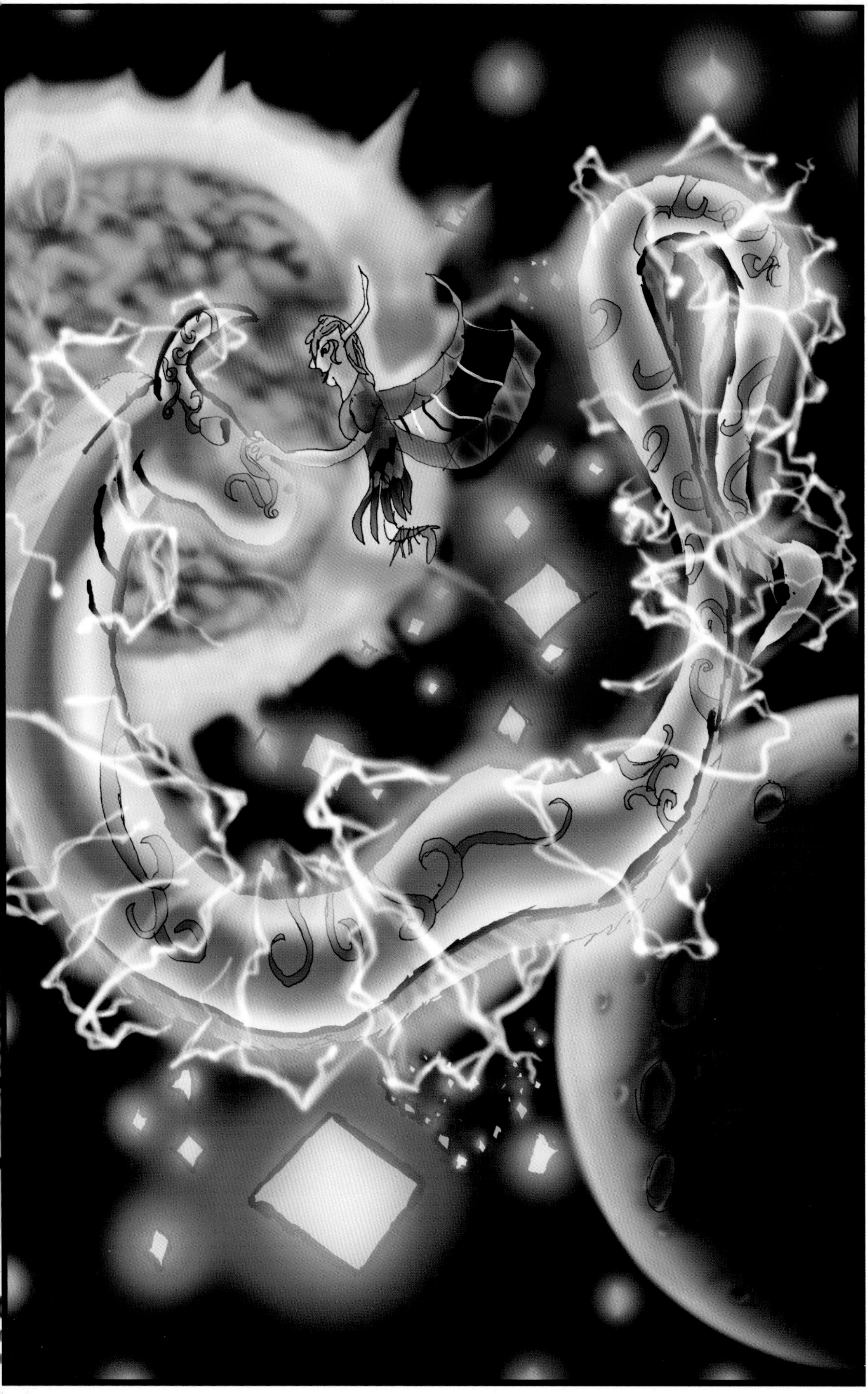

Art by Anna Bowie (under 18 Contributor) • Colors by Sarah Elkins

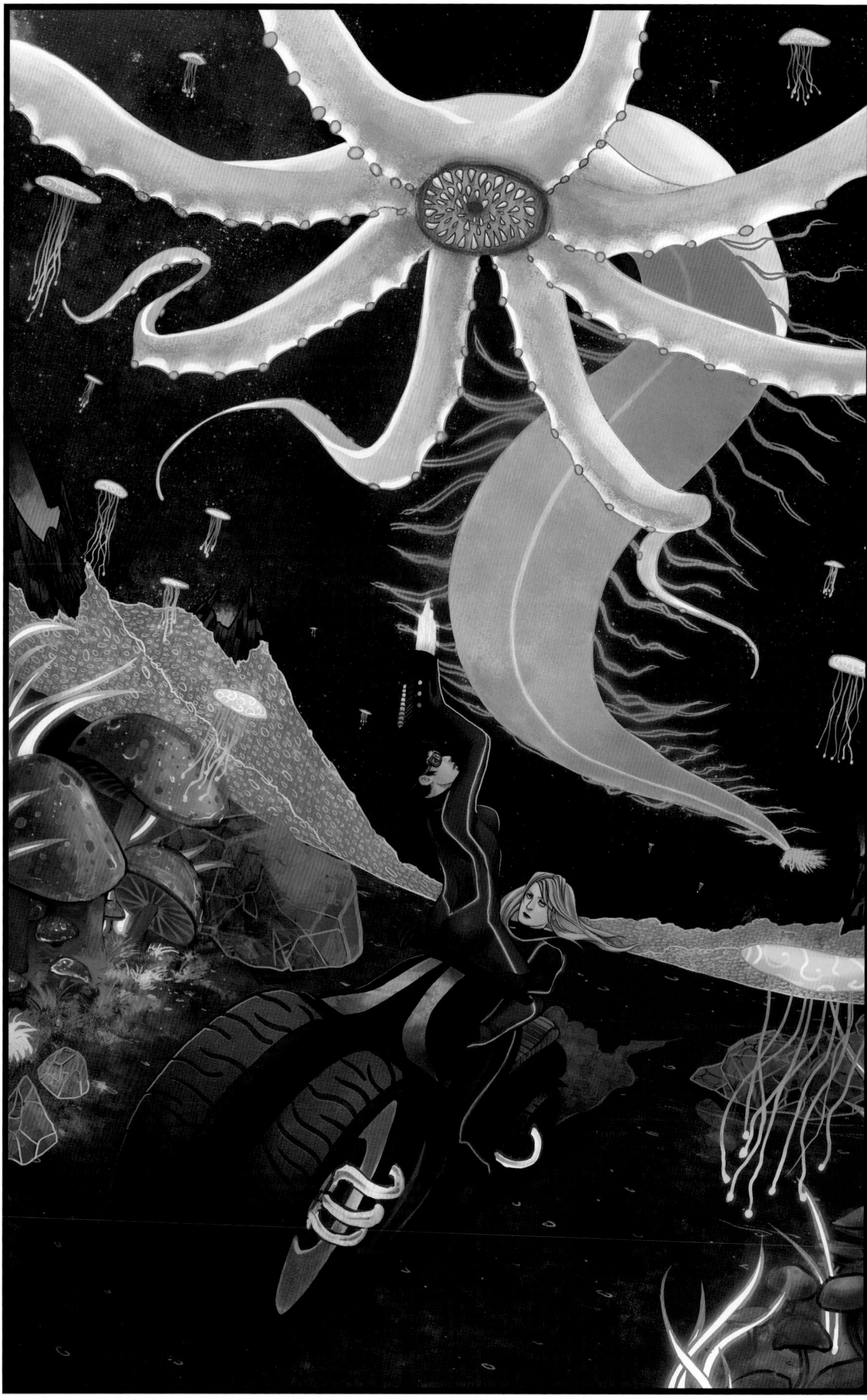

Art by Alice Fox

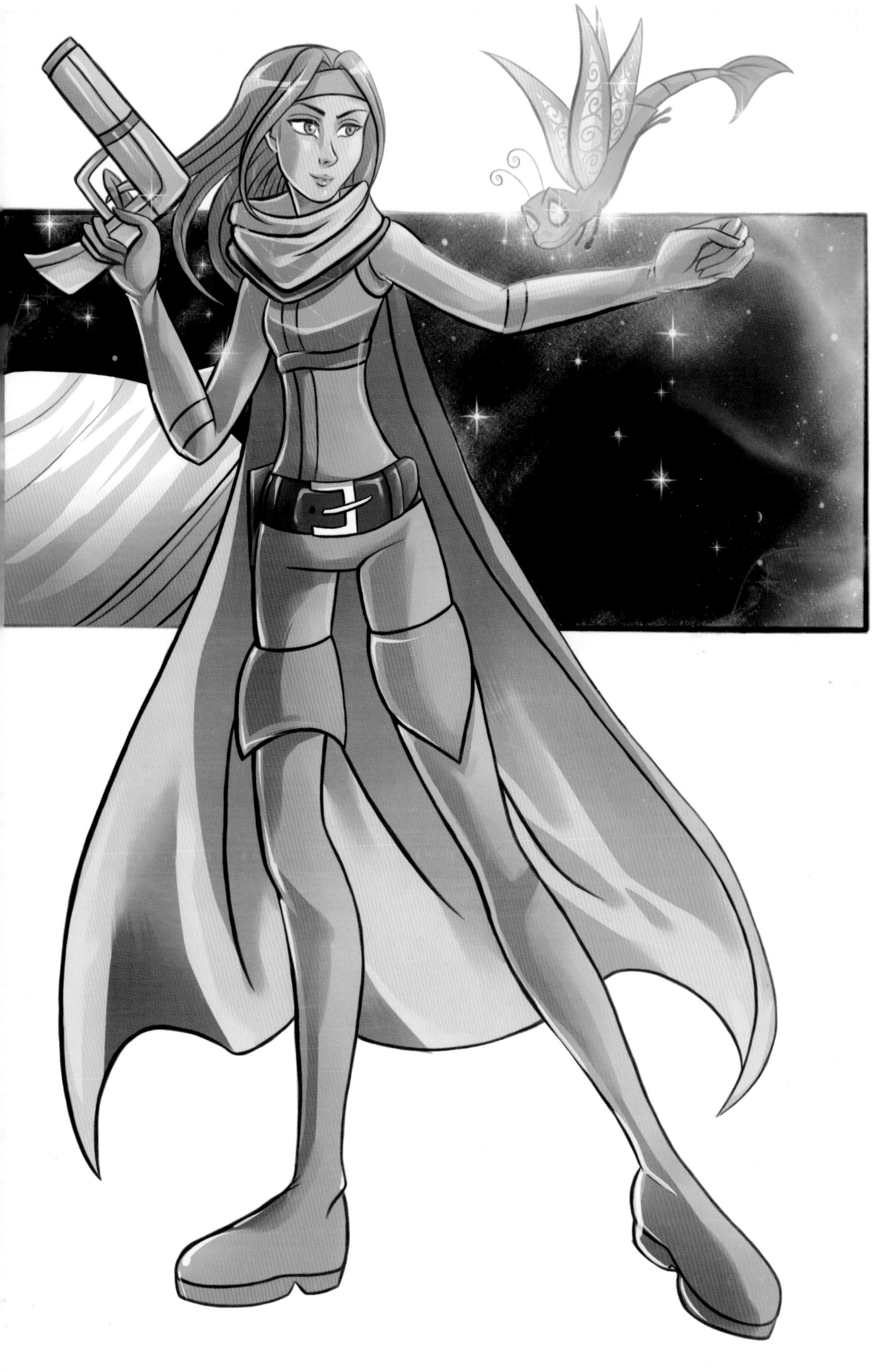

Art by Sherri Rose

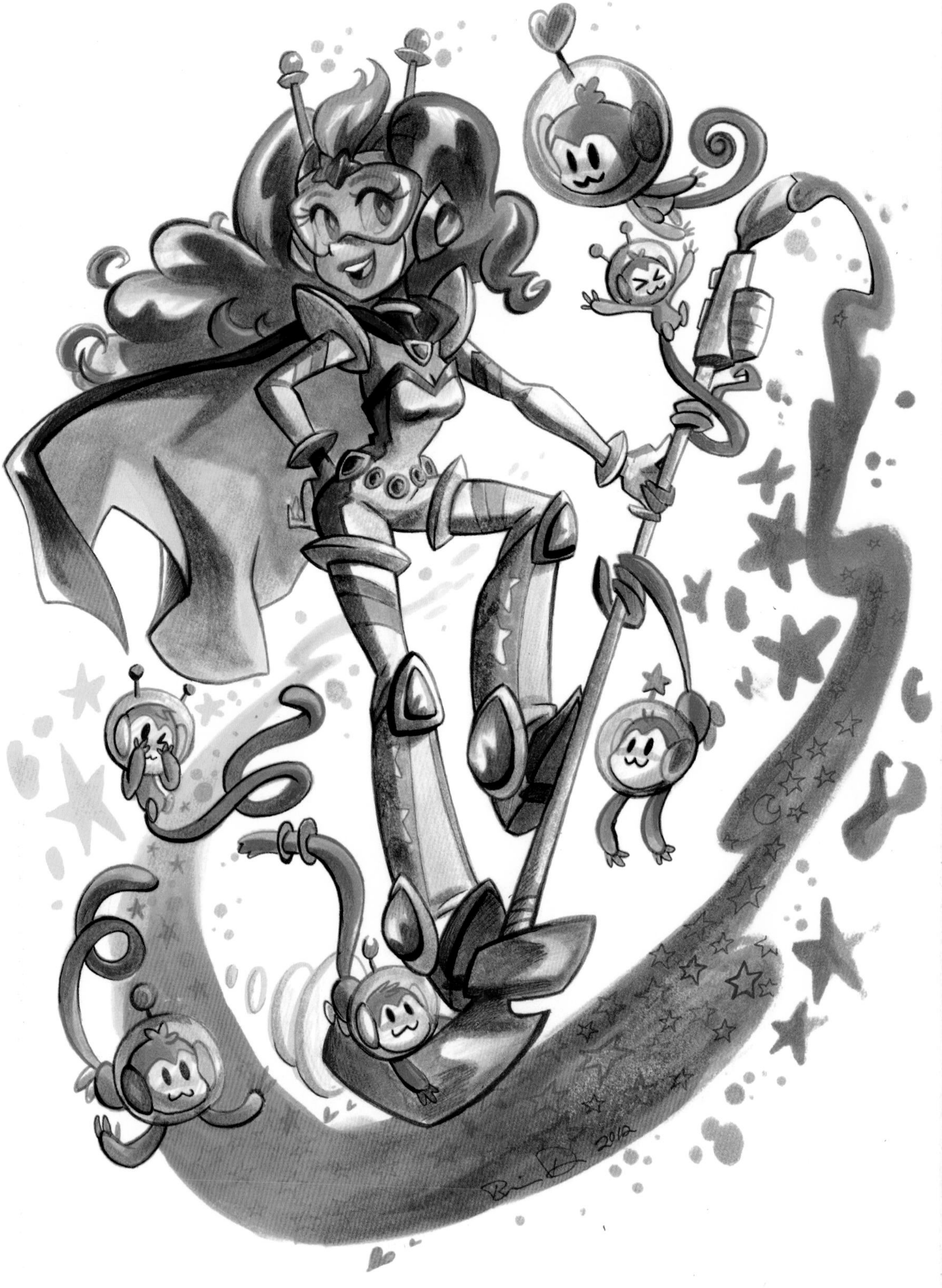

Art by Brianne Drouhard

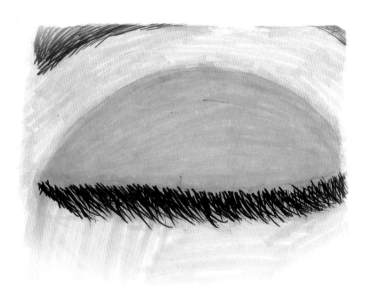

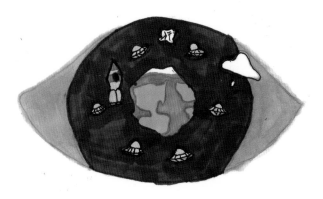

Art by Chloe Young (under 18 Contributor)

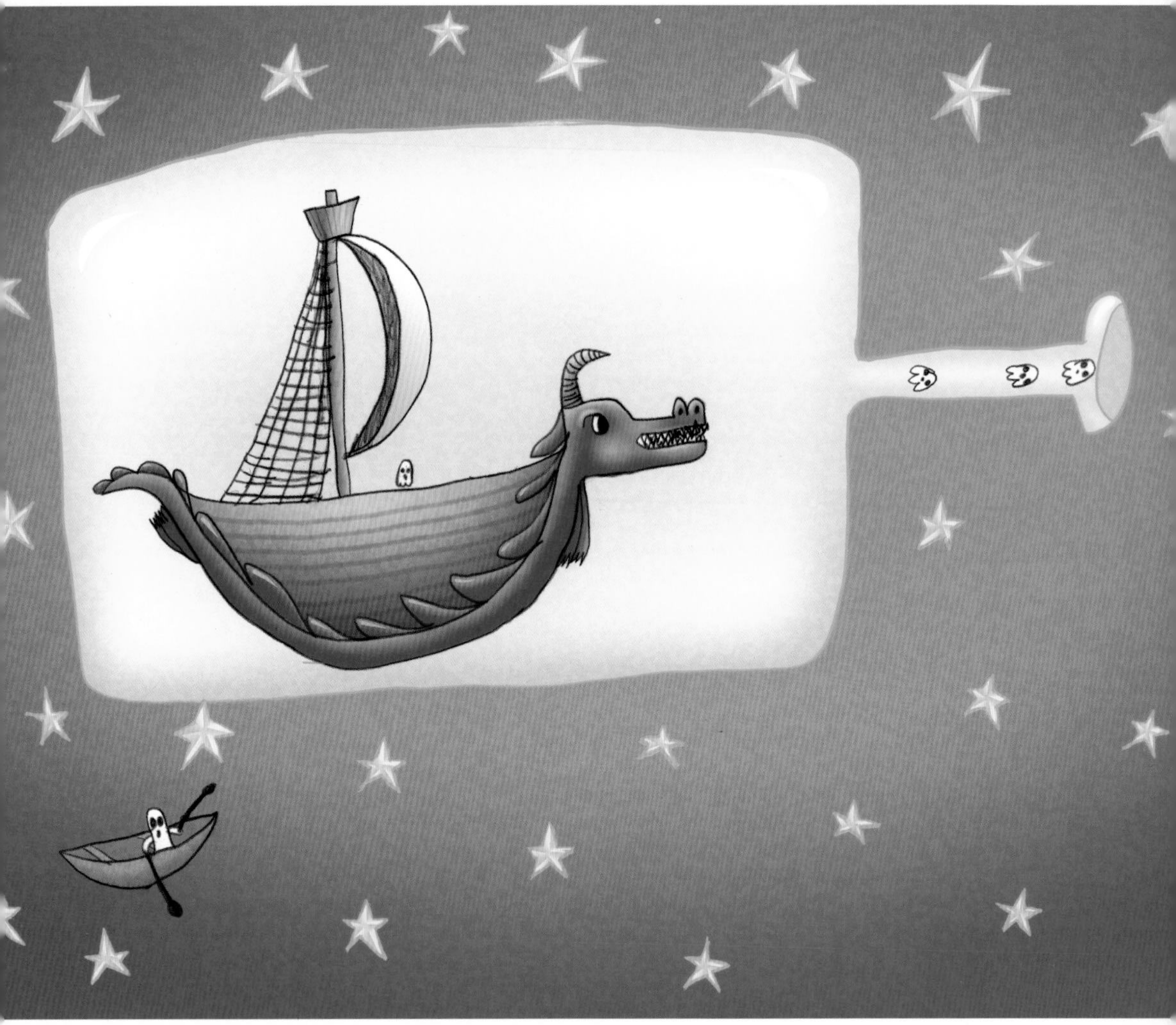

Art by Maysa O'Connor (Under 18 Contributor)

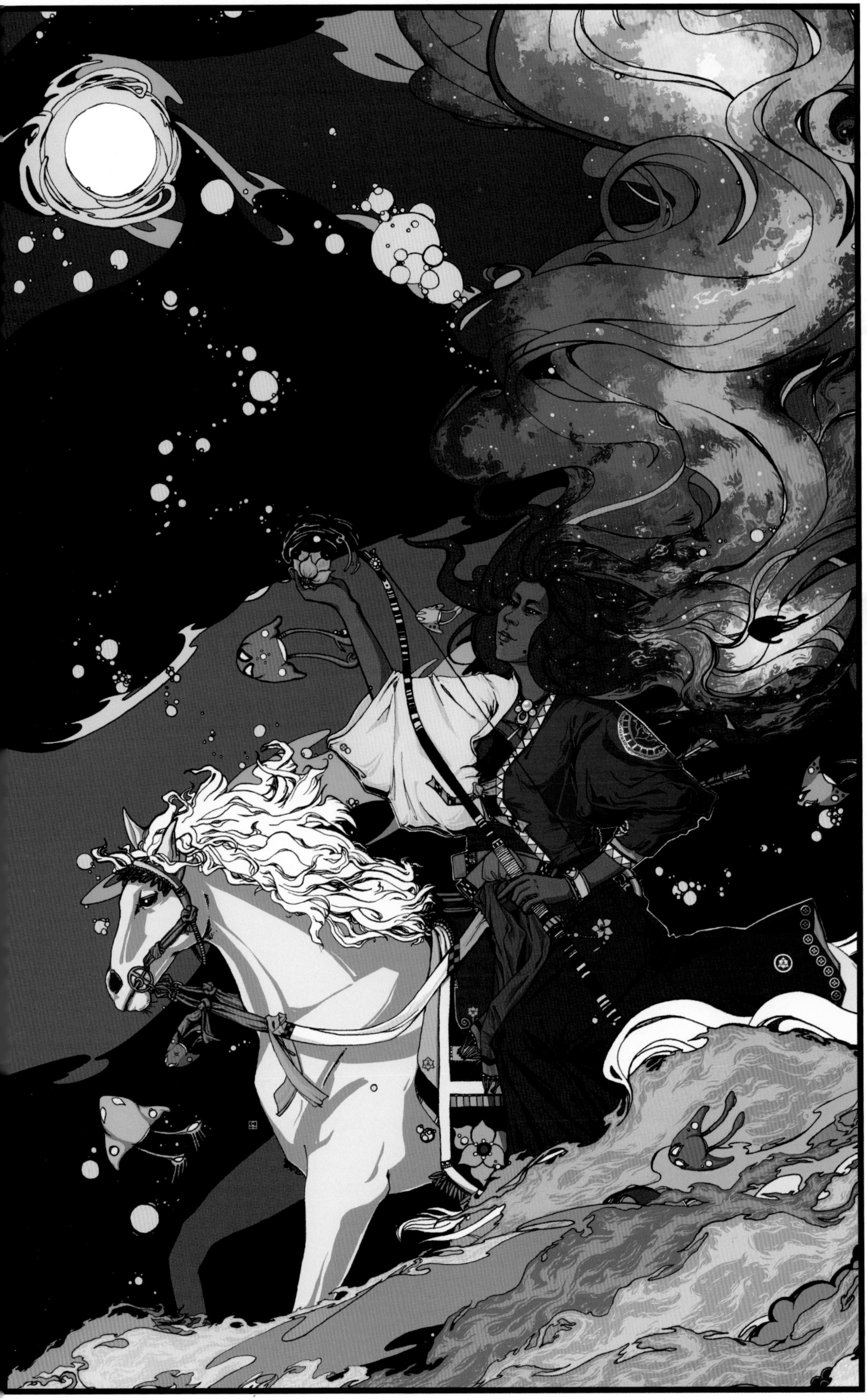

Art by Catherine Miller

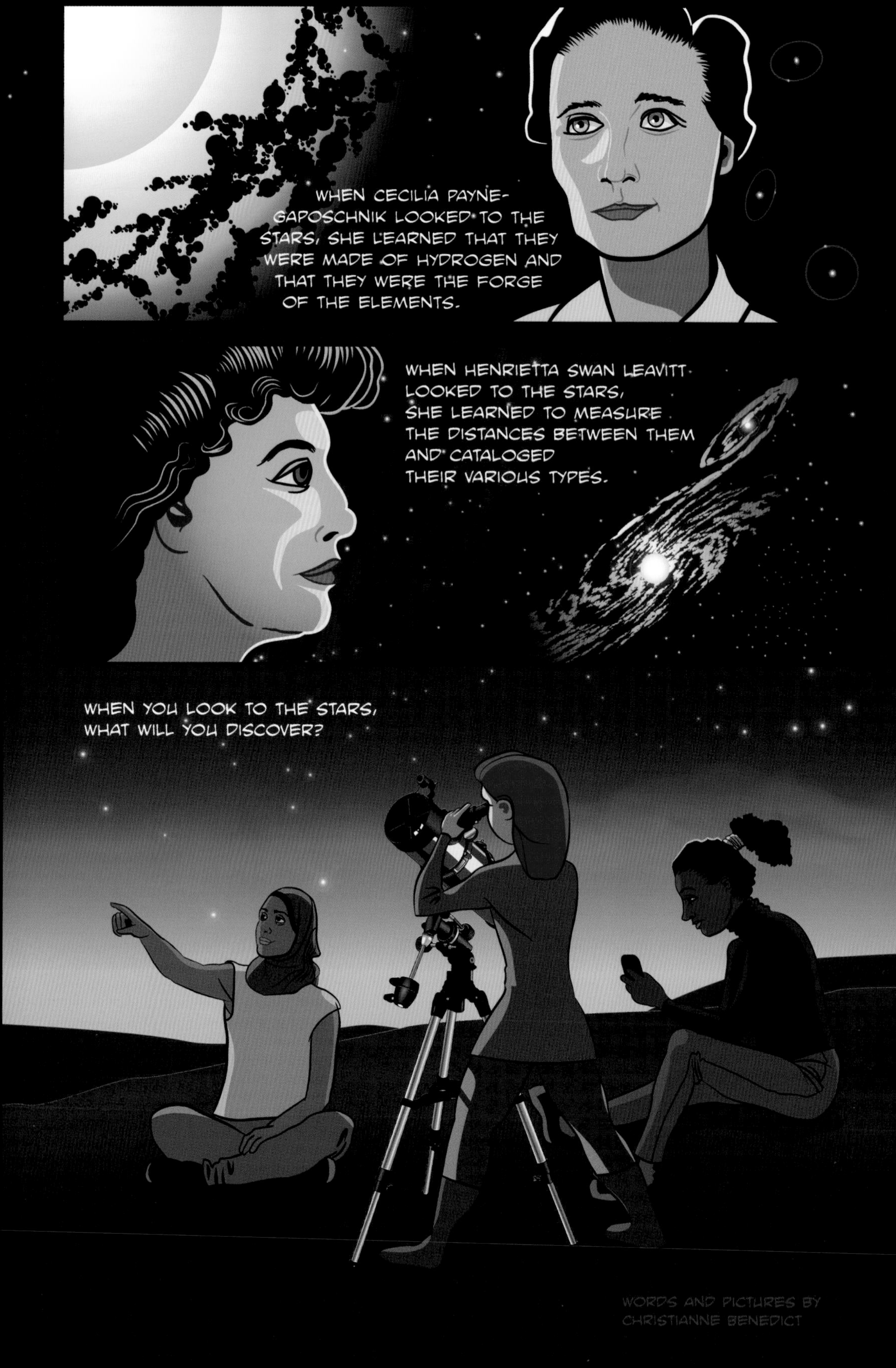
WHEN CECILIA PAYNE-GAPOSCHNIK LOOKED TO THE STARS, SHE LEARNED THAT THEY WERE MADE OF HYDROGEN AND THAT THEY WERE THE FORGE OF THE ELEMENTS.
WHEN HENRIETTA SWAN LEAVITT LOOKED TO THE STARS, SHE LEARNED TO MEASURE THE DISTANCES BETWEEN THEM AND CATALOGED THEIR VARIOUS TYPES.
WHEN YOU LOOK TO THE STARS, WHAT WILL YOU DISCOVER?
WORDS AND PICTURES BY CHRISTIANNE BENEDICT

Words and Pictures by Christianne Benedict

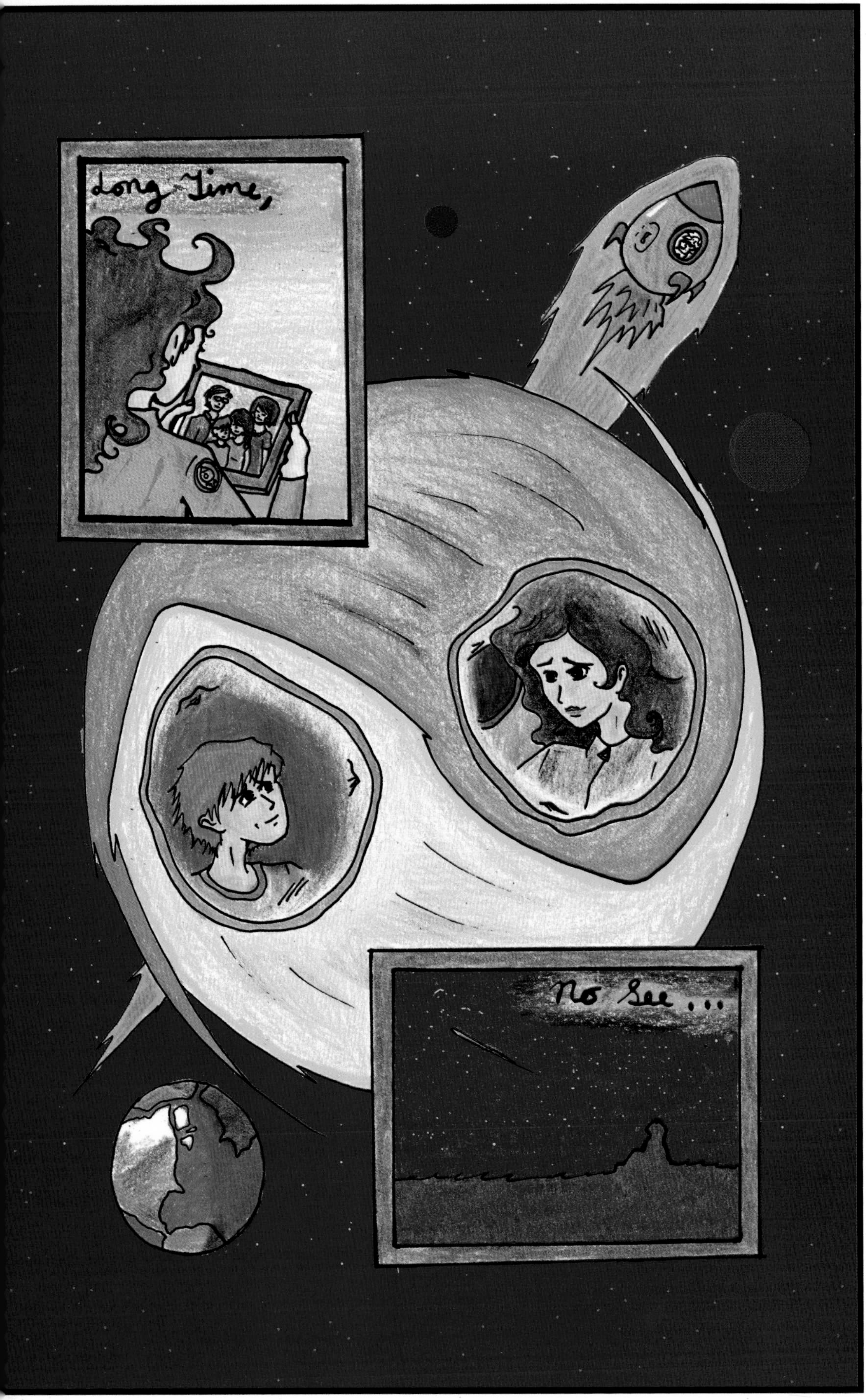
Long Time,
No See...

Art by Ceili Conway (Under 18 Contributor)

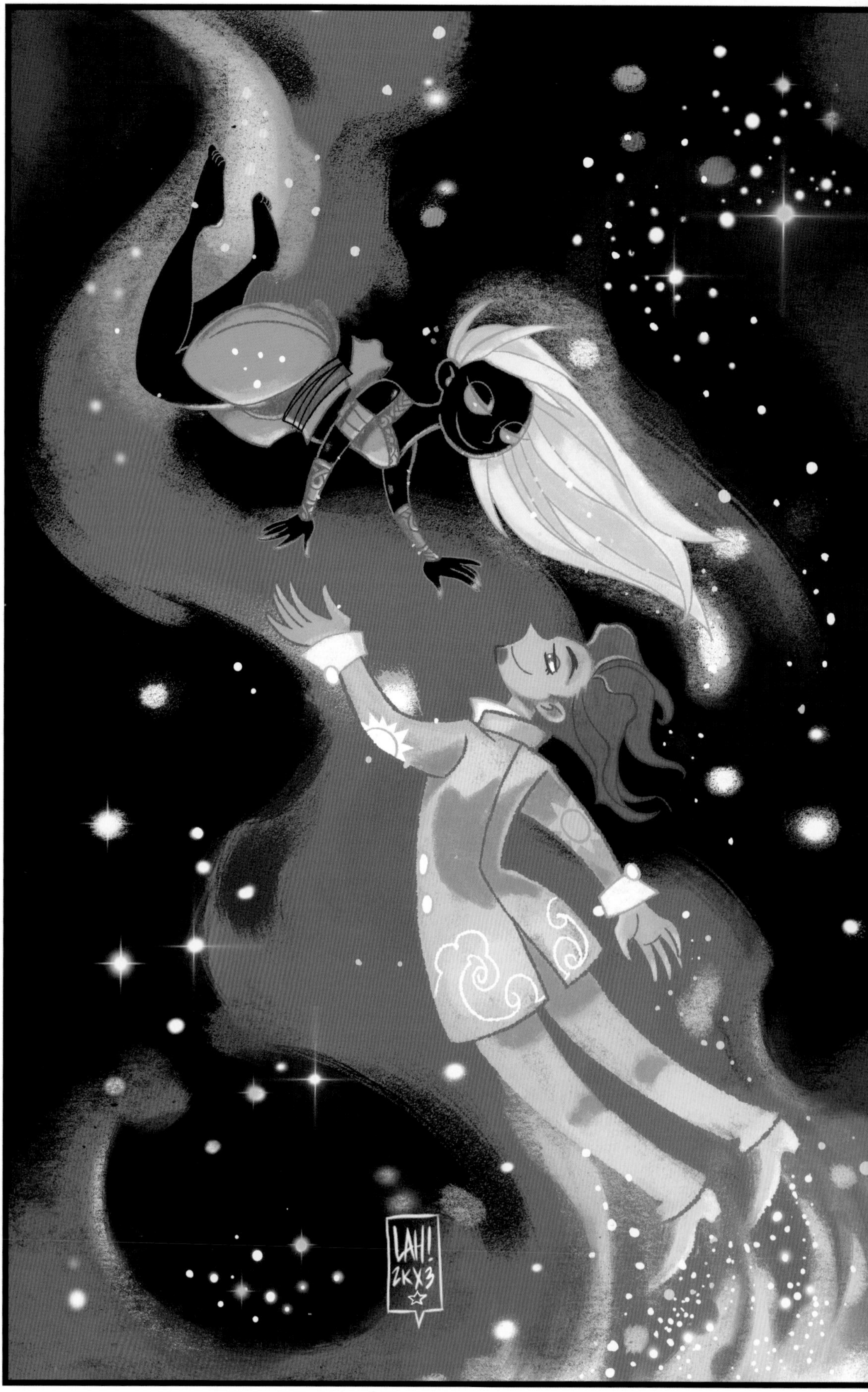
LAH! 2KX3

Art by Lea Hernandez

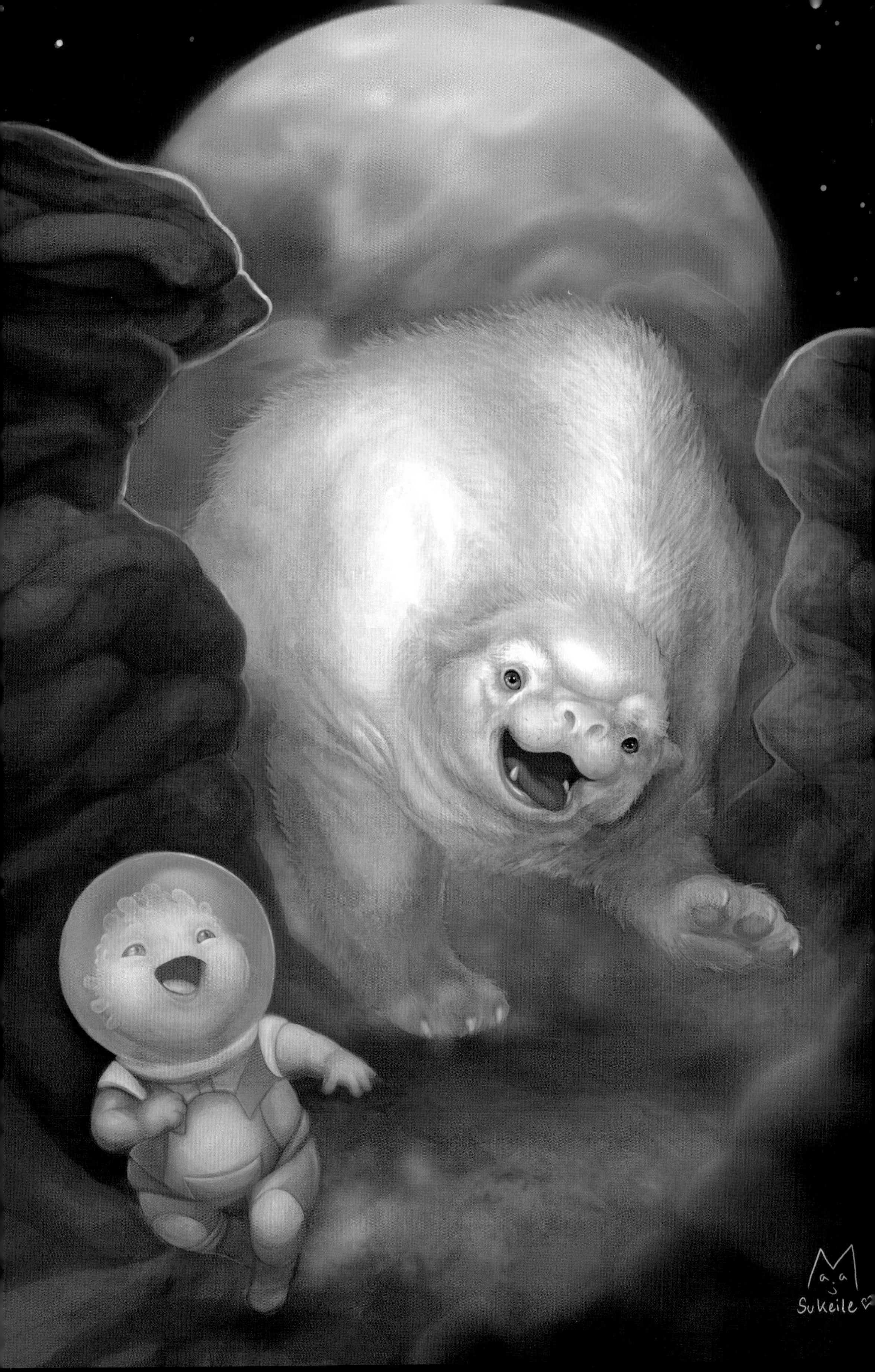
Maja
Sukeile

Art by Maja Sukeile

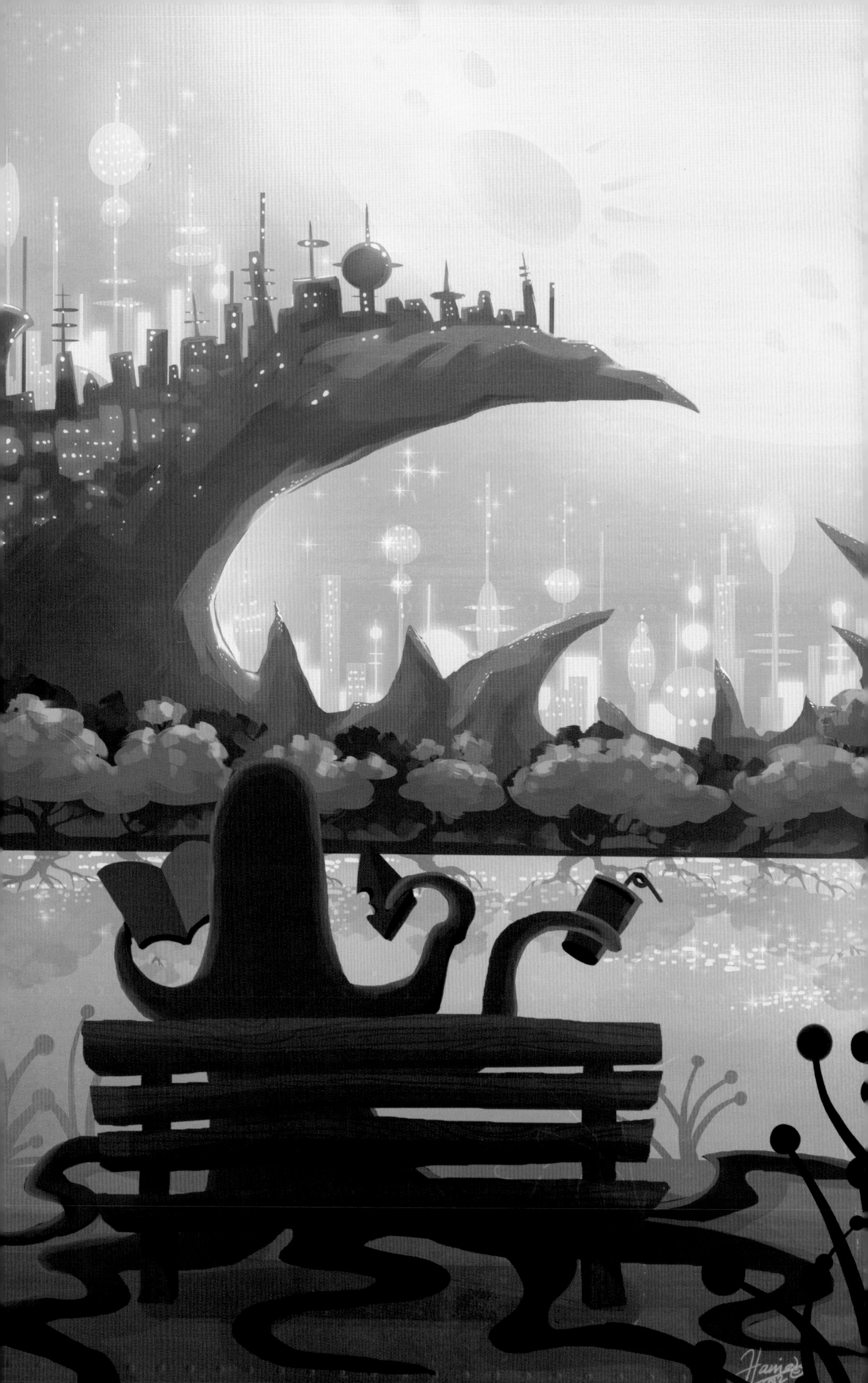

Art by Hanie Mohd

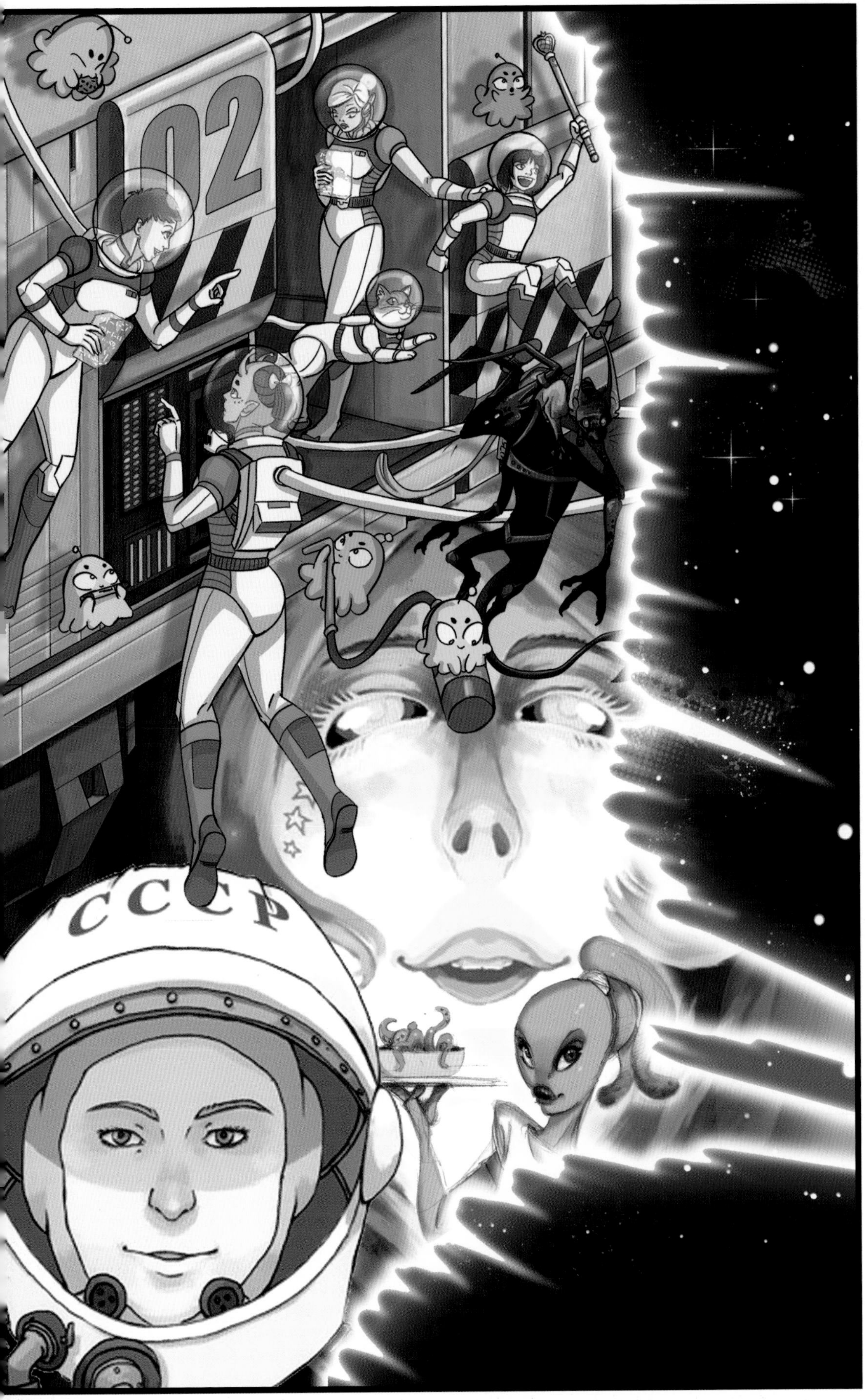
102
CCCP

Art by Alicia Fernandez, Jean Kang, Maarta Laiho, Jessica Hickman, and Hanie Mohd

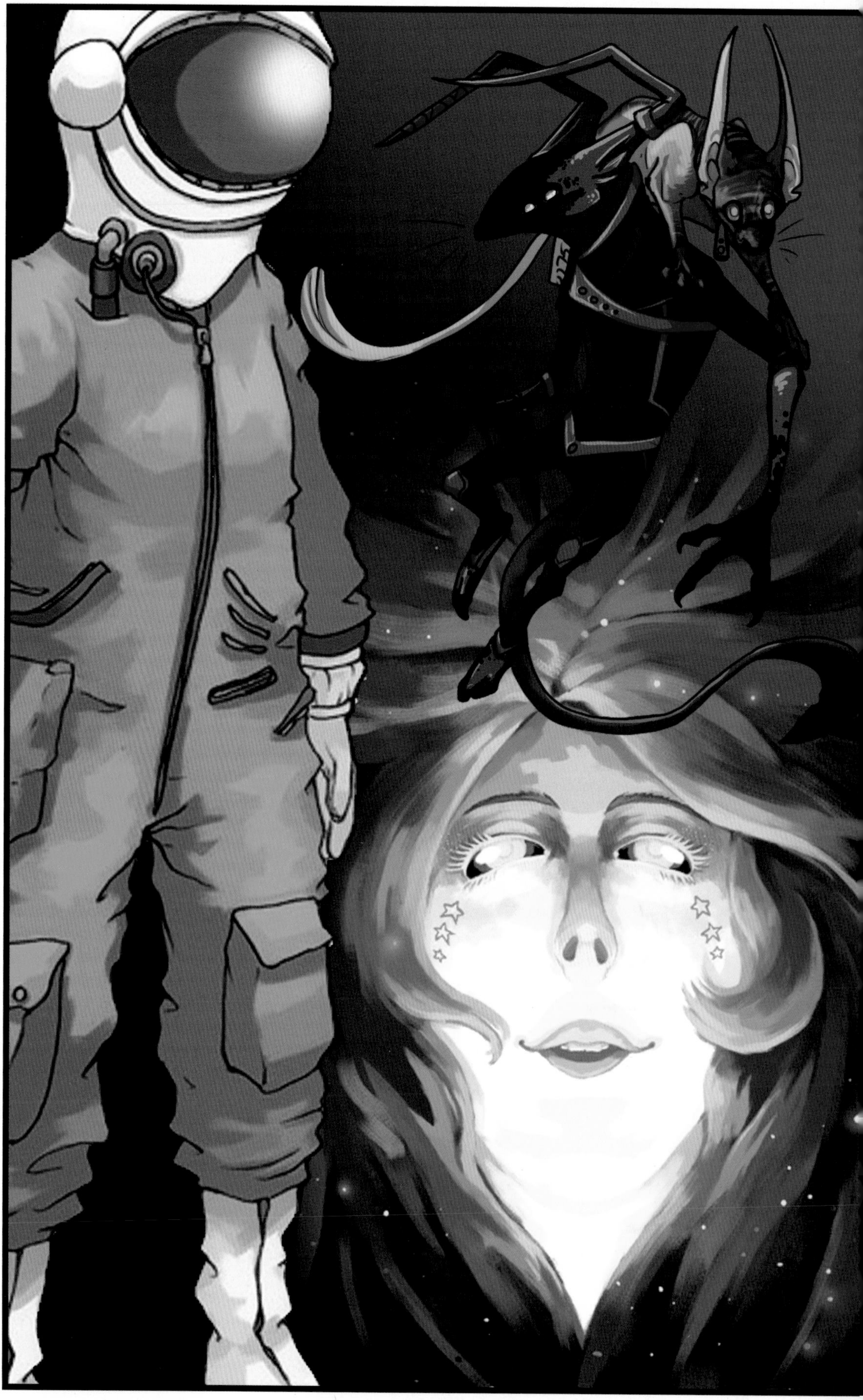

Art by Alicia Fernandez, Jean Kang, and Maarta Laiho

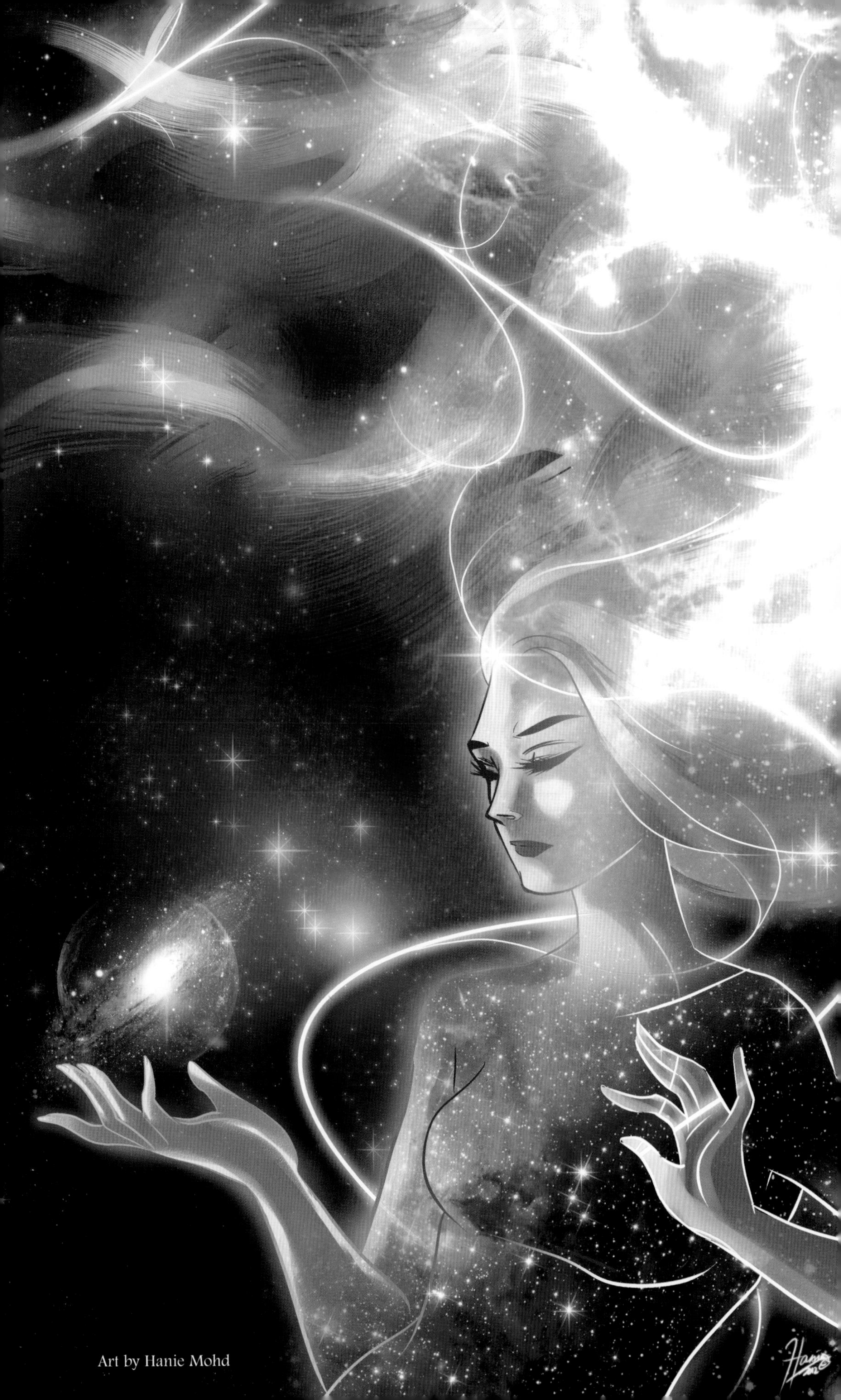

Art by Hanie Mohd

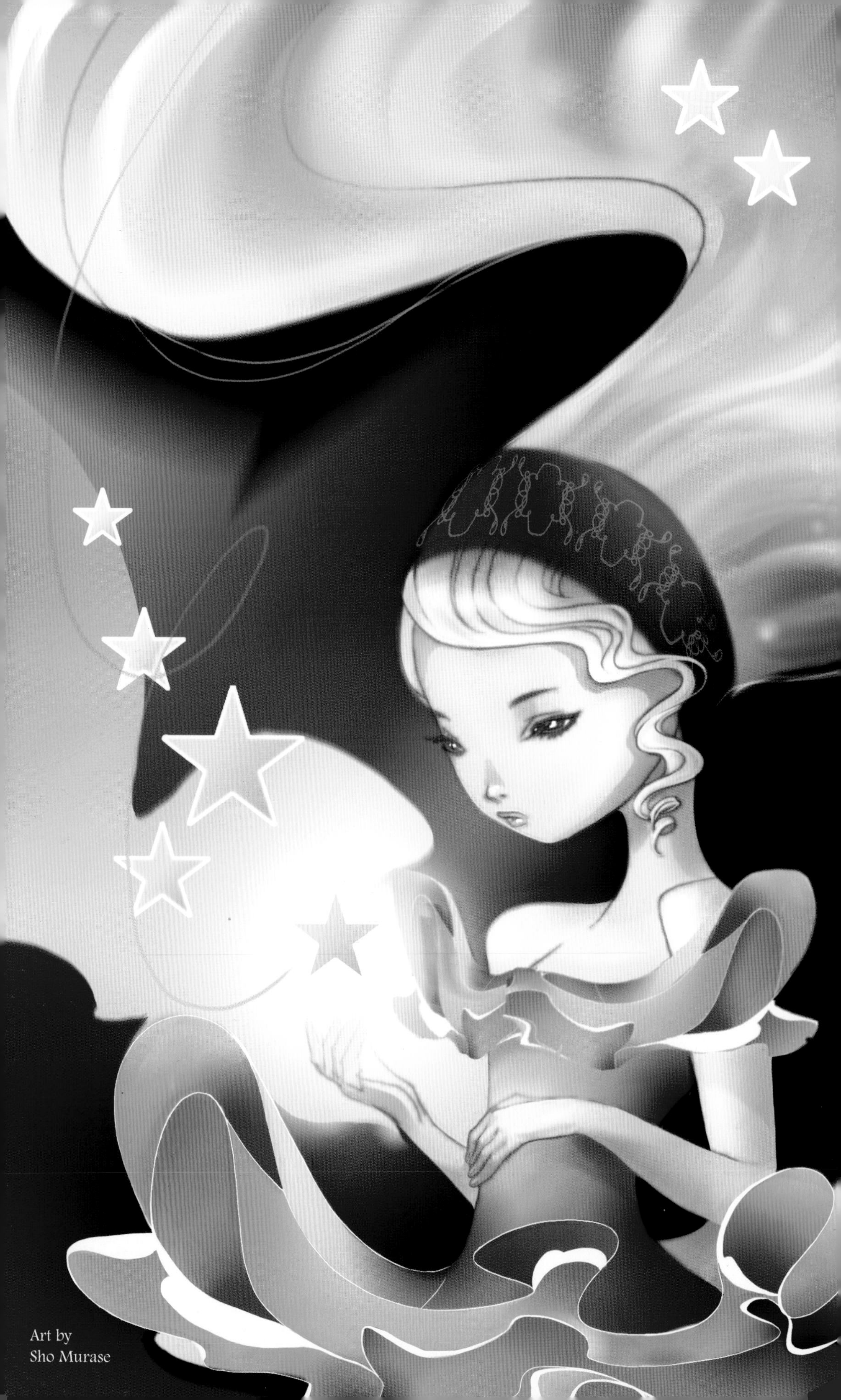

Art by
Sho Murase

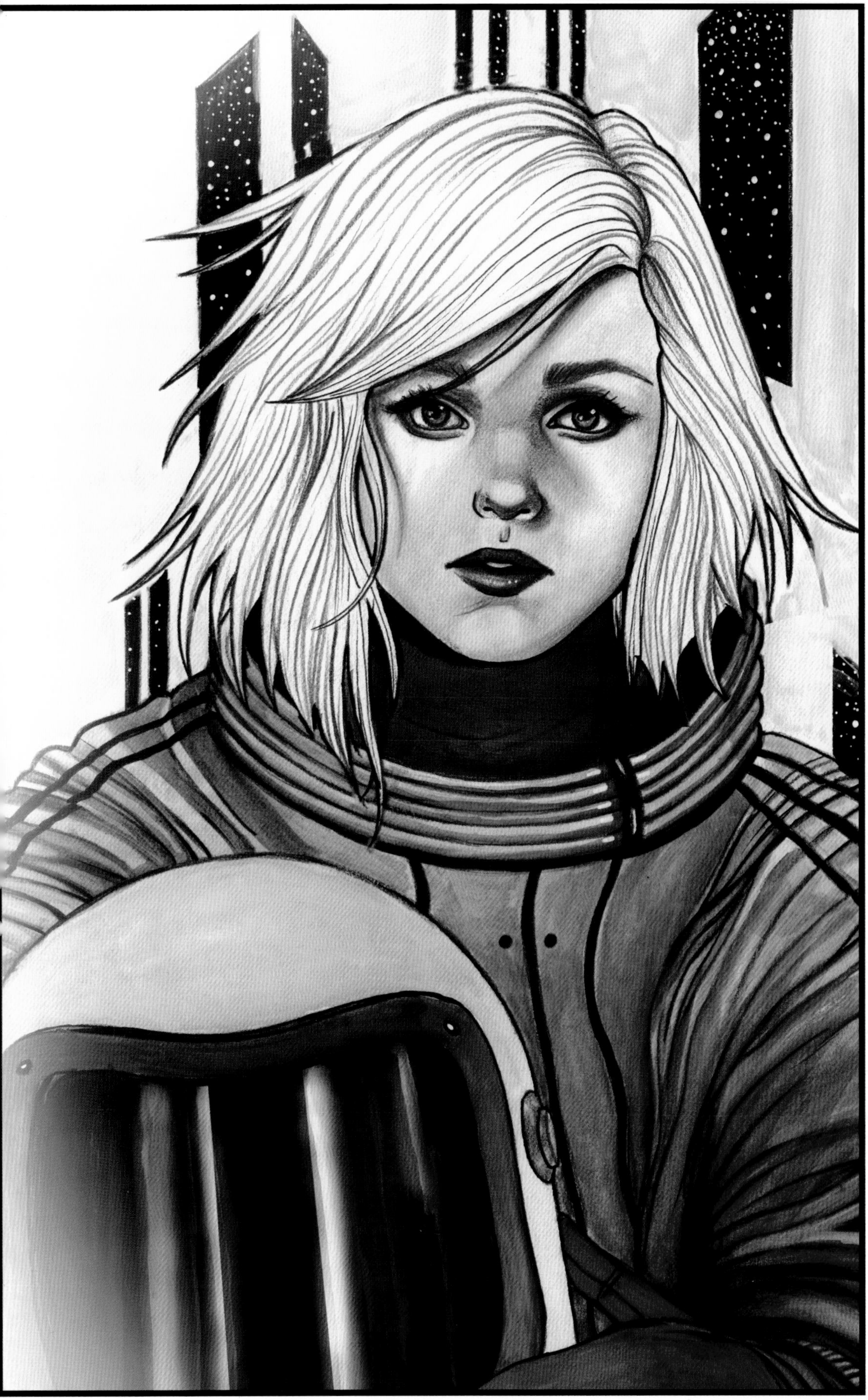

Art by Chrissie Zullo

H O W   T O
SCRIPT
COMICS!

by Devin Grayson

PAGE 1, splash
> Open on a blank piece of paper—an actual piece of paper would work, but let's be realistic and go with a freshly opened, blank computer document with a cursor visible in the upper left-hand corner of the page.

> NO COPY

PAGE 2, panel one
> Pull back just far enough so that we can see that the document—still completely blank—is on a laptop computer perched on a small desk.

> NO COPY

Page 2, panel two
> Now a pair of (female) human hands settle on the keyboard. No nail polish (in fact, the fingernails are short and uneven, albeit clean) and just one simple silver ring with a small sky-blue topaz set between two teeny-tiny diamonds adorning the ring finger of the right hand.

> NO COPY

Page 2, panel three
> And finally, as the hands begin to move, text appears in the upper left corner of the blank page.

> 1 COPY: Page 1, panel one

Page 2, panel four
> Pull back for an over-the-shoulder (OTS) shot of our writer, the document she's working on still visible in close background. Her medium-length auburn hair is pulled back by a single silver barrette into a haphazard pony tail and she's wearing a brightly colored but wrinkled t-shirt that she most likely slept in. A steaming cup of coffee is now visible on a small green coaster to the right of the keyboard (white mug with Batman™ logo), as is a wireless mouse on a pad featuring a Japanese Woodblock print. To the left of the laptop, we see a young brown mackerel tabby. The cat is lying on her back alongside the entire length of the laptop, upside-down, eyes closed.

2 CAPTION: This is a script.
3 CAPTION: It can be filmed or, if you're making a comic, sent to an artist to pencil.

PAGE 3, panel one
        Our writer turns to address the cat, which opens its eyes to regard the writer sleepily.

        1 WRITER: Do you think this is enough?
        2 WRITER: I mean, people who want to be writers…someone's bound to have told them they need to read a lot and study story structure and everything already, right?

Page 3, panel two
        As the writer ponders and/or waits for an answer, the cat closes its eyes in a kitty smile (see also: "Super Kawaii Japanese Cat Smile").

        3 WRITER: Maybe I should put in something about freelancing…like the reality of facing deadlines or living check to check…

Page 3, panel three
        The writer, still talking out loud—presumably to the cat—turns back to her document as the cat gets up to indulge in a deep back stretch.

        4 WRITER: …or how hard it can be to get started.
        5 WRITER: Yeah, that's good. I can talk about the challenge of finding inspiration and staring down the blank page…

Page 3, panel four
        The writer freezes, hands held aloft as the cat flops back down happily…this time across the keyboard, eagerly waiting for her furry white tummy to be pet.
        The document on the laptop monitor is instantly replaced by a seemingly unending series of "g"s.

        6 COPY:
gggggggggggggggggggggggggggggggggggggggggggggggggggggggggggggggggggggggggggg
                        ggggggggggggggggggggggggggggggggggggggggggggggggggggggggggggggggggg
            gggggggggg

        7 SFX/writer: =sigh=

Page 3, panel five
        Elbows on the desk to either side of the keyboard, the writer drops her head into her hands. Sensing her distress, the cat stands up (on the keyboard) to nuzzle against her lovingly.

        8 COPY: ggggggggggggggggggggggggggrewTO'wa
                       P:L,eqgrf wlkn<>?
                       ]\i.lvv AdXHN';OI   EFfwelkojp;/lmfedwds; j/31e

        9 WRITER: Or maybe I'll just remind them to hit "Save" a lot.

        10 COPY: THE END

HOW TO:
MAKING AN ATMOSPHERIC DIGITAL PAINTING

by Lois Van Baarle

In this 'how to' article, I'll be sharing the process behind one of my digital paintings, 'bus ride.' The piece was drawn in Photoshop CS3 with an Inuos3 tablet, but it is actually not very important which version of photoshop you have or which tablet you use. When I created this piece, I wanted to create a potrait of a character lost in her own moment, daydreaming while travelling with her pet fish. The focus was to create an atmospheric image with hazy, soft lighting. I usually draw character pinups which are not situated in any specific setting, so creating a character in a proper setting was the focus. I wanted the final image to have a soft, painted look and evoke a certain timeless, poetic mood. Here is how I went about this process:

Step 1: starting out with a rough sketch

Even though I work digitally, I sketch just like I would with pencil on paper - that is, loose, not too detailed and in a lighter color. The advantage of sketching digitally is that applying colors to the sketch is really easy if you keep the sketch on a separate layer, and you can gradually 'paint over' the sketch as you continue painting detail. Because of this, I keep the sketch pretty simple since I will end up painting over it anyway. I see it more as a guide for the overall composition and gesture of the character than a definite indication of how the final piece will look. So, when sketching, keep it loose and rough!

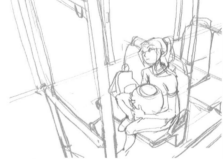

step 1

Step 2 - Adding rough colors

When my sketch is complete, I slap down some rough, messy colors. At this phase, it's important to know what effect the colors will have on the composition. The contrast, balance of cool and warm shades, and positioning of brighter color accents - such as here with the beams of the bus - have a big effect on the way the image is balanced and positioned. Just like in the previous phase, I like to keep the coloring rough so that I can work intuitively and make changes throughout the painting process. The more detailed and precise the coloring becomes, the less inclined you will be to make changes later on, so keep it loose in the early phases of the drawing. I use a lot of color editing tools - Hue/Saturation, color balance and replace color - to change the colors after I have already painted them on. Trust your intuition to 'feel' whether the colors are working out.

step 2

Step 3 - Rough painting

When the basic colors are applied, I start painting. By this I mean flattening all of the layers and applying color over my existing image to flesh in more detail, such as lighting and shapes. This is the point when I start painting over the lineart and working more with color than line. In the early painting phases, I like to use a nice thick brush, which can be any shape/texture but usually set to 70% opacity and 50% flow. During this phase I'm basically just adding more detail to the picture - I'm particularly focusing on adding highlights and shadows to emphasize the lighting and create more shape and mass in the artwork - but also staying open to changes. As you can see I've changed the colors to make them warmer. By keeping the artwork rough, it's still possible to make many changes to the artwork without compromising any details I may have already added.

step 3

Step 4 - Painting with a softer brush

I now select a softer brush - in this case, the standard round photoshop brush with an 8% flow and 100% opacity - and add softer shading to the picture. I feel like the picture is far enough for me to start moving towards more detailed shading. What I focus on during this phase is adding more volume to the work, and softening the harder blocks of color that I laid down in the previous phase. I also added a gradient to emphasize the light flowing in from the windows. You can do this by putting a light yellow gradient on a separate layer and then setting the layer mode to 'screen' or 'overlay' and playing around with the opacity settings for the layer. These kinds of tricks are very useful for emphasizing certain parts of the image more than others.

step4

Step 5- Finalizing the composition and cropping

Many artists make sure the composition is finalized in an earlier phase, but I find that during the painting process, the composition tends to change slightly from the original sketch. With the addition of color and lighting, certain aspects of the drawing become more important than others. This is why I cropped and modified the composition a bit at such a late phase, bringing the viewer slightly closer to the character and tilting the image a little. This makes the space look a bit less empty and makes the composition more harmonious, in my opinion. Sometimes I use the warp or liquify tool a bit to distort aspects of the image, but I try not to over-use this tool as this can look very wonky and be quite obvious, especially if you use these tools at such a late phase of the painting process.

step 5

Step 6 - Softening the colors and fleshing out the detail

As you may have noticed, I was pushing the saturation and warmth of the images more and more in each step. Oddly enough, at this point I feel like a less saturated image would work better to bring out the lighting. I do this quite often when I am painting digitally - the picture can evolve in unexpected ways if you work intuitively. I take an even softer round brush - this time around 4% flow, but still 100% opacity - and start working in the detail. Since I already got the harder shadows and bolder colors in during earlier phases, there's no need for a harder brush and I can just work with a soft one to smooth out most of the shading. Be careful not to make your picture too blurry or smooth - this can cause an overly shiny and digital look which can take away the character and personality of your rougher brush strokes. I try to keep certain details sharp and chunky, while I soften other things, such as the hazy lighting.

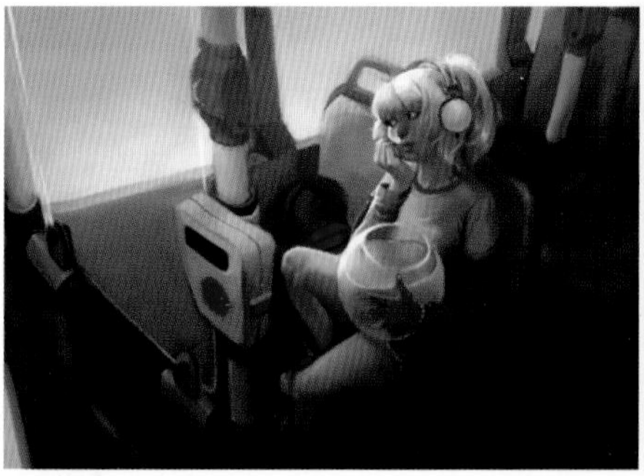

step 6

Step 7 - finishing the paintwork

Admittedly, this is the most boring part of the painting process. Once I am totally settled on the exact colors and composition of the picture, there's nothing left to do but finish off all the detail. This involves a lot of zooming in and painting in little details, or smoothing out the rougher shading and brushwork. Adding tiny details like strands of hair or sharp shiny highlights can really complete the picture. Because the colors are more or less set, I can use the shortcut Alt+click (for windows) to paint. This makes the eyedropper tool appear temporarily so you can pick a color and start painting with it right away. It always feels a bit like sculpting with color at this point. This phase takes the longest but it is definitely worth it in the end!

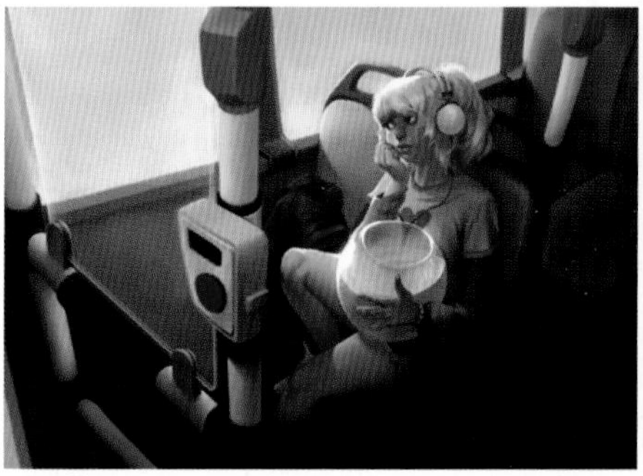

step 7

Step 8 - Finishing touches

When I'm done painting, I always add some finishing touches to complete the picture. It usually boils down to adding a gradient here or there or tweaking the colors just a tiny bit so that I feel the image is complete. This is always quite easy and fun to do digitally. What I did was make the light coming from the window a bit brighter and also slightly blurred so that it is a bit more hazy. I do this by selecting this part of the drawing, filling this up with a yellow color on a separate layer, blurring it and then playing with the layer modes until I like what I see. I also darken the shadows a bit to create more contrast, and emphasize the bright glow on the girl's hair and fishbowl by selecting these with a blurred lasso tool (set to about 150px) and amping the levels in these areas.

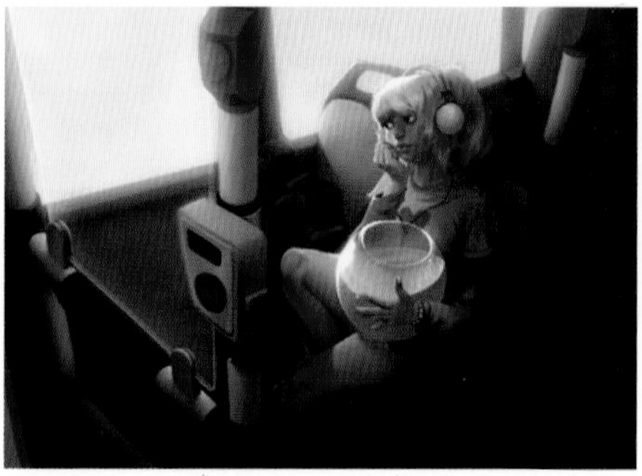

step 8

When painting digitally, there's no limit to how much you can paint on your canvas. You never run out and the colors never mix into a big brown blob. That is why I like to just start rough and let the picture evolve from there, changing slowly as I paint in more and more detail. Of course, it's important to have a concept when you begin, but it's also good to just let go of this as you draw and see where the picture takes you.

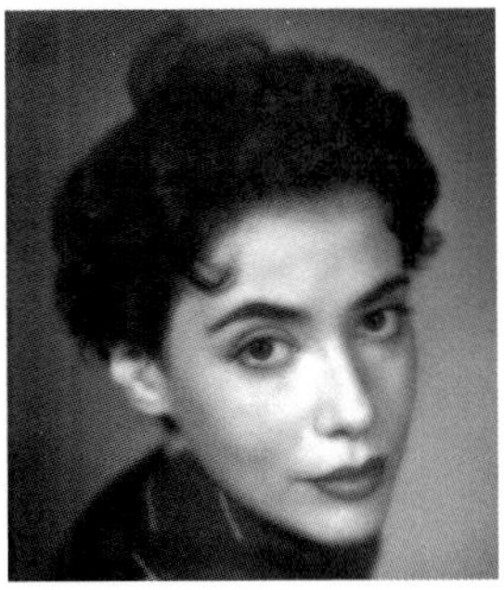

LILY RENEE:
She Fought Nazis With Pen and Ink

by Trina Robbins

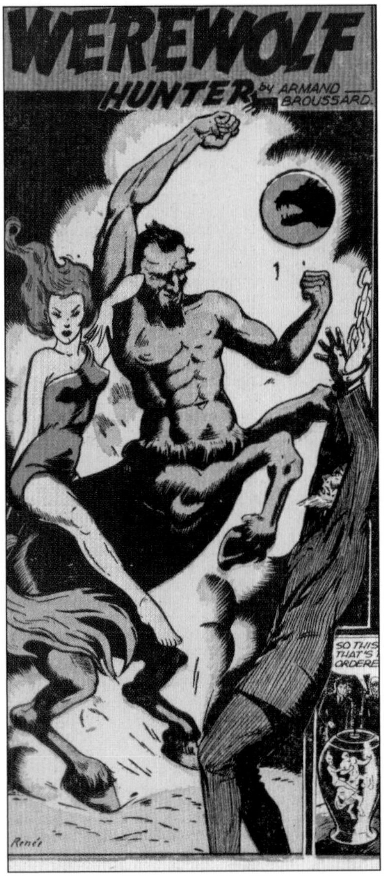
WEREWOLF HUNTER
BY ARMAND BROUSSARD

During World War II, the young men in the American comics industry, as in all other industries, were either drafted or enlisted in the military, and as in other industries, women stepped up to take their places. The result was more women working on comic books than ever before. Of all the comic book publishers, the one that hired the most women was Fiction House, known for its pulpy action stories featuring strong, beautiful women. And of the women who drew for Fiction House—Lily Renee, Marcia Snyder, Ruth Atkinson, and Fran Hopper—the star of the bunch was unquestionably Lily Renee, the only woman who drew covers for the company. During the 1940s, she drew the post-apocalyptic science fiction series, *The Lost World*, the supernatural series, *Werewolf Hunters*, the Nazi-fighting flying nurse, *Jane Martin*, and the series that best used her elegant sense of design, *Senorita Rio*, about a beautiful counterspy masquerading as a Brazilian nightclub entertainer.

For years I had hoped to find Lily Renee and I had despaired of finding her alive, when I received an email from her granddaughter who, knowing that her grandmother had drawn comics, Googled her name and kept coming up with my name. I learned that Lily Renee Wilheim Phillips was—and is—alive and well, an elegant and gracious women living in Manhattan's upper East side, and I visited her for the first time in May, 2006.

What Lily had to tell me was a story right out of the comics she drew. Lily had been a talented Jewish teenager from a well-to-do, cultured family in Vienna when the Nazis marched in, in 1938, and changed her life. After a harrowing year and a half under Nazi rule, she escaped to England via Kindertransport, a large scale rescue operation on the part of England, credited with saving the lives of about 10,000 Jewish children from Nazi-occupied countries.

But there was no happy ending for Lily – yet. She had gone to live with her pen-pal in a suburb of Leeds, but she soon found that her pen-pal's mother had expected a ragged, grateful refugee whom she could turn into an unpaid servant. After England declared war on Germany and Lily lost all contact with her parents back in Vienna, she walked out of her pen-pal's house without a penny to her name, hiked into Leeds and found work, first as a mother's helper,

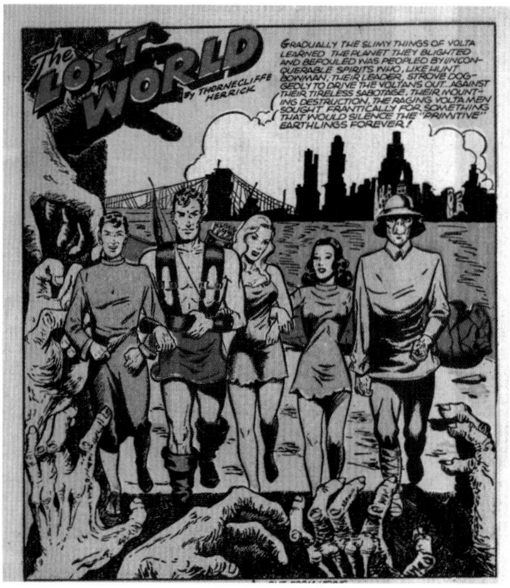
The LOST WORLD
BY THORNECLIFFE HERRICK
GRADUALLY THE SLIMY THINGS OF VOLTA LEARNED THE PLANET THEY BLIGHTED AND BEFOULED WAS PEOPLED BY UNCONQUERABLE SPIRITS WHO, LIKE HUNT BOWMAN, THEIR LEADER, STROVE DOGGEDLY TO DRIVE THE VOLTANS OUT...AGAINST THEIR TIRELESS SABOTAGE, THEIR MOUNTING DESTRUCTION, THE RAGING VOLTAMEN SOUGHT FRANTICALLY FOR SOMETHING THAT WOULD SILENCE THE "PRIMITIVE" EARTHLINGS FOREVER!

then as a nurse's assistant in Leeds Maternity Hospital, where she ferried babies down to the bomb shelter every night during the Blitz.

Shortly after that, England classified all refugees between the ages of 16 and 70 as "Enemy aliens." To avoid being put into an internment camp, Lily fled to London, where a cousin lived. She was put up in an abandoned school (all the children had been evacuated to the countryside to escape the bombing), and convinced to turn herself over to the police. At the police station she learned that her parents had escaped to America, had been searching for her, and finally found her, thanks to Bloomsbury House, the London central office that reunited Jewish refugees with their families.

Lily sailed to America on the last Kindertransport ship and was reunited with her parents. They'd had to leave everything behind, and now were living in a cramped apartment in New York, with other refugees, scrambling for a living. Lily's father, who had managed the Holland-America steamship line, found work as an elevator operator. Her mother took in piecework, crocheting dresses with other refugee women, and Lily painted Tyrolean designs on wooden boxes and drew for Woolworths catalogues for 50 cents an hour. Then one day Lily's mother saw an ad in the newspaper: a comic book company was looking for artists. Lily had never read a comic in her life, but she bought a couple of comic books, studied them, and drew some sample panels. Long story short, she got the job, drawing for Fiction House comics.

Jane Martin, the flying nurse, fought Nazis. Senorita Rio fought Nazis. And in her elegant style, often influenced by Austrian *Jugendstil*, Lily Renee, who as a helpless teenager had been persecuted by the Nazis, got to fight back with pen and paper.

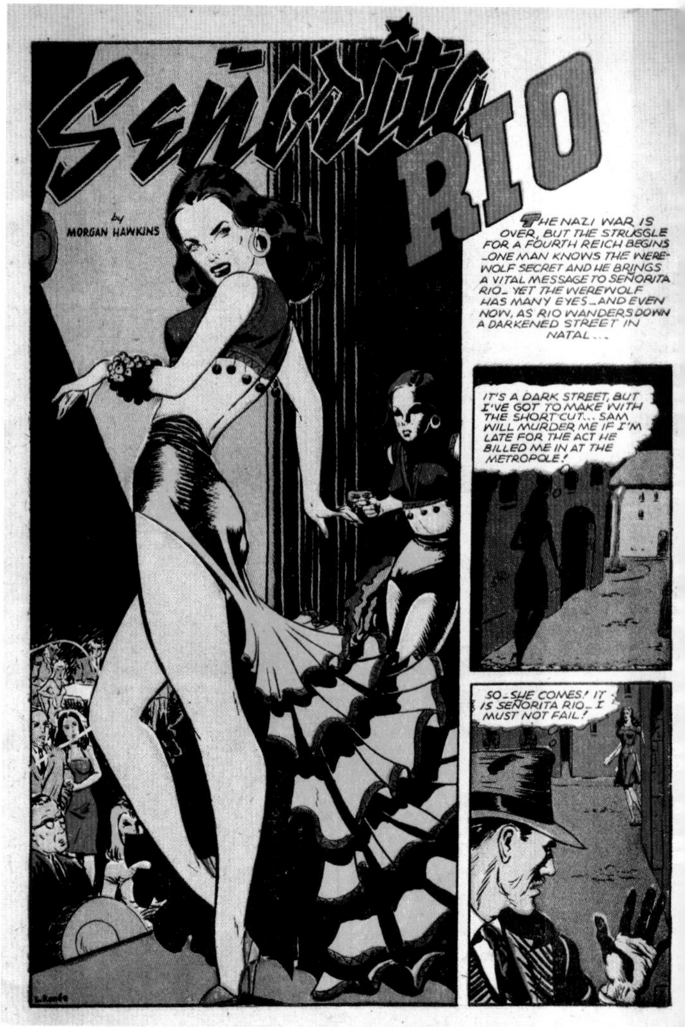
Señorita RIO
by MORGAN HAWKINS
THE NAZI WAR IS OVER, BUT THE STRUGGLE FOR A FOURTH REICH BEGINS —ONE MAN KNOWS THE WEREWOLF SECRET AND HE BRINGS A VITAL MESSAGE TO SEÑORITA RIO— YET THE WEREWOLF HAS MANY EYES—AND EVEN NOW, AS RIO WANDERS DOWN A DARKENED STREET IN NATAL...
IT'S A DARK STREET, BUT I'VE GOT TO MAKE WITH THE SHORT CUT... SAM WILL MURDER ME IF I'M LATE FOR THE ACT HE BILLED ME IN AT THE METROPOLE!
SO—SHE COMES! IT IS SEÑORITA RIO—I MUST NOT FAIL!

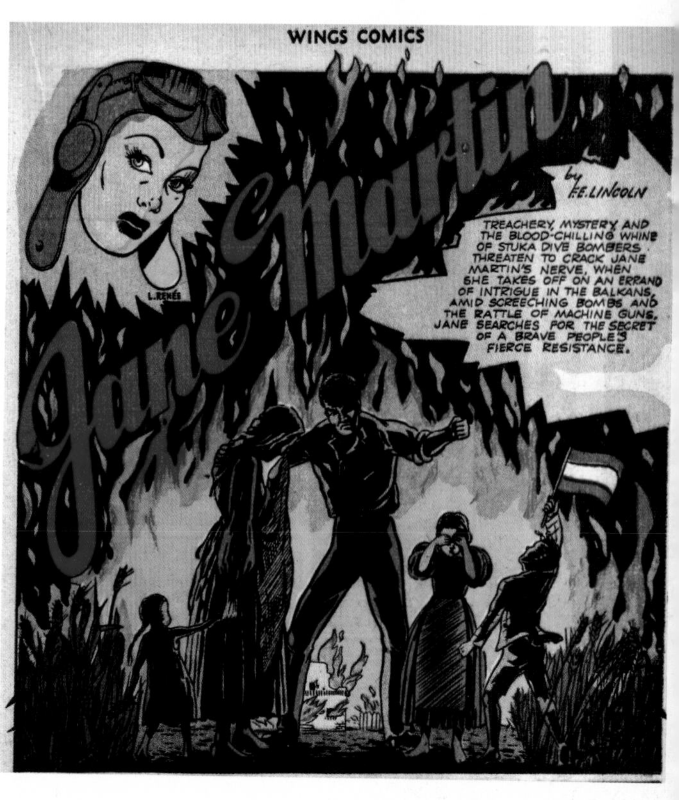
WINGS COMICS
Jane Martin
by F.E. LINCOLN
TREACHERY, MYSTERY AND THE BLOOD-CHILLING WHINE OF STUKA DIVE BOMBERS THREATEN TO CRACK JANE MARTIN'S NERVE, WHEN SHE TAKES OFF ON AN ERRAND OF INTRIGUE IN THE BALKANS, AMID SCREECHING BOMBS AND THE RATTLE OF MACHINE GUNS, JANE SEARCHES FOR THE SECRET OF A BRAVE PEOPLE'S FIERCE RESISTANCE.
L. RENÉE

Creator Biographies

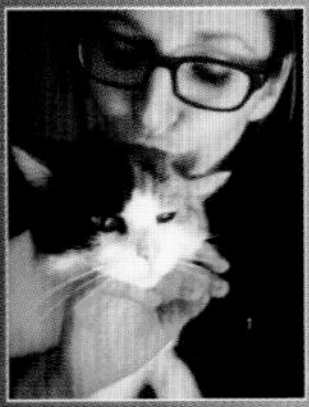

Jordie Bellaire

Jordie Bellaire's recent projects include *Doctor Strange* and *Hulk: Season One, John Carter Gods of Mars, The Rocketeer: Cargo of Doom* and she's currently working on *Manhattan Projects*. Upcoming projects include *Mara* (alongside beautiful collaborator Ming Doyle) and *Nowhere Men* (Nate Bellegarde, Eric Stephenson).

She lives with her cat Buffy and watches *X-Files* everyday in Dublin, Ireland.

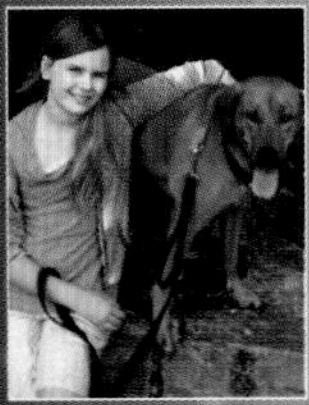

Anna Bowie

Anna is a 10 year old (at the time of this drawing) kid from North Carolina. She enjoys creating: whether it be drawing, sculpting, or taking pictures with her camera. She has a great love for animals and the outdoors. When she isn't creating she is teaching her dogs (she has three) tricks or finding creative ways to feed the birds and squirrels around her house. She also enjoys her iPod and racing games on the XBox. She is very excited to be a part of *Womanthology*!

Little known fact:
Anna is a child black belt in Tae Kwon Do

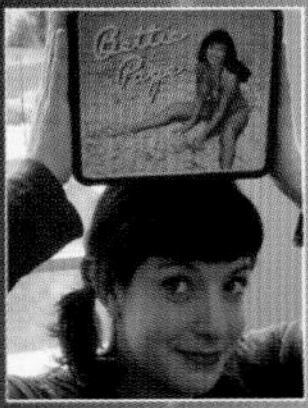

Bonnie Burton

Bonnie Burton is a book author, web show host, social media strategist & geek! Author of the books: *The Star Wars Craft Book, Draw Star Wars: The Clone Wars, The Clone Wars: Planets in Peril, Girls Against Girls: Why We Are Mean to Each Other, You Can Draw: Star Wars* and *Never Threaten To Eat Your Co-Workers: Best of Blogs*.

Host of "Geek DIY" craft show on Stan Lee's World of Heroes channel and "Ask Bonnie" on Youtube. Co-host of the "Vaginal Fantasy Hangout" Book Club Web Series with Felicia Day, Kiala Kazebee and Veronica Belmont. Appeared on the web series "The Guild" and "Tabletop."

Editor/Contributor on the *Womanthology* comic book anthology from IDW. Columnist for *SFX* magazine. Written for *Wired, Geek Monthly, Craft, BUST, Star Wars Insider*, CNN.com, HuffPost, AOL, & Blastr. She can be found at Grrl.com and on Twitter at twitter.com/bonniegrrl

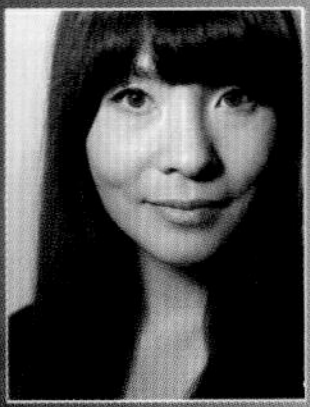

Ming Doyle

Ming Doyle's art has been featured in anthology pieces ranging from IDW's *Womanthology* to Image's *Popgun Vol.2* and *Comic Book Tattoo* as well as in longer format works such as Candlewick Press's young adult graphic novel *Tantalize: Kieren's Story* and BOOM! Studio's adaptation of *Jennifer's Body*. Recent work has been featured in Marvel's *Fantastic Four #600* and Vertigo's *Mystery in Space*. Her upcoming miniseries *Mara*, written by Brian Wood and published by Image Comics, is due out in early 2013.

Ming currently lives in Somerville, MA with her boyfriend Neil Cicierega, several Harry Potter Puppet Pals, and a traditional Siamese cat named The Big Kahuna, AKA "Maui."

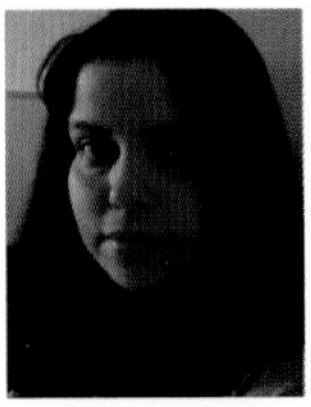

Jessica Hickman

Jessica's worked with several companies including IDW, Disney, Lucasfilm, and Image, to name a few. She's currently working on her creator-owned comics.

Little known fact:
She has a thing for coffee mugs

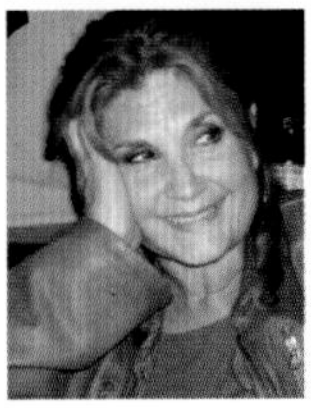

Sandy King

Artist, writer, film producer and president of Storm King Productions.

With a background in art, photography and animation, Sandy King's filmmaking career has included working with John Cassavetes, Francis Ford Coppola, Michael Mann, Walter Hill, John Hughs and John Carpenter.

She has produced films ranging from public service announcements on Hunger Awareness to a documentary on astronaut/teacher Christa McAuliffe, and major theatrical hits like *John Carpenter's Vampires*. From working underwater with sharks in the Bahamas to converting 55 acres of New Mexican desert into the vast red planet of Mars, new challenges interest and excite her. The world of comic books is no exception. It allows her to bring her art and story telling experience to a new discipline with an expanded group of collaborators.

She is married to director John Carpenter and lives in Hollywood, California.

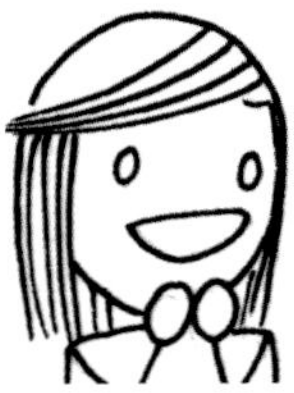

Stacie Ponder

When Stacie isn't tackling the writing and art duties of Space Girls or her webcomic RPG (www.rpgcomic.com), she inks other peoples' comics. In her off-time, she indulges in video games, horror movies, '80s nighttime soaps, and shows featuring geriatric detectives. She enjoys a good laugh, harbors an unholy love of cheese, and spends an inordinate amount of time thinking about kittens.

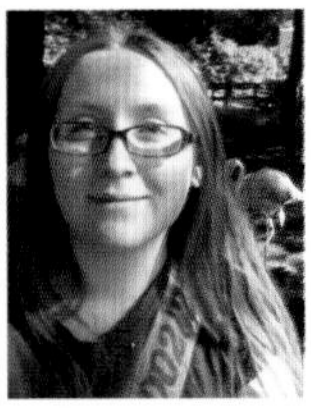

Alison Ross

Alison lives in rain-tastic Vancouver with her fiance and their two bunnies. She works in production for animated television and does some freelance writing on the side. This is Alison's first published comic and she's hoping there will be more in the future. In her spare time, Alison spins her own yarn, designs patterns, and knits like crazy.

Little known fact:
Alison's future plans involve 10+ acres and a herd of alpacas.

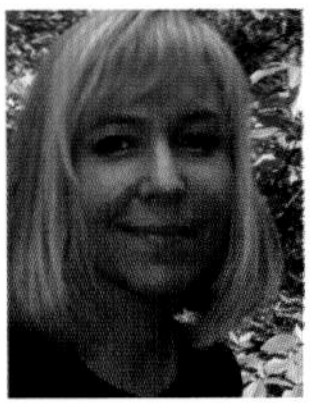

Tanja Wooten

Artist contributor for *Womanthology*. Creative background includes children's book illustration as well as toy and novelty product design.

Little known fact:
During high school worked as a portrait artist at Six Flags Amusement Park.

Blair Butler

Blair Butler is a television writer based in Los Angeles. She is also a correspondent for the G4 program, "Attack of the Show," and wrote the mini-series *Heart* at Image Comics. She is honored to be included in *Womanthology*.

Bibliography stuff: Russian Spaceflight transcripts from here:
Siddiqi, Asif .A. "The first woman in Earth orbit." Spaceflight, Vol. 51. Jan. 2009: pp. 18-27.

Siddiqi, Asif .A. "The first woman in Earth orbit. - Part 2." Spaceflight, Vol. 51. Feb. 2009: pp. 64-71.

JEAN KANG

Jean Kang is an artist and illustrator based Los Angeles. She has a BA in Illustration from A Center College of Design and has been workir in the field of animation, games and comics. H work has been seen in *Womanthology: Hero* MTV's "Good Vibes" and "Popzilla," and in vario galleries across Southern California. Mo information and a portfolio of her work can b found on her website: www.jeandrawsstuff.com

ELLISE HEISKELL

Ellise Heiskell grew up so far out in the middle nowhere that it might as well have been oute space. She's worked as a DJ, a bookseller, edite manga and worked in the anime industry. She love writing strange stories, '70s-'80s scifi/fantas movies, small dolls with large heads and may hav seen *The Cat from Outer Space* one too many time at an impressionable age.

ALICIA FERNANDEZ

Ohmybug is Alicia Fernandez (Barcelona, 1990), a young illustrator and comic artist based in Barcelona, Spain and a student at the prestigious Joso School of Comic and Graphic Arts.

Her interest in the perception of reality and the dream world also defines her illustration work. Interested in comics, she also studied one year in a script school.

Samples of her work have been published in some books, but if you feel curiosity for her illustrations, you can take a look here:
http://ohmybug.deviantart.com/

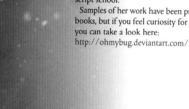

MAARTA LAIHO

Maarta was born and raised in the midcoas mountains of Maine, where she spent her childhood befriending the local wildlife population and obsessing over dinosaurs. She later graduated from The Savannah College of Art and Design with degree in Sequential Art, where she further expanded her love for visual storytelling and worldbuilding. Currently she works as a freelance artist, and eventually hopes to one day self-publish her webcomic MadWillow.

JOELLE SELLNER

Joelle Sellner began her career as an advertising copywriter, writing award-winning print, radio and television ads for clients such as Lexus, In-N-Out Burger, and Kleenex. While working fulltime, Joelle also began writing animation, starting with an animated series featuring the Olsen Twins: Mary-Kate and Ashley in Action.

Since then, she's written for shows including Teen Titans, Jackie Chan Adventures, Shin Chan, Secret Saturdays, Avengers: Earth's Mightiest Heroes and Ben 10: Omniverse. Her animated web series work includes Mattel's Monster High and Samurai! Daycare, for Smosh's Shut Up! Cartoons channel. She's also written comics for DC, Marvel and is currently writing her first graphic novel.

Joelle graduated from the University of Pennsylvania. She is also a graduate of the Warner Bros Sitcom Writers Workshop, Best Screenplay winner at the 2010 La Femme Film Festival and a WGA member.

MARY BELLAMY

Mary has been an artist and creator in indie comics since 2001, working with Antarctic Press, Radio Comix, Slave Labor, and more. Currently she works as a trading card artist for 5finity, Cryptozoic, Breygent, and Rittenhouse Archives. She also self-publishes her own books: *Ah Heck!! —The Angel Chronicles*, and *Faux Facts – The Truth Can Be Strange!*

JENNIFER DE GUZMAN

Jennifer de Guzman, world traveler and dream caretaker, was born during a drought-ending rainstorm in the San Francisco Bay Area. She has worked as a professional writer and in the comics industry for more than a decade, spending many of those years as editor-in-chief at SLG Publishing. In 2007, she received the Friends of Lulu Woman of Distinction Award. Currently, she is the PR and Marketing Director at Image Comics. Her comics work can be found in two anthologies from that publisher, *Take the Book Off the Shelf* and *This Is a Souvenir*. She wears a portrait of Morrissey around her neck.

Picture by Shari Chankhamma

LEIGH DRAGOON

Leigh Dragoon, an instructional designer by day, writer and comics creator by night... and weekends, lunch breaks, early mornings, and what should be vacations. Her credits include comic scripts for *Fraggle Rock* and the *Vampire Academy* graphic novel adaptations. She lives in Sacramento with her loving husband, a houseful of adorable cats, and three pet chickens. You can visit her blog at www.leighdragoon.com.

RACHEL EDIDIN

Rachel Edidin is a writer and editor. She lives in Portland, Oregon, with her husband Miles and a lumpy cat, and abuses twitter as @RaeBeta.

ROBIN FURTH

Robin Furth is the coauthor of Marvel's bestselling *Dark Tower* comic book series. The first two collections, *The Gunslinger Born* and *The Long Road Home* both won YALSA's Great Graphic Novel Award for 2008. *The Gunslinger Born* was also nominated for an Eisner and a Harvey Award. She has adapted Sherrilyn Kenyon's *Lords of Avalon* series into graphic novel form and has contributed to Marvel's *Legion of Monsters* and to several other anthologies. She is the author of *Stephen King's The Dark Tower: A Concordance, Volume I* (nominated for a Locus Award), *Stephen King's The Dark Tower: A Concordance, Volume II*, and *Stephen King's The Dark Tower: The Complete Concordance*, all of which grew out of her long-time work as Stephen King's research assistant. As well as continuing to do freelance work for the Master of Horror, she is finishing up a novel.

SOPHIA FOSTER-DIMINO

Sophia Foster-Dimino is an illustrator living in San Francisco with her husband, Roman. She has a BFA in Illustration from the Rhode Island School of Design. Her favorite films set in outer space are *Moon*, *Alien*, and *Solaris*. Her favorite comic set in space is Chris Ware's *Acme Novelty Library* #19.

CARLI IHDE

Carli Ihde is a relatively new member of the comic book community. A recent graduate of the Kubert School's class of 2011, Carli has been published in Vertigo comics and has worked with a number of companies as a freelance illustrator. Her work can be found in a number of different mediums and venues and her style changes depending on the project. Carli is constantly trying to widen her artistic horizon with new and unique projects such as pumpkin carving and henna tattoo design, but her true passion will always be in the art of comic books and sequential illustration. Carli hopes that one day her passions will grow into a lifelong career that will open the door to sharing her love of the arts with the rest of the world.

TRINA ROBBINS

Award-winning herstorian and writer Trina Robbins has been writing books, comics, and graphic novels for over forty years. Her 2009 book, *The Brinkley Girls: the Best of Nell Brinkley's Cartoons from 1913-1940* (Fantagraphics), and her 2011 book, *Tarpe Mills and Miss Fury*, were nominated for Eisner awards and Harvey awards. Her 2010 all-ages graphic novel, *Chicagoland Detective Agency: The Drained Brains Caper*, first in a 6-book series, was a Junior Library Guild Selection. Her graphic novel, *Lily Renee: Escape Artist*, was awarded a gold medal from Moonbeam Children's Books and a silver medal from Sydney Taylor Awards.

Pic by Ann Sanfedele

creator biographies

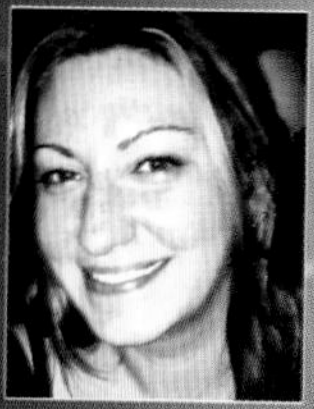

Christine Ellis

Christine Ellis is a writer living in New York City. She works mostly in film and television and received her MFA in Dramatic Writing from NYU Tisch Asia. She enjoys drinking wine in exotic places and traveling the world on a budget slightly bigger than a bread box, learning how to swear in foreign languages, and getting lost everywhere she goes. Her favorite novel of all time is the *Count of Monte Cristo* (ask her about her copy). This is her first time writing comics but she hopes it won't be the last.

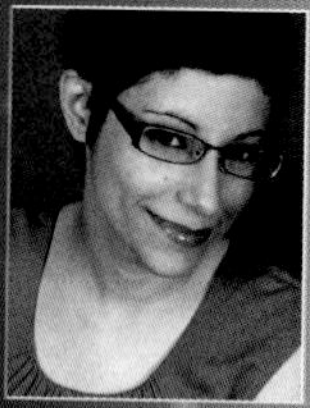

Jody Houser

A writer and third-generation geek, Jody Houser received her MFA at Emerson College and currently resides in Los Angeles where she focuses on comics and screenwriting. She is the creator of the webcomics "Cupcake POW!" and "Brickgirl & Oscar" and a contributor to several comic anthologies including *Womanthology: Heroic, Dead Roots* and *The Gathering*. Links to her work can be found at MindEclipse.com.

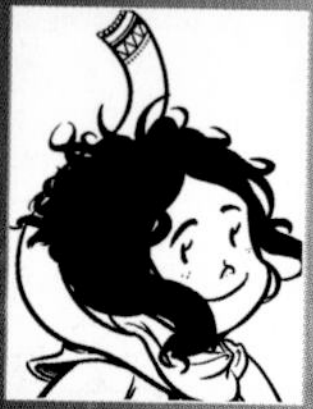

Catherine Miller

Catherine currently lives in Florida, and blames the locale for the flights of fancy found in her illustrative work. Her contribution to *Womanthology* is her first experience with a major publisher, having previously provided guest work for independent comics. When not working on freelance or personal projects, Catherine enjoys perusing history books or playing the odd video game.

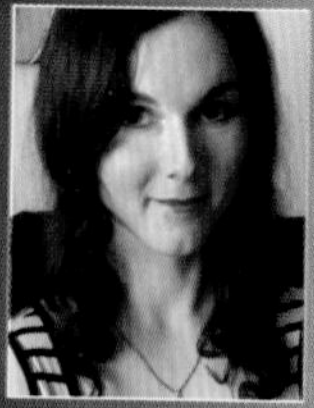

Lindsay Walker

Lindsay Walker always knew she was going to be an artist. She grew up with a love for dinosaurs, monsters, fantasy, scifi, cartoons and super-heroes. Some of her biggest influences include Terry Pratchett's *Discworld, Labyrinth, Dark Crystal, Lord of the Rings, The Phantom, Goon* and *Judge Dredd*. She has work published on *The Phantom, Kolchak: Night Stalker/Sherlock Holmes, Zombies Vs. Cheerleaders, Voltron, Street Fighter* and *Darkstalkers*. Lindsay is also open about being transgender. She and her partner Kimberley have been together for more than ten years and have three daughters. Ariel, Heloise and Evelyn. Their rainbow family have been looked up to as an inspiration for some LGBT people. Lindsay's official website is... www.puggdogg.com

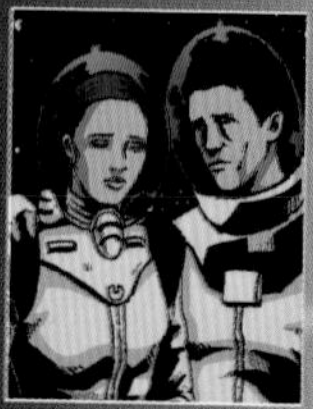

Devin Grayson

Best known as a mainstream comic book writer for DC's *Batman* titles, Devin is also a novelist, video game scripter, RPG enthusiast and essay writer. An insulin-dependent diabetic since the age of fifteen, Devin is the lucky partner of an amazing diabetic alert dog, Cody, and a passionate volunteer for Early Alert Canines. She is also an LGBTQ rights advocate and a firm believer in the ability of fiction to illuminate truth.

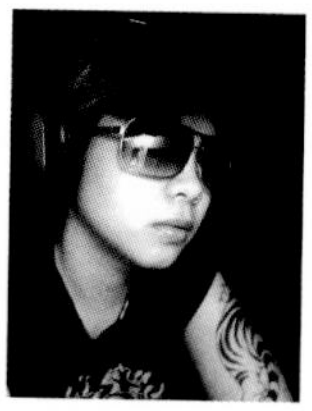

Kathryn Layno

Kathryn is a freelance illustrator based in t Philippines. She has worked on various sketch ca sets, some independent comic work as an illustrat as well as coloring for comics since she started h freelance career in 2007.

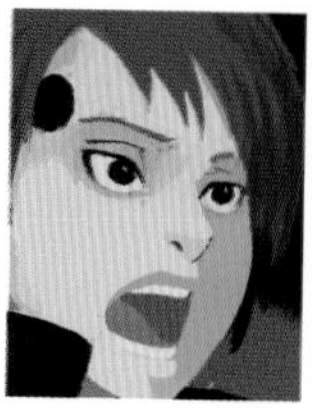

Elva Wang

My name is Elva Wang, a freelance illustrator ar animator, who lives in Canada. Strongly influence by all the animations and comics around the worl I chose to be an animator as my career. I lo drawing and can't live without it. Although I a happy with doing concept and background f animations, my life goal is to complete a comic th I put all my effort in.

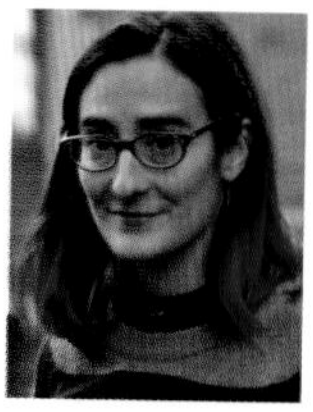

Cecil Castellucci

Cecil Castellucci is the author of books an graphic novels for young adults including *The Ye of the Beasts Boy Proof, The Plain Janes*, and *First Da on Earth*. She is the YA editor of the Los Angele Review of Books and Children's Correspondenc Coordinator for The Rumpus. For mor information, go to www.misscecil.com

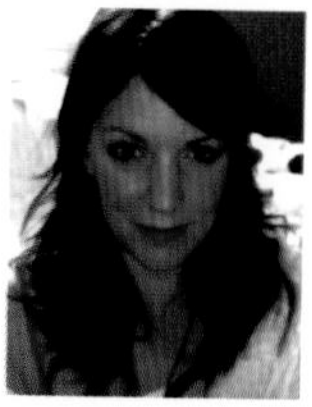

Kiala Kazebee

Kiala Kazebee is a writer on the internet and co-host of Felicia Day's web show/book clu "Vaginal Fantasy." She apologizes in advance fo making you google that.

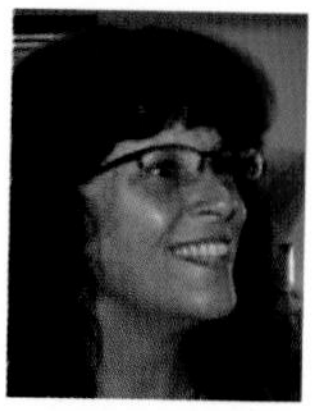

Barbara Randall Kesel

Barbara Randall Kesel has written or edited a whole lot of comics with women (and men!) in them and is busy writing more stuff. She's working with Digger T. Mesch on *Baby Boodas* and promises to eventually finish the YA novel she's been chipping away at between interesting assignments for other people.

KEL MCDONALD

Kel McDonald spends her time drawing comics all day everyday. You can read those comics at www.sorcery101.net. She enjoys silly supernatural stories and musicals.

LAURA MORELY

Laura Morley writes comics about out-of-shape crime-fighters, comatose sleeper agents, and Walter Mitty characters way out of their depths. She lives in Cambridge, UK, with a zoologist, a banana palm, and a five-month-old with superpowers.

ALLISON PANG

Allison Pang is the author of the Abby Sinclair urban fantasy series. Her latest book, *A Trace of Moonlight*, was released by Pocket Books in October 2012. She also writes the online graphic novel *Fox & Willow*, found at www.sadsausagedogs.com and has a penchant for Hello Kitty, sparkly shoes and gorgeous violinists. Find her at www.heartofthedreaming.com

ISABELLE MELANÇON

Isabelle Melançon is a French-Canadian artist who grew up in a family of literature and comic lovers, which began her interest in the genre. She is currently working on *Namesake*, a fantasy online graphic novel that publishes three days a week with one book released in print. Isabelle's drawing style is heavily influenced by American and Japanese animation, as well as older Victorian and French illustration work. She is madly in love with fairy tales and literature and enjoys playing with the classics in her comics and written work.

MAJA SUKELLE

Maja Sukelle lives in a small village in northern Sweden and is inspired greatly by the wildlife and nature there.

SARA RICHARD

Sara Richard is an American illustrator who loves looking at artwork from the Art Nouveau and Art Deco eras (can't you tell?) She is the illustrator of the kid's book *Kitty & Dino* and loves watching sci-fi and dreaming of building her own TARDIS, cosplaying with her besties and hang gliding when it's warm. As of late Sara is also getting into the hobby of ghost hunting. You can see more of her swirly works and upcoming appearance schedule on her website, www.SaraRichard.com. Stay Classy!

CEILI CONWAY

Ceili Conway is a freshman in high school who loves drawing. She enjoys participating in Art Alliance at school and also delights in taking various art classes over the summer. Ceili has been published in several previous *Womanthology* collections. She wishes to continue to develop her artistic skills and to someday have a career in art education. To see more of her work, you can visit www.ceiliconway.com.

CHRISSIE ZULLO

Chrissie Zullo has worked for DC, Dark Horse, IDW, Devil's Due, and Archie Comics, including cover work for "Cinderella: From Fabletown with Love", "Cinderella: Fables are Forever", "Hack/Slash", "Creepy", "Womanthology", and "New Crusaders", and interiors for "Fables", "Madame Xanadu", "Womanthology", and "Creepy". Her work can be seen online at chrissiez.blogspot.com.

LEA HERNANDEZ

Lea Hernandez makes webcomics and print comics and has won a few awards. She writes and draws the vampire family comedy *The Garlicks* (TheGarlicks.net). Lea loves *Sailor Moon*, *My Little Pony*, and *Amethyst, Princess of Gemworld*.

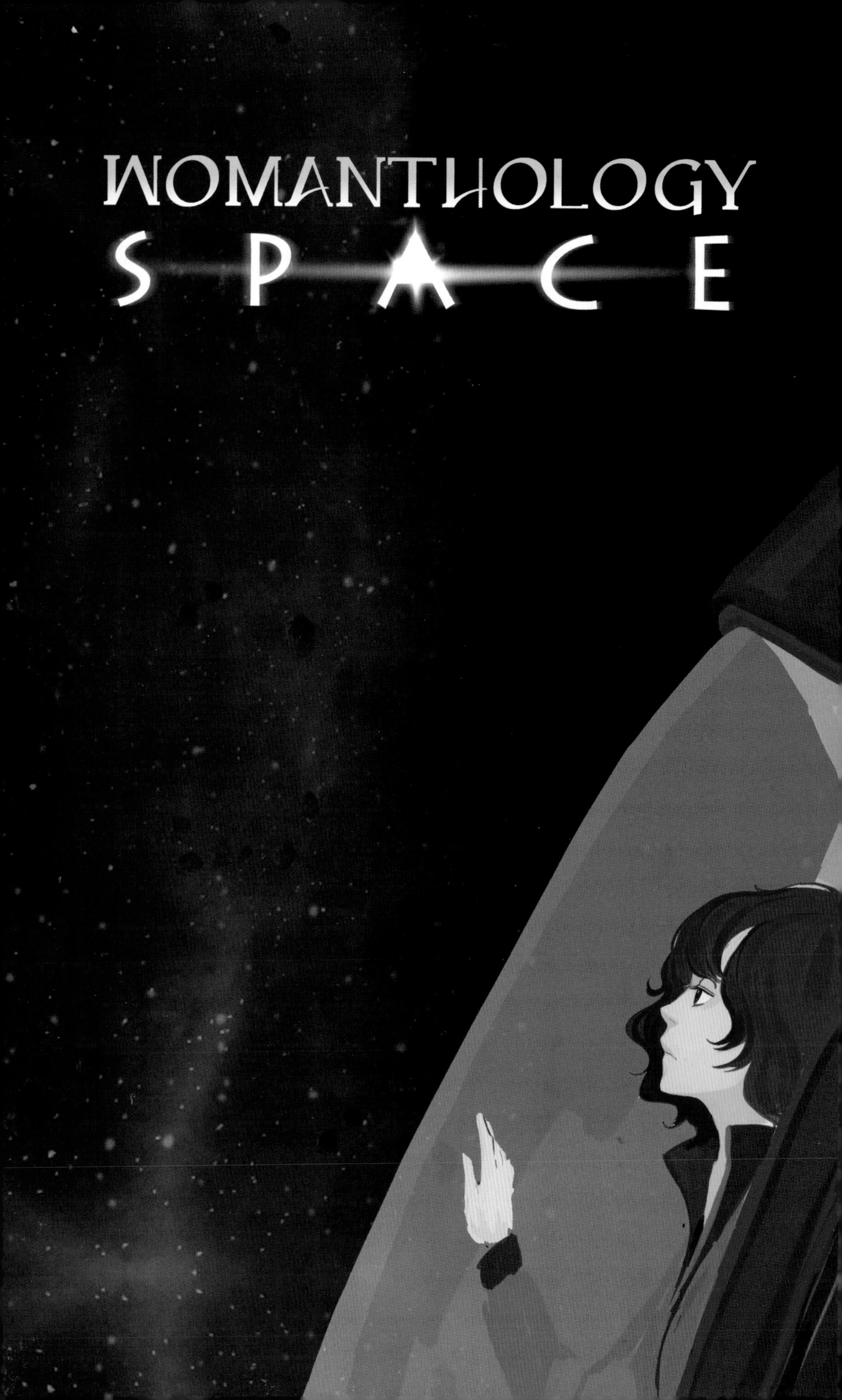
WOMANTHOLOGY
SPACE